MISSISSIPPI REAL ESTATE LICENSE LAW

Welcome to the Real Estate Training Institute

Our Mission

Our mission is to provide our adult learners with the highest quality instruction in classroom and online real estate courses to prepare them for a successful professional career in the real estate industry.

Our Vision

The Real Estate Training Institute will flourish as a distinctive Mississippi institution of learning that fosters a culture of diversity, values, and student-centered experiences. As the premier real estate licensee support system, RETI will remain dedicated to the positive development of Mississippi's real estate community.

Our Statement of Diversity

The Real Estate Training Institute is dedicated to creating an intellectual, cultural, and social climate that allows everyone the opportunity to contribute to the educational experiences at the school.

The people at the Real Estate Training Institute promote acceptance and appreciation of all individuals regardless of age, sex, race, color, marital status, familial status, physical or mental disability, religious creed, national origin or sexual preference and identity.

Our Philosophy of Education

Quality education is paramount.

Collaboration

Nurturing an environment grounded in common goals and trust enable our school members to reach beyond the jurisdictional and educational minimums. Together we search for what our adult learners need and deserve both educationally and individually and foster a safe environment where our instructors and learners become explorers and risk-takers of innovation. Removing the fear to participate begins the concrete foundation on which the Real Estate Training Institute operates. A quality education grows from a positive school environment.

Inclusiveness

Fostering social networks, friendships, and support to enhance the personal growth of our adult learners is essential. Communication between the adult learners to instructors and learner to learner provides social interaction to many learners who may not have had the opportunity of group inclusiveness unless participating in RETI's adult programs. The individual's desire to be included is respected. Our backs never turn towards our learners.

Continuous Improvement

Continuous school improvement is a necessary component of the Real Estate Training Institute's quality education. Improvements begin with our instructor's commitment to life-long learning and exploring. Participation in the Real Estate Educators Association is mandatory to foster instructor growth and development for the continuous improvement of the Real Estate Training Institute.

Open Door Policy

By opening the doors to our classrooms through both physical and virtual environments, we have the opportunity to improve real estate consumer safety and experiences with our graduates. We open up our classrooms to educators not only in our schools but to schools creating a positive impact in the community.

Leadership

Leadership starts at the top. We value our instructor's expertise by focusing on their strengths first. We then help them develop in other areas to foster their leadership skills. We continuously inspire our instructors to be leaders.

Our instructors inspire our learners not to be followers but to lead. Our learners are encouraged to be leaders in their communities.

Communication

Through the school's use of Zoom, www.goretionline.com, Google Classroom, and chat, we open up our classrooms to digital communication.

Headings; Gender

The headings in this book and all reference material and statements by representatives of the Real Estate Training Institute are for convenience of reference. Unless the context clearly indicates otherwise, each pronoun herein shall be deemed to include the masculine gender, feminine gender, neutral gender, singular gender, vice-versa and plural forms.

Locations

Biloxi

2650 Beach Blvd. #35
Biloxi, MS 39531 (across from the Edgewater Mall)

Southaven

Community Mortgage
3964 Goodman Rd E
Southaven, MS 38672

Oxford

The Enterprise Center

9 Industrial Park Dr.
Oxford, MS 38655

Hattiesburg

Woodall Center at Pearl River Community College
906 Sullivan Dr.
Hattiesburg, MS 39401

Contact

(228) 354-8585 email:
information@msrealtycourses.com

MREC COURSE SUPPLEMENTS ADDED October 2021

MREC COMPLAINT PROCESS
MREC DISCIPLINARY PROCESS---STEP BY STEP
MREC Disciplinary Action Matrix - July, 2021

MREC COMPLAINT PROCESS

The Complaint Process typically begins when the MREC receives either a formal complaint (signed and notarized) from an individual or legal entity (§73-35-23) or when the MREC receives reliable information of unlawful real estate activity which might necessitate the MREC Administrator beginning an Investigation.

At that point in time the procedure is as follows, to wit: A letter is mailed to the Complainant (if applicable) informing them that the MREC has received the complaint, an investigation has been initiated and the Complainant is given the name of the MREC Investigator for future reference. A letter is mailed to the real estate licensee(s) informing them that a formal complaint has been received by the MREC and that an investigation has been initiated with respect to a real estate transaction which involved the licensee(s).

The licensee(s) are provided a copy of the complaint and any documents submitted by the Complainant and requested to tender the following information to the MREC, to wit:

1) A formal written response to the Complaint by the licensee(s). The licensee is instructed to provide a written statement specifically addressing the allegations of the complaint, with a notarized signature. The licensee's legal counsel (attorney) may assist in any way the licensee chooses but the response must be from the licensee (in their own words) and it should be signed with a notarized signature.

2) An Affidavit which stipulates that complete, accurate and true copies of "all documents" which are germane to the real estate transaction being investigated are being tendered to the MREC. The affidavit should be signed by the licensee(s) and their signatures should be notarized. The submission should include the following:

The "ENTIRE WORK FILE" (every piece of paper in the file).

Upon the receipt of all the documentation from the licensee's work file, the MREC will begin the investigative process with the following protocol, to wit:

1) The MREC Investigator will immediately send the Complainant the response and all documentation from the licensee's work file to verify the authenticity of each document which has been submitted as part of the transaction that is being investigated. The Complainant is asked to respond to the documents within a ten (10) day period.

2) The MREC Investigator will compare any/all documents which were originally submitted (by the complainant) with those documents which were submitted by the licensee(s) and are certified to be complete, accurate and true copies of the work file.

3) After the response/rebuttal is received from the Complainant (if applicable), the response will be sent to the licensee(s) so that each party is fully aware of the allegations and know which documents are considered germane and are being reviewed by the MREC.

4) If any major discrepancies are noted by the investigator, they will request a written (signed) response from each of the parties to the transaction so they may clarify how, if at all, the documents were used during the transaction. The investigator may conduct a personal interview with each of the parties to clarify the documents.

Following the review and analysis of the documentation secured from the complainant and the licensee(s), the investigator will issue an Investigative Summary (opinion) indicating whether they discovered licensable activities which might be violations of the Real Estate Brokers Act of 1954, as amended and/or the Administrative Rules of the Real Estate Commission.

The Investigative Summary, including the original Complaint, the response from the licensee(s), the rebuttal from each of the parties (if any), the entire licensee's work file and the data secured by the MREC Investigator (including notes) are then reviewed and discussed (in detail) with the MREC Legal Counsel, the MREC Senior Attorney and the MREC Administrator in attendance.

During the meeting the parties will agree on the facts that have been discovered, discuss the merits of the investigation and attempt to reach a consensus for one of the following courses of action:

1) Additional Information may be required to clarify some specific details and the Investigator will be given specific instructions concerning what is required to bring the case to fruition.

2) No violations of MREC guidelines were evident from the facts of the investigation and the recommendation from the participants is that the case be dismissed.

3) Minor violations appear to be present in the documentation and the recommendation from the participants is that the case be "dismissed" but, with either a written Letter of Caution (not a disciplinary action) or a Formal Letter of Reprimand being presented to the licensee(s) based on the violations (must be approved by the Commissioners).

4) Possible Major Violations appear to exist in the documentation and either the MREC Legal Counsel or the MREC Senior Attorney is charged with taking the investigative file and drafting a "Formal Complaint" to be presented to the licensee(s) based on the evidence that has been discovered.

When the "Formal Complaint" is drafted and presented to the licensee(s), the MREC will provide a written explanation indicating how the investigation will continue and a statement will be given to the licensee(s) informing them whether the MREC is willing to consider negotiating an "Agreed Order" with the licensee(s) and their legal counsel (attorney), if any, rather than conducting an Administrative Hearing.

If the terms of an "Agreed Order" are negotiated to the satisfaction of the licensee(s) and their attorney and the MREC Legal Counsel, the Agreed Order will be drafted, signed by the licensee (with advice from counsel) and presented to the Real Estate Commissioners (typically at the next monthly meeting) for approval prior to the "Order" becoming effective. If the MREC Investigator, the MREC Legal Counsel, the MREC Senior Attorney and the MREC Administrator believe the violations are so egregious that a "License Revocation" might be a possibility, an Administrative Hearing will be recommended. Similarly, if the licensee(s) are unwilling to negotiate or accept an "Agreed Order", an Administrative Hearing will be set at the convenience of the MREC and the legal counsel for the licensee(s).

MREC DISCIPLINARY PROCESS---STEP BY STEP

The MREC disciplinary process typically begins with an individual or a legal entity filing a formal (written) complaint with the MREC Office but, statutorily, a complaint may be initiated by the MREC based on information which appears to indicate that a licensee has been involved in a violation of the License Law or the Administrative Rules of the MREC.

In either instance, a letter is drafted to the Principal Broker of the Brokerage Firm and all licensees who are believed to be involved, they are notified of the complaint and each licensee is asked to respond with all information in their possession within the **next ten (10) days**.

Upon receipt of the notice of a complaint, the Broker and the licensees should have a conversation with and receive direction from their Errors and Omissions Insurance Carrier; including a discussion about securing an attorney who specializes in real estate license law and/or handles complaints involving licensed professionals.

Each of the licensees (individually) will be required to provide an explanation of the events which may be in question.

The individual response is required even if a real estate attorney provides a rebuttal to the formal complaint.

The MREC Investigative Staff will compile all information, review documents which are pertinent to the investigation, interview witnesses (if necessary), subpoena documents from third parties and conduct a complete administrative investigation.

If the Investigative Staff and Legal Counsel believe there may have been a violation, a formal complaint indicating the specific violations of MREC Guidelines will be issued to the various licensees.

Once the formal complaint has been issued, the licensees have the opportunity (if they choose to do so) to agree with the investigative findings and negotiate a tentative settlement of the case with the MREC Investigative Staff--- subject to the final approval of the entire Real Estate Commission---or they may choose to have an Administrative Hearing before the Real Estate Commissioners.

At an Administrative Hearing the licensees may (actually, should) be represented by legal counsel and the MREC will also have an attorney(s) present. The proceeding is very much like a court trial but with relaxed rules of evidence. The final adjudication is made by the Real Estate Commissioners.

The Commissioners are individuals who are highly informed in the practice of real estate and are not bureaucrats or employees of the MREC.

Each Commissioner is a peer of the licensees, is an active real estate broker and was appointed by the Governor of the state and confirmed by a vote of the Mississippi Senate to serve on the MREC.

Any adverse decision of the MREC Commissioners may be appealed by a licensee, **within thirty (30) days** of the action, by filing the appeal in Circuit Court in the home county of a licensee or in Hinds County.

Decisions from those courts may also be appealed to the Mississippi Supreme Court or the State Court of Appeals.

Except in rare situations, all appeals are decided "on the record" from the Hearing.

DISCIPLINARY ACTIONS USED BY THE MREC

The MREC has a multitude of disciplinary actions from which to choose when a licensee or a brokerage firm has violated MREC Guidelines; most of which do not lead to the permanent revocation of a license. They are as follows, to wit:

1) **Letter of Caution:**

This is not a disciplinary action but is a "written warning" addressing minor misconduct being committed by the licensee which does not warrant the imposition of a sanction. The letter is not considered in any subsequent disciplinary proceedings against the licensee unless the prior warning(s) in the letter is relevant to the misconduct alleged in the later proceeding(s).

2) Letter of Reprimand:

This is a disciplinary action and a formal letter of censure which is a public document that is issued by the MREC and informs a real estate licensee or a brokerage firm that the licensee's or the firm's conduct violates state law or the Administrative Rules of the MREC and will require the Commission to monitor the licensee or firm. It informs the licensee or firm that future violations will lead to more severe sanctions. It is placed in the licensing file of the recipient but does not negatively impact the ability of the licensee or the firm to continue with licensable real estate activities.

The initial Letter of Reprimand is typically for a minor Administrative Rule violation.

3) Letter of Reprimand with Continuing Education:

This is a disciplinary action which is practically identical to a Letter of Reprimand but is typically issued when the licensee is a repeat violator of a minor misconduct or commits a more severe violation.

The continuing education is used for remedial training of the violator.

The recipient of the letter is allowed to continue with licensable real estate activities.

4) License Suspension held in Abeyance:

This is a disciplinary action which is typically imposed when a licensee or brokerage firm violates a state law which stipulates that a violator's license may be suspended or revoked or their actions are such that members of the public, clients and/or customers suffer financial harm as a direct result of their actions.

This action is generally going to include an additional probationary period for the licensee and will require them to complete some remedial training in the form of several continuing education courses.

The violator is allowed to continue to engage in licensable real estate activity but any additional misconduct during the period of their sentence may lead to a full license suspension or other sanctions.

5) Full License Suspension:

This is a disciplinary action which is typically imposed when a licensee of brokerage firm has shown total disregard for the state statute or an administrative rule or the licensee has made substantial misrepresentations to customers and clients during a real estate transaction.

In the majority of the instances, the statutory violations are shown to be egregious and the licensee's actions or the brokerage's actions border on *fraud and improper dealing*.

The violator is forbidden to engage in any licensable activities for a specifically defined time frame when their license is suspended.

The licensee or brokerage firm will normally appear before the Commissioners prior to their licenses being reinstated and licensees will be required to complete remedial training during the term of their license suspension and probationary period.

6) License Revocation:

This is a disciplinary action which directly impacts the licensee's ability to work, diminishes their earnings potential and hinders their ability to advance their real estate career.

The licensee no longer has the right to practice real estate.

It is very common for the Commissioners to allow a licensee the right to petition the MREC for the opportunity to become licensed again. However, the state statute requires at least **a five (5) year** hiatus for the licensee.

Often a licensee who has their license revoked is also involved in criminal activity.

Corrective or Remedial Education is designed to improve a licensee's deficient skills to achieve expected competencies in specific areas of their real estate activities.

Period of Probation is a time during which a licensee and/or a licensee's real estate abilities may be more closely scrutinized and observed.

MREC Disciplinary Action Matrix
July, 2021

This Matrix provides guidance to assist the MREC Commissioners, the Investigative Staff and the MREC Legal Counsel in enforcement cases.

PURPOSE AND NATURE OF SANCTIONS

The purpose of discipline is to protect the public from licensees who have not or will not competently perform their fiduciary obligations to their clients and/or treat their customers honestly and fairly. The ultimate disposition of any disciplinary action should be made public in cases of licensee reprimand, suspension or revocation.

POSSIBLE SANCTIONS

Letter of Caution
1. Formal Letter of Reprimand
2. Formal Letter of Reprimand with Continuing Education
3. License Suspension held in Abeyance

4. Full License Suspension	
A. Short Suspension	Up to 3 months
B. Medium Suspension	3-6 months
C. Significant Suspension 　　a. Continuing Education 　　b. Probation	More than 6 months

License Revocation

This chart is provided to be used in conjunction with the **Aggravating and Mitigating Circumstances** listed below.

The potential sanctions outlined in this chart is an <u>average sanction</u> where aggravating and mitigating circumstances balance each other. Where aggravating circumstances outweigh mitigating circumstances, the level of sanction would increase, and vice versa.

This chart is provided to be used in conjunction with the **Aggravating and Mitigating Circumstances** listed below.

The potential sanctions outlined in this chart is an average sanction where aggravating and mitigating circumstances balance each other. Where aggravating circumstances outweigh mitigating circumstances, the level of sanction would increase, and vice versa.

Levels of Sanctions

LEVEL	VIOLATION	SANCTION
I	Minor violations that do not involve clients or the outcome of the transaction.	Letter of caution; corrective education (CE); or both.

II	Technical errors or carelessness where licensee would benefit from education.	Reprimand or equivalent; corrective education (CE that cannot be used for renewal); short probation; monitoring; or any combination of above.
III	Minor violations of the MREC Rules and/or State Statutes that rise to the level of affecting the outcome of the transaction.	License suspension; corrective education that cannot be used for CE for renewal; short suspension; medium probation; or any combination of above.
IV	Significant violations of the Rules and/or state statutes.	Significant suspension; significant amount of corrective education (that cannot be used for CE for renewal); significant probation; or any combination of above.
V	Significant willful violations of MREC Rules or State Statutes.	Revocation or Voluntary Surrender in lieu of disciplinary action.

AGGRAVATING CIRCUMSTANCES

An aggravating circumstance consists of factual information or evidence regarding the licensee(s) or the violation that might result in an increased sanction. Aggravating circumstances include:

- o Prior disciplinary history
- o Number of transactions involved in the case
- o Number of total violations involved in the case
- o Pattern of similar violations
- o Significant financial harm to a lending institution, a consumer or others
- o Evidence that the violation was willful or intentional
- o Evidence that the violation was grossly negligent
- o Failure to exercise due diligence in the supervision of others
- o Refusal to acknowledge violation
- o Lack of cooperation with investigation
- o Submission of false statements or evidence, or other deceptive practices (e.g., creating or adding to work file after complaint filed)
- o Intimidation of or threats to witnesses or others involved with the investigation

MITIGATING CIRCUMSTANCES

A mitigating circumstance consists of any information or evidence regarding the licensee or the violation that might result in a decreased sanction. Mitigating circumstances include:

- o Length of time since the date of violation
- o No prior disciplinary history
- o No other complaints currently pending against licensee
- o No pattern of similar offenses
- o No evidence that the violation was willful or intentional
- o No evidence that the violation was grossly negligent
- o License level at the time of violation
- o Licensee was under the supervision of another licensee at the time (e.g., agents)
- o Additional education taken and/or experience gained after violation occurred
- o Cooperation with investigation
- o Little or no financial harm to consumer or others

- o Timely mitigation of financial loss
- o Understanding and acknowledgement of violation
- o Personal problems such as physical, mental or emotional problems at the time of the violation that have since been addressed

EXAMPLE OF THE APPLICATION OF LEVELS AND AGGRAVATING AND MITIGATING CIRCUMSTANCES

The following are generic examples of how to apply sanction levels and aggravating and mitigating circumstances:

When determining an appropriate sanction, the highest level of sanction should be considered unless

substantial mitigating circumstances exist.

Example 1:

A licensee conducts a transaction in an area where he is not competent, failed to notify the broker that he was not competent and failed to take the necessary steps to become competent. As a result, he produced a transaction that failed or experienced unnecessary difficulty.

With no aggravating or mitigating circumstances, the sanction would be Level 1ll.

Example 1A:

Assume in the above scenario that there are no aggravating circumstances and that the following mitigating circumstances exist:

- o The transaction was done 3 years ago and the licensee now has achieved competency in the market. b. The licensee has no prior disciplinary history.
- o The licensee cooperated with the investigation.
- o Since the transaction was completed, the licensee has taken additional education that will help avoid this issue in the future.
- o Based on these circumstances, the sanction would be Level 1 or Level 1l.

Example 1B:

Assume in the above scenario that there are no mitigating circumstances and that the following aggravating circumstances exist:

- o The licensee has been disciplined for similar conduct in the past.
- o The licensee had already taken education designed to address this issue before the transaction in question.
- o As a result of the violation, there was significant financial harm to the consumer.
- o Based on these circumstances, the sanction would be Level IV or Level V.

Example 2:
- o A licensee conducts a transaction in an area where he is not competent, failed to notify the broker that he was not competent and failed to take the necessary steps to become competent. As a result, he produced a transaction that failed or experienced unnecessary difficulty.
- o With no aggravating or mitigating circumstances, the sanction would be Level IV.

Example 2A:
Assume in the above scenario that there are no aggravating circumstances and that the following mitigating circumstances exist:
- o The licensee was under severe emotional stress at the time the transactions were performed due to the illness of a child.

- o The licensee had been licensed for less than a year.
- o Based on these circumstances, the sanction would be Level 1l or Level 1ll.

Example 2B:
Assume in the above scenario that there are no mitigating circumstances and that the following aggravating circumstances exist:
- o There are 10 transactions involved in this case.
- o The licensee altered documents in the work files before sending them to MREC.
- o The licensee did not cooperate with the investigation, refusing to meet with the investigator or to provide more information when requested.

Based on these circumstances, the sanction would be Level V.

Example 3: states in his response on a transaction that he inspected the interior and exterior of the subject property, when in fact he only drove by the property. As a result, he stated that the subject property was in average condition when it was actually in poor condition and essentially uninhabitable. He did not use any extraordinary assumptions or hypothetical conditions. He knew that the lender required an interior inspection.
- o With no aggravating or mitigating circumstances, the sanction would be Level IV.

Example 3A:
Assume in the above scenario that there are no aggravating circumstances and that the following mitigating circumstances exist:
- o The licensee took CE courses after the transaction was done but before the complaint was received.
- o The licensee cooperated with investigation and acknowledged his error.
- o The sale never went through, so there was little or no financial harm to the consumer or others.
- o Based on these circumstances, the sanction would be Level 1ll.

Example 3B:
Assume in the above scenario that there are no mitigating circumstances and that the following aggravating circumstances exist:
- o The violation was intentional.
- o The licensee has been licensed for over 20 years.
- o When confronted with the issue by the client, the licensee refused to review or correct the issue.
- o Based on these circumstances, the sanction would be Level V.

Example 3C:
Assume in the above scenario that there are both the mitigating circumstances in Example 3A and the aggravating circumstances in Example 3B.
- o The sanction, therefore, would be anywhere from Level 1ll to Level V.
- o Based on these circumstances, the aggravating circumstances are more serious and outweigh the mitigating circumstances, thus the sanction would be Level IV or Level V.
- o In determining an appropriate sanction, one would start at the lowest level violation (Level 1l for record keeping) and consider the highest level violation (Level V for preparing a fraudulent transaction or communicating results in a misleading or fraudulent manner).

Example 4A:
Assume in the above scenario that there are no aggravating circumstances and that the following mitigating circumstances exist:
- o There are no other complaints pending or previous disciplinary actions against the licensee and there is no indication that there has been a pattern of similar offenses.
- o It appears that the agent altered the report after the client signed it. It also appears that the agent deleted the transaction and supporting documentation from the work file.
- o The licensee acknowledged that he failed to supervise his agent.

Based on these circumstances, the sanction would be Level IV or possibly even Level 1ll.

4B: Assume in the above scenario that there are no mitigating circumstances and that the following aggravating circumstances exist:

- o There were several violations in the case.
- o The loan was made and went into foreclosure. The lender subsequently sold the property for $65,000.
- o Failure to supervise his agent was grossly negligent as he knew his agent had altered his reports in the past.
- o Based on these circumstances, the sanction would be Level V.

§73-35-1 Citation of chapter; license requirement

§73-35-3 Definitions; applicability of chapter

§73-35-4 Broker's price opinion; preparation, contents and use of opinion

§73-35-4.1 Disclosure of information concerning size or area of property involved in real estate transaction; liability; remedy for violation of section

§73-35-5 Real estate commission created; organization; seal; records

§73-35-6 Licenses for business entities

§73-35-7 Qualifications for license

§73-35-8 Nonresident's license; application

§73-35-9 Application for license

§73-35-10 Background investigation required of applicants for real estate broker's, real estate salesperson's, or nonresident's license

§73-35-11 Nonresident may not act except in cooperation with licensed broker of state

§73-35-13 Written exam requirement; exemption for license of another state; reciprocity

§73-35-14 Real estate schools; regulation by commission

§73-35-14.1 Standards for real estate schools

§73-35-14.2 Standards for instructors

§73-35-14.3 Course content

§73-35-14.4 Distance learning courses

§73-35-14.5 Temporary licenses; post-license education

§73-35-15 Location of business and responsible broker to be designated

§73-35-16 Real estate licensees required to obtain errors and omissions insurance coverage; persons required to submit proof of errors and omissions insurance; minimum requirements of group policy issued to the commission; public bid for group insurance contract; requirements for independent coverage; rules and regulations

§73-35-17 Fees

§73-35-18 License renewal; continuing education requirements; exemptions; rules and regulations; Reinstatement of expired license

§73-35-19 Real estate license fund

§73-35-21 Grounds for refusing to issue or suspending or revoking license; hearing

§73-35-23 Powers of commission as to violations; hearings upon revocation; subpoena

§73-35-25 Appeals

§73-35-27 Duties of commission

§73-35-29 Administrator to give bond

§73-35-31 Penalties for violations of chapter

§73-35-33 License required to sue for compensation; suit by salesperson in own name

§73-35-35 Commission to adopt rules and regulations

§73-35-101 Short title

§73-35-103 Definitions

§73-35-105 Interest on Real Estate Broker's Escrow Accounts (IREBEA) program

§89-1-501 Applicability of real estate transfer disclosure requirement provisions

§89-1-503 Delivery of written statement required; indication of compliance; right of transferee to terminate for late delivery

§89-1-505 Limit on duties and liabilities with respect to information required or delivered

§89-1-507 Approximation of certain information required to be disclosed; information subsequently rendered inaccurate

§89-1-509 Form of seller's disclosure statement

§89-1-511 Disclosures to be made in good faith

§89-1-513 Provisions not exhaustive of items to be disclosed

§89-1-515 Amendment of disclosure

§89-1-517 Delivery of disclosure

§89-1-519 Agent; extent of agency

§89-1-521 Delivery of disclosure where more than one agent; inability of delivering broker to obtain disclosure document; notification to transferee of right to disclosure

§89-1-523 Noncompliance with disclosure requirements not to invalidate transfer; Liability for actual damages

§89-1-525 Enforcement by Mississippi Real Estate Commission

§89-1-527 Failure to disclose nonmaterial fact regarding property as site of death or felony crime, as site of act or occurrence having no effect on physical condition of property, or as being owned or occupied by persons affected or exposed to certain diseases; failure to disclose information provided or maintained on registration of sex offenders to define real estate brokers and real estate salespersons; and providing for the licensing, regulation, and supervision of resident or nonresident real estate brokers and real estate salespersons and their business; and providing penalties for violation.

BE IT ENACTED BY THE LEGISLATURE OF THE STATE OF MISSISSIPPI: TITLE 73. PROFESSIONS AND VOCATIONS CHAPTER 35. REAL ESTATE BROKERS IN GENERAL

§73-35-1. Citation of chapter; license requirement

This chapter shall be known, and cited, as "the Real Estate Brokers License Law of 1954"; and from and after May 6, 1954.

It shall be unlawful for any person, partnership, association or corporation to engage in or carry on, directly or indirectly, or to advertise or to hold himself, itself or themselves out as engaging in or carrying on the business, or act in the capacity of, a real estate broker, or a real estate salesperson, within this state, without first obtaining a license as a real estate broker or real estate salesperson.

§73-35-3. Definitions; applicability of chapter

"real estate broker" shall include all persons, partnerships, associations and corporations, foreign and domestic, who for a fee, commission or other valuable consideration, or who with the intention or expectation of receiving or collecting the same, list, sell, purchase, exchange, rent, lease, manage or auction any real estate, or the improvements thereon, including options; or who negotiate or attempt to negotiate any such activity; or who advertise or hold themselves out as engaged in

such activities; or who direct or assist in the procuring of a purchaser or prospect calculated or intended to result in a real estate transaction.

The term **"real estate broker"** shall also include any person, partnership, association or corporation employed by or on behalf of the owner or owners of lots or other parcels of real estate, at a stated salary or upon fee, commission or otherwise, to sell such real estate, or parts thereof, in lots or other parcels, including timesharing and condominiums, and who shall sell, exchange or lease, or offer or attempt or agree to negotiate the sale, exchange or lease of, any such lot or parcel of real estate.

(2)   The term **"real estate"** includes leaseholds as well as any and every interest or estate in land, including timesharing and condominiums, whether corporeal or incorporeal, freehold or non-freehold, and whether said property is situated in this state or elsewhere.

"Real estate" as used in this chapter shall not include oil, gas or mineral leases, nor shall it include any other mineral leasehold, mineral estate or mineral interest of any nature whatsoever.

(3)   One (1) act in consideration of or with the expectation or intention of, or upon the promise of, receiving compensation, by fee, commission or otherwise, in the performance of any act or activity.

(4)   The term **"real estate salesperson"** shall mean and include any person employed or engaged by or on behalf of a licensed real estate broker.

(5)   The term **"automated valuation method"** means any computerized model used by mortgage originators and secondary market issuers to determine the collateral worth of a mortgage secured by a consumer's principal dwelling.

(6)   The term **"broker price opinion"** means an estimate prepared by a real estate broker, agent, or salesperson that details the probable selling price of a particular piece of real estate property and provides a varying level of detail about the property's condition, market, and neighborhood, and information on comparable sales, but **does not include an automated valuation model.**

Exemptions from licensing requirements

(7)   Exempt from the licensing requirements shall be any person, partnership, association or corporation, who, as a bona fide owner, shall perform any aforesaid act with reference to property owned by them, or to the regular employees thereof who are on a stated salary, where such acts are performed in the regular course of business.

(8)   The provisions of this chapter shall not apply to: (a) Attorneys at law in the performance of primary or incidental duties as such attorneys at law.

(b) Any person holding in good faith a duly executed power of attorney from the owner, authorizing the final consummation and execution for the sale, purchase, leasing or exchange of real estate.

(c) The acts of any person while acting as a receiver, trustee, administrator, executor, guardian or under court order, or while acting under authority of a deed of trust or will.

(d) Public officers while performing their duties as such.

(e) Anyone dealing exclusively in oil and gas leases and mineral rights.

(9) Nothing in this chapter shall be construed to prohibit life insurance companies and their representatives from negotiating or attempting to negotiate loans secured by mortgages on real estate, nor shall these companies or their representatives be required to qualify as real estate brokers or agents.

(10) The provisions of this chapter shall not apply to the activities of mortgagees approved by the Federal Housing
Administration or the United States Department of Veterans Affairs, banks chartered under the laws of the State of Mississippi or the United States, savings and loan associations chartered under the laws of the State of Mississippi or the United States, licensees under the Small Loan Regulatory Law, and under the Small Loan Privilege Tax Law, being through, small business investment companies licensed by the Small Business Administration and chartered under the laws of the State of Mississippi, or any of their affiliates and subsidiaries,

related to the making of a loan secured by a lien on real estate or to the disposing of real estate acquired by foreclosure or in lieu of foreclosure or otherwise held as security.

No director, officer or employee of any such financial institution shall be required to qualify as a real estate broker or agent under this chapter when engaged in the aforesaid activities for and on behalf of such financial institution.

§73-35-4. Broker's price opinion; preparation, contents and use of opinion

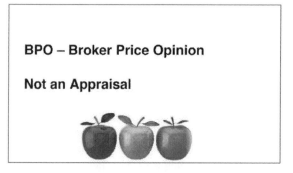

(1) A person licensed under this chapter **may prepare a broker's price opinion and charge and collect a fee** for such opinion if:

(a)   The license of that licensee is active and in good standing; and

(b)   The broker's price opinion meets the requirements of subsections (3) and (4) of this section.

(2) Notwithstanding any provision to the contrary, a person licensed under this chapter may prepare a broker's price opinion for:

(a) An existing or potential seller for the purposes of listing and selling a parcel of real property;

(b) An existing or potential buyer of a parcel of real property;

(c) A third-party making decisions or performing due diligence related to the potential listing, offering, sale, exchange, option, lease or acquisition price of a parcel of real property; or

(d) An existing or potential lienholder or other third party for any purpose other than as the basis to determine the value of a parcel of real property, for a mortgage loan origination, including first and second mortgages, refinances, or equity lines of credit.

(e) The provisions of this subsection do not preclude the preparation of a broker's price opinion to be used in conjunction with or in addition to an appraisal.

(3) A broker's price opinion prepared under the authority granted in this section shall be in writing and shall conform to the standards and guidelines published by a nationally recognized association of providers of broker price opinions.

The Mississippi Real Estate Commission shall promulgate regulations that are consistent with, but not limited to, the standards and guidelines of a nationally recognized association of providers of broker price opinions.

(4) A broker's price opinion shall be in writing and contain the following:

(a) A statement of the intended purpose of the price opinion;

(b) A brief description of the subject property and property interest to be priced;

(c) The basis of reasoning used to reach the conclusion of the price, including the applicable market data and/or capitalization computation;

(d) Any assumptions or limiting conditions;

(e) A disclosure of any existing or contemplated interest of the broker or salesperson issuing the opinion;

(f) The effective date of the price opinion;

(g) The name and signature of the broker or salesperson issuing the price opinion;

(h) The name of the real estate brokerage firm for which the broker or salesperson is acting; (i) The signature date;

(j) A disclaimer stating that, "This opinion is not an appraisal of the market value of the property and may not be used in lieu of an appraisal.

If an appraisal is desired, the services of a licensed or certified appraiser must be obtained.

This opinion may not be used by any party as the primary basis to determine the value of a parcel of real property for a mortgage loan origination, including first and second mortgages, refinances or equity lines of credit."; (k) A certification that the licensee is covered by errors and omissions insurance, to the extent required by state law, for all liability associated with the preparation of the broker's price opinion.

(5) If a broker's price opinion is submitted electronically or on a form supplied by the requesting party:
(a) A signature required by paragraph (g) of subsection (4) may be an electronic signature.
(b) A signature required by paragraph (g) of subsection (4) and the disclaimer required by paragraph (j) of subsection
(4) may be transmitted in a separate attachment if the electronic format or form supplied by the requesting party does not allow additional comments to be written by the licensee.
The electronic format or the form supplied by the requesting party must:
(i) Reference the existence of a separate attachment; and
(ii) Include a statement that the broker's price opinion is not complete without the attachment.

(6) Notwithstanding any provisions to the contrary, a person licensed pursuant to this chapter may not prepare a broker's price opinion for any purpose in lieu of an appraisal when an appraisal is required by federal or state statute.

A broker's price opinion which estimates value or worth of a parcel of real estate rather than sales price shall be deemed to be an appraisal and may not be prepared by a licensed broker or sales agent under the authority of their licensee but may only be prepared by a duly licensed appraiser and must meet the regulations promulgated by the Mississippi Real Estate Appraiser Licensing and Certification Board.

A broker's price opinion may not under any circumstances be referred to as a valuation or appraisal.

§73-35-4.1. Disclosure of information concerning size or area of property involved in real estate transaction; liability; remedy for violation of section

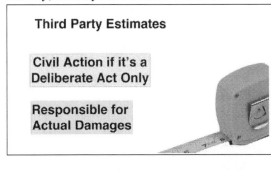

Third Party Estimates

Civil Action if it's a Deliberate Act Only

Responsible for Actual Damages

(1)(a) In connection with any real estate transaction, the size or area, in square footage or otherwise, of the subject property, if provided by any real estate licensee in accordance with paragraph (b)(i) and (ii), shall not be considered any warranty or guarantee of the size or area information, in square footage or otherwise, of the subject property.

(b)(i) If a real estate licensee provides any party to a real estate transaction with third-party information concerning the size or area, in square footage or otherwise, of the subject property involved in the transaction, the licensee shall identify the source of the information.

(ii) **"third-party information"** means:
1. An appraisal or any measurement information prepared by a licensed appraiser;
2. A surveyor developer's plan prepared by a licensed surveyor;
3. A tax assessor's public record; or
4. A builder's plan used to construct or market the property.

(c)   A real estate licensee has no duty to the seller or purchaser of real property to conduct an independent investigation of the size or area, in square footage or otherwise, of a subject property, or to independently verify the accuracy of any third-party information.

(d)   A real estate licensee who has complied with the requirements of this section, as applicable, shall have no further duties to the seller or purchaser of real property regarding disclosed or undisclosed property size or area information, and shall not be subject to liability to any party for any damages sustained with regard to any conflicting measurements or opinions of size or area, including exemplary or punitive damages.

(2)(a) If a real estate licensee has provided third-party information to any party to a real estate transaction concerning size or area of the subject real property, a party to the real estate transaction may recover damages from the licensee in a civil action only when a licensee knowingly violates the duty to disclose the source of the information as required in this section.

However, nothing in this section shall provide immunity from civil liability to any licensee who knowingly misrepresents the size or area of the subject real property.

(b)   The sole and exclusive civil remedy at common law or otherwise for a violation of this section by a real estate licensee shall be an action for actual damages suffered by the party as a result of such violation and shall not include exemplary or punitive damages.

(c)   For any real estate transaction commenced after July 1, 2013, any civil action brought pursuant to this section shall be commenced within two (2) years after the date of transfer of the subject real property.

Up to two years to sue an agent.

(d)   In any civil action brought pursuant to this section, the prevailing party shall be allowed court costs and reasonable attorney fees to be set by the court and collected as costs of the action.

(e)   A transfer of a possessory interest in real property subject to the provisions of this section may not be invalidated solely because of the failure of any person to comply with the provisions of this section.

(f)   The provisions of this section shall apply to, regulate and determine the rights, duties, obligations and remedies, at common law or otherwise, of the seller marketing the seller's real property for sale through a real estate licensee, and of the purchaser of real property offered for sale through a real estate licensee, with respect to disclosure of third-party information concerning the subject real property's size or area, in square footage or otherwise, and this section hereby supplants and abrogates all common-law liability, rights, duties, obligations and remedies of all parties therefor.

§73-35-5. Real estate commission created; organization; seal; records

(1) There is hereby created the Mississippi Real Estate Commission.

The commission shall consist of five (5) persons, to be appointed by the Governor with the advice and consent of the Senate.

Each appointee shall have been a resident and citizen of this state for at **least six (6) years prior to his appointment, and his vocation for at least five (5) years shall have been that of a real estate broker.**

One (1) member shall be appointed for the term of one (1) year; two (2) members for terms of two (2) years; two (2) members for terms of four (4) years; thereafter, the term of the members of said commission shall be for four (4) years and until their successors are appointed and qualify.

There shall be at least one (1) commissioner from each congressional district, as such districts are constituted as of July 1, 2002.

The commissioners appointed from each of the congressional districts shall be bona fide residents of the district from which each is appointed.

One (1) additional commissioner shall be appointed without regard to residence in any particular congressional district.

Members to fill vacancies shall be appointed by the Governor for the unexpired term.

The Governor may remove any commissioner for cause.

The State of Mississippi shall not be required to furnish office space for such commissioners.

This section shall not affect persons who are members of the Real Estate Commission. Such members shall serve out their respective terms, upon the expiration of which the provisions of this section shall take effect.

Nothing shall be construed as prohibiting the reappointment of any member of the said commission.

(2) The commission shall organize by selecting from its members a chairman and may do all things necessary and convenient for carrying into effect the provisions of this chapter and may from time to time promulgate rules and regulations.

Each member of the commission shall receive per diem and his actual and necessary expenses incurred in the performance of duties pertaining to his office.

(3) The commission shall adopt a seal by which it shall authenticate its proceedings.
Copies of all records and papers in the office of the commission, duly certified and authenticated by the seal of said commission, shall be received in evidence in all courts equally and with like effect as the original.

All records kept in the office of the commission under authority of this chapter shall be open to public inspection except pending investigative files.

§73-35-6. Licenses for business entities

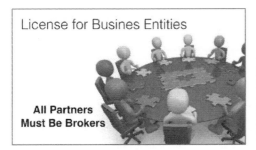

A corporation, partnership, company or association shall be granted a license when individual broker's licenses have been issued to every member, owner, partner or officer of such partnership, company, association or corporation who actively participates in its brokerage business and when any required fee is paid.

Qualifications for license

Licenses shall be granted only to persons who present, and to corporations, partnerships, companies or associations whose officers, associates or partners present satisfactory proof to the commission that they are trustworthy and competent to transact the business of a real estate broker or real estate salesperson in such manner as to safeguard the interests of the public.

Resident license as a real estate broker

Except as otherwise provided in this section, every person who applies for a resident license as a real estate broker: (a) shall be age twenty-one (21) years or over, and have his legal domicile in the State of Mississippi at the time he applies; (b) shall be subject to the jurisdiction of this state, subject to the income tax laws and other excise laws thereof, subject to the road and bridge privilege tax laws thereof;	**Trustworthy and Competent** **21 Years or Over** **Pay Taxes and Vote in Mississippi** **120 Hours** **Pass the Exam** 

(c) shall not be an elector in any other state;

(d) shall have held a license as an active real estate salesperson for twelve (12) months prior to making application for the broker's examination hereafter specified;

(e) shall have successfully completed a minimum of one hundred twenty (120) hours of courses in real estate as hereafter specified; and

(f) shall have successfully completed the real estate broker's examination as hereafter specified; and

(g) shall have successfully been cleared for licensure by the commission's background investigation

(h) sign a form under penalty of perjury stating that the applicant will not hire any real estate salespersons for thirtysix (36) months from the date of approval of his or her active real estate salesperson's license.

NOTICE

APPLICANTS FOR REAL ESTATE BROKER'S LICENSE

Miss. Code Ann. §73-5-7 (Amended, Effective July 1, 2020)

In its 2020 Regular Session, the Mississippi Legislature enacted an amendment to Miss. Code Ann. §73-5-7 which made changes to the experience requirements for persons seeking to be licensed as a real estate broker in Mississippi, including certain restrictions on new broker licensee employment of real estate salespersons. The legislation was approved by Governor Tate Reeves and became effective July 1, 2020. As amended, the relevant statutory provisions for obtaining a real estate broker's license now include:

12 months licensure as Salesperson prior to application for Broker's license and 36 month restriction on employment of Salespersons

- An applicant for a broker's license must have held an active license as a real estate salesperson for a minimum of twelve (12) months **prior** to making application. The required period of active licensure as a real estate salesperson may be satisfied by evidence of **cumulative** period(s) of active licensure as a real estate salesperson totaling a minimum of twelve (12) months prior to application for licensure as a real estate broker.

  - *Broker Certification Form*
    Applicant must execute the Broker Certification Form (available on Commission website) and swear/affirm, under penalty of perjury, the broker will not hire any real estate salespersons for a period of thirty-six (36) months following the date of approval of the broker's original (active) salesperson's license.

Exclusions

- The thirty-six (36) month restriction on employment of real estate salespersons shall not apply to brokers who have held a license as an active real estate salesperson for a **cumulative** period of thirty-six (36) months **prior** to making application for the broker's license examination.

- The thirty-six (36) month restriction on employment of real estate salespersons shall not apply to brokers who have completed a minimum of one hundred fifty (150) classroom hours of real estate courses, which courses are acceptable for credit toward a degree at a college or university as approved by the Southern Association of Colleges and Schools.

The real estate commission shall create a standard form to comply with the requirements.

(h) the real estate broker is authorized to employ any number of real estate salespersons.

(i) shall not apply to an applicant who seeks to hire a real estate salesperson in less than thirty-six (36) months from the date of approval of his or her active real estate salesperson's license.

Any person who desires to hire a real estate salesperson in less than thirty-six (36) months from the date of approval of his or her active real estate salesperson's license shall:

(a) be age twenty-one (21) years or over, and have his or her legal domicile in the State of Mississippi at the time he or she applies;

(b) be subject to the jurisdiction of this state, subject to the income tax laws and other excise laws and subject to the **road and bridge privilege tax laws**;

(c) not be an elector in any other state;

(d) have held a license as an active real estate salesperson for thirty-six (36) months prior to making application for the broker's examination;

(e) have successfully completed a minimum of one hundred twenty (120) hours of courses in real estate;

(f) have successfully completed the real estate broker's examination as hereafter specified; and

(g) have successfully been cleared for licensure by the commission's **background investigation** .

An applicant who has not held an active real estate salesperson's license for a period of at least thirty-six (36) months prior to submitting an application shall have successfully completed a minimum of **one hundred fifty (150) classroom hours in real estate courses**, which courses are acceptable for credit toward a degree at a college or university as approved by the Southern Association of Colleges and Schools.

Resident license as a real estate salesperson

Every applicant for a resident license as a real estate salesperson shall be **age eighteen (18) years or over,** shall be a bona fide resident of the State of Mississippi prior to filing his application, shall have successfully completed a minimum of sixty (60) hours in courses in real estate as hereafter specified, and shall have successfully completed the real estate salesperson's examination as hereafter specified.

The residency requirements set forth in this section shall not apply to those licensees of other states who qualify and obtain nonresident licenses in this state.

The commission is authorized to exempt from such prelicensing educational requirements, in whole or in part, a real estate licensee of **another state** who desires to obtain a license under this chapter, provided that the prelicensing educational requirements in the other state are determined by the commission to be equivalent to prelicensing educational requirements in this state and provided that such state extends this same privilege or exemption to Mississippi real estate licensees.

The issuance of a license by reciprocity to a military-trained applicant or military spouse shall be approved.

§73-35-8. Nonresident's license; application

(1) A nonresident may apply for a nonresident's license in Mississippi provided the individual is

(i) a licensed broker in another state or

(ii)   is a broker/salesperson or salesperson affiliated with a resident or nonresident Mississippi broker or

(iii) is a nonresident who applies for a broker's license and who will maintain an office in Mississippi.

The nonresident broker need not maintain a place of business within Mississippi provided he is regularly actively engaged in the real estate business and maintains a place of business in the other state.

The nonresident licensee or applicant shall be subject to all the provisions of MREC except for the residency requirement and approved equivalent pre-licensing education.

(2)   Every nonresident applicant shall file a statement of irrevocable consent with the Real Estate Commission that legal actions may be commenced against him in the proper court of any county of this state in which a cause of action may arise or in which the plaintiff may reside by service of process or pleading authorized by the laws of this state, by the Secretary of State of Mississippi, or by any member of the commission or chief executive officer thereof, the consent stipulating that the service of process or pleading shall be taken in all courts to be valid and binding as if personal service had been made upon the nonresident licensee in this state.

The consent shall be duly acknowledged.

Every nonresident licensee shall consent to have any hearings conducted by the commission at a place designated by the commission.

(3)   Any service of process or pleading shall be served on the executive officer of the commission by filing duplicate copies, one (1) of which shall be filed in the office of the commission and the other forwarded by certified mail to the last known principal address of the nonresident licensee against whom such process or pleading is directed.

No default in any such action shall be taken except upon an affidavit of certification of the commission or the executive officer thereof that a copy of the process or pleading was mailed to the defendant as herein provided, and no default judgment shall be taken in any such action or proceeding until thirty (30) days after the mailing of process or pleading to the defendant.

(4)   An applicant shall sign an agreement to cooperate with any investigation of the applicant's real estate brokerage activities which the commission may undertake.

(5)   Each applicant for a nonresident license must qualify in all respects, including education, examination, and fees, as an applicant who is a resident of Mississippi with the exception of the residency requirement and approved equivalent pre-licensing education.

(6)   A certification from the Executive Officer of the Real Estate Commission in the state in which the nonresident maintains his principal place of business shall be required.

An applicant shall disclose all states in which he has held a real estate license and furnish a certification of licensure from that state or states.

(7)   The applicant/broker shall obtain an appropriate Mississippi license for the firm through which he intends to operate as a broker.

(8)   Any nonresident broker, broker-salesperson and salesperson shall meet Mississippi continuing education requirements after becoming licensed just as any resident licensee.

(9)   A broker or salesperson licensed in this state, on inactive status in good standing and no longer a resident of this state, may, after meeting other requirements for nonresident licensees, make application for a nonresident license without being required to meet current prelicensing educational requirements at the time of application or having to sit for the examination in order to obtain the equivalent nonresident license.

(10)   A nonresident licensee in good standing who changes his legal domicile to the State of Mississippi may obtain a resident license equivalent to his nonresident license without meeting the current educational requirements or sitting for the examination, provided other requirements set forth for residents of the state are met.

(11)   A nonresident licensee may utilize the inactive status for his license under the same requirements as a resident licensee, including but not limited to, continuing education requirements, and ceasing active status under a licensed nonresident broker.

§73-35-9. Application for license

(1) Every applicant for a real estate broker's license shall apply therefor in writing upon blanks prepared by the commission and shall provide such data and information as the commission may require.

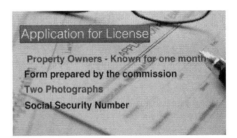

(2) Such application shall be accompanied by the **recommendation of at least three (3) citizens who have been property owners for at least three (3) years, who have known the** *applicant for three (3) years, and who are not related to the applicant*, **certifying that the applicant bears a good reputation for honesty and trustworthiness and recommending that a license be granted to the applicant.**

(3) Every applicant for a salesperson's license shall apply therefor in writing **upon blanks prepared by the commission** and shall provide such data and information as the commission may require.

(4) Each application for license shall also be accompanied by **two (2) photographs** of the applicant in such form as the commission may prescribe.

(5) Each application or filing made under this section shall include **the social security number(s)** of the applicant.

(6) Beginning on July 1, 2019, each application for a license must include a current email address for the applicant.

§73-35-10. Background investigation required of applicants for real estate broker's, real estate salesperson's, or nonresident's license

(1)(a) To qualify for a Mississippi real estate broker's license or a Mississippi resident license as a real estate salesperson, or a nonresident's license in Mississippi, an applicant must have successfully been cleared for licensure through an investigation that shall consist of a determination that the applicant does not possess a background which calls into question public trust.

(2), and verification that the prospective licensee is not guilty of or in violation of any statutory ground for denial of licensure.

(b)   To assist the commission in conducting its licensure investigation, from and after July 1, 2016, all applicants for a Mississippi real estate broker's license, or a Mississippi resident license as a real estate salesperson, or a nonresident's license in Mississippi, and all applicants for renewal of any real estate license shall undergo a fingerprint-based criminal history records check of the Mississippi central criminal database and the Federal Bureau of Investigation criminal history database.

Each applicant shall submit a full set of the applicant's fingerprints in a form and manner prescribed by the commission, which shall be forwarded to the *Mississippi Department of Public Safety* (department) and the *Federal Bureau of Investigation Identification Division.*

(c)   Any and all state or national criminal history records information obtained by the commission that is not already a matter of public record shall be deemed nonpublic and confidential information restricted to the exclusive use of the commission, its members, officers, investigators, agents and attorneys in evaluating the applicant's eligibility or disqualification for licensure, and shall be exempt.

Except when introduced into evidence in a hearing before the commission to determine licensure, no such information or records related thereto shall, except with the written consent of the applicant or by order of a court of competent jurisdiction, be released or otherwise disclosed by the commission to any other person or agency.

(d)   The commission shall provide to the department the fingerprints of the applicant, any additional information that may be required by the department, and a form signed by the applicant consenting to the check of the criminal records and to the use of the fingerprints and other identifying information required by the state or national repositories.

(e)   The commission shall charge and collect from the applicant, in addition to all other applicable fees and costs, such amount as may be incurred by the commission in requesting and obtaining state and national criminal history records information on the applicant.

(2)(a) The commission must ensure that applicants for real estate licenses do not possess a background that could call into question public trust. An applicant found by the commission to possess a background which calls into question the applicant's ability to maintain public trust shall not be issued a real estate license.

(b) The commission shall not issue a real estate license if:
(i) The applicant has had a real *estate license revoked in any governmental jurisdiction within the five-year period immediately preceding the date of the application;*

(ii) The applicant has been convicted of, or pled guilty or nolo contendere to, a felony in a domestic or foreign court:
1. During the five-year period immediately preceding the date of the application for licensing;
or 2. At any time preceding the date of the application, if such felony involved an act of *fraud, dishonesty or a breach of trust, or money laundering.*

(c) The commission shall adopt rules and regulations necessary to implement, administer and enforce the provisions.

(d) The requirement of a criminal background check shall not apply to persons who have held a broker's or salesperson's license in this state for at least twenty-five (25) years and who are older than seventy (70) years of age.

Salesperson's Application

INSTRUCTIONS FOR COMPLETING THE RESIDENT SALESPERSON LICENSE APPLICATION

NOTE: This form is ONLY to be used by MISSISSIPPI residents.

Questions 1 – 3: This is the applicant's personal information. All correspondence from MREC is sent to the applicant's home address until they become licensed. If you cannot receive mail at your residence, you **must** provide your mailing address IN ADDITION TO your residential address. You must provide a working phone number for yourself. We must also have your email address. Be sure to provide a valid email address you have access to and regularly check in the event MREC should need to contact you.

Question 4: The broker's name must be listed. If the broker has a company license, also list it.

Question 5: If you have ONLY been licensed in Mississippi, **DO NOT** request a certificate of licensure. **ONLY** send a certificate of licensure if you are or were licensed in another state! All certificates of licensure submitted to MREC must be received by MREC within 60 days of the notary date.

Question 6: Should be self-explanatory.

Questions 7 – 8: If you have applied before, and were not licensed because your application expired or you failed the state exam, that does NOT constitute being denied a license or a license being revoked.

Questions 9 – 11: Should be self-explanatory. If you plan to have a job in addition to real estate, you must list it on question 11.

Question 12: FULL addresses should be listed along with the business person's name (not their company name). Do not use relatives.

Questions 13 – 14: If you answer 'yes' to any of these questions, you **MUST** provide a SEPARATE statement regarding why you answered 'yes.'
Regarding arrests and judgments, "all facts" include:
- The date of arrest and result. Any jail time and/or probation should be listed with dates of when it was or will be completed. Both **misdemeanors** and **felonies** should be disclosed.
- The date of the judgment, the amount, and when it was or will be paid in full.

Questions 15 - 21: Note that some questions have multiple parts. Be sure to answer all questions fully.
- If you are currently in bankruptcy, you must send a copy of your petition/schedule. If you have been discharged, you ONLY need to send a copy of the discharge paper.

Question 22: This is for your PERSONAL bank accounts.

Recommendation of Three Real Estate Owners: If you do not live in the state of Mississippi or haven't lived in Mississippi for long, you are not expected to know three Mississippi real estate owners. You should have people who have owned property for at least three (3) years sign this. It is preferable that they be in your state, but not required. You may copy this section if you need to mail it to someone. Just be sure to include all ORIGINALS with your application to MREC. DO NOT USE THE SAME INDIVIDUALS USED IN QUESTION 12!!

Rev. 12/2016

To Be Completed by Employing Broker: The broker must be licensed in Mississippi, and MUST complete the section for comments regarding the applicant's qualifications, integrity and character. One word, the applicant's license number, and the like are NOT acceptable.

Photos of applicant: You MUST include a full face and a profile (side view) face photo with your application. The photos are not required to be any certain size, but the MUST be clear.

BEFORE MAILING, BE SURE THE FOLLOWING HAVE BEEN ADDRESSED:

■ Application **MUST** be typed or printed. If it is printed, be sure handwriting is VERY CLEAR. MREC is not responsible for any misprints due to illegible handwriting.

■ **ALL** questions have been answered in their entirety.

■ The application fee is included.

■ Your qualifying education certificates or an original college transcript (that includes real estate education) are attached. If you did not take college real estate courses, it is not necessary to send a college transcript.

■ The application must be notarized and must be received by MREC within 60 days of the notary date.

■ If you are currently in bankruptcy, you must send a copy of your petition/schedule. If you have been discharged, you ONLY need to send a copy of the discharge paper.

Rev. 12/2016

Mississippi Real Estate Commission

LeFleur's Bluff Tower, Suite 300
4780 I-55 North, Jackson, MS 39211
OR
Post Office Box 12685
Jackson, MS 39236-2685
(601) 321-6970 – Telephone * (601) 321-6955 – Fax
www.mrec.ms.gov

$120.00 FEE

APPLICATION FOR RESIDENT SALESPERSON LICENSE
(TYPE OR PRINT CLEARLY)

1. Legal name of Applicant _____ Age_____ Sex_____

   Name as you want to appear on your license: _____

2. Residence Address of Applicant_____
   _____(Number/Street)_____(City)_____

   ____(County)_____(State)_____(Zip)_____(Home Phone)_____(Other Phone)____

   Email address _____

3. Marital Status _____ Spouse's Name _____

4. Name Of Employer to be designated on license_____
   _____(Broker, Company, etc.)_____

4A. Physical address of Employer_____
   _____(Street and Number)_____

   _____(P.O. Box)_____

   ____(City)_____(County)_____(State)_____(Zip Code)_____(Telephone Number)____

5. Have you ever held a real estate License in Mississippi or any other state? Yes_____ No_____
   (If answer is yes, please attach certification of licensure.)

   A Broker_____ Where_____
   _____(Street and No.)____(City)____(County)____(State)__(From)__(To)__
   A Salesperson_____ Where_____
   _____(Street and No.)____(City)____(County)____(State)__(From)__(To)__

6. Have you ever before applied for a real estate License in the State of Mississippi? Yes_____ No_____

7. Have you ever been denied a real estate license in this or any other state? Yes____ No____ (If answer is "Yes" furnish statement of details)

8. Has ANY license ever held by you been revoked or suspended, in this or any other state? Yes____ No____ (If answer is "Yes" furnish statement of details) (This refers on any license for any business or profession regulated by law in this or any other state, or district or possession of the United States.)

9. What has been your business or occupation for past five years? Give places where employed for sixty days or more, and account for entire time. If self-employed, list nature of business and address.

   _____ From_____ To_____
   (Employer) (Street & Number) (City) (State) (Mo. & Yr.) (Mo. & Yr.)

   _____ From_____ To_____
   (Employer) (Street & Number) (City) (State) (Mo. & Yr.) (Mo. & Yr.)

   _____ From_____ To_____
   (Employer) (Street & Number) (City) (State) (Mo. & Yr.) (Mo. & Yr.)

   _____ From_____ To_____
   (Employer) (Street & Number) (City) (State) (Mo. & Yr.) (Mo. & Yr.)

Rev. 12/2016

Page 1

10. Years Education (Circle highest school year completed)   1 2 3 4 5 6 7 8 9 10 11 12 13 14 15 16 17 18 19 20

11. What business other than real estate, do you expect to engage in, and what is the address of such business? ____
_____

12. Give the **names and address of three** business persons who have known you for the last five years. Relatives should not be listed.
_____
_____
_____

13. Have you ever been convicted of any criminal offense or entered a plea of guilty/nolo contend ere? Yes_____ No_____
                                                                (If answer is "**Yes**" furnish a detail statement of all facts)
14. Has anyone every obtained a judgment against you? Yes_____ No_____
              (If answer is "**Yes**" furnish a detail statement of all facts)
15. Are you an American Citizen? Yes_____ No_____

16. Have you ever declared bankruptcy? Yes_____ No_____ (If answer is "**Yes**" furnish petition for voluntary bankruptcy schedules
                                    and discharge)
17. When were you born? _____ Where? _____
              (Mo.   Day   Yr.)   (City)   (County)   (State)

18. How long, immediately prior to date of the execution of this application, have you been a resident of Mississippi? _____

19. Social Security Number: _____

20. Did you file a Mississippi Income Tax return last year? Yes_____ No_____
      If answer is "No" please explain: _____

21. Do you have a Mississippi Driver's license? Yes_____ No_____ If "**Yes**" furnish number_____

22. Give the name and addresses of the banks you have accounts with.

_____
        (Bank)   (Street & Number)   (City)   (Zip Code)

( ) Checking   ( ) Savings   ( ) Loans   ( ) Credit Cards

_____
        (Bank)   (Street & Number)   (City)   (Zip Code)

( ) Checking   ( ) Savings   ( ) Loans   ( ) Credit Cards

AFFIDAVIT
(Read Carefully)

The undersigned, in making this application to the Mississippi Real Estate Commission for license to carry on the business of real estate Salesperson under the provisions of the Mississippi Real Estate Broker's License Act of 1954, as Amended, swears (or affirms) that he or she has read and is thoroughly familiar with the provisions of the aforementioned Act, and Rules and Regulations issued by the Commission, and agrees to comply fully with them. The undersigned further swears (or affirms) that all of the information given in this application is true and correct to the best of his or her knowledge and belief. Under Section 73-35-5 (3) all records kept in the office of the Commission are a matter of Public Record. Therefore, this application and other information submitted to this Commission may be reviewed by members of the general public under reasonable rules and regulations as shall be prescribed the Commission. I hereby authorize financial institutions, educational institutions, or other agencies, public or private, federal or state, to release any information contained in their files to the Mississippi Real Estate Commission.

Signature of Applicant _____

Subscribed and sworn to before me, this _____ day of _____ 20 _____

My commission expires:_____   _____
                                                        Notary Public   County   State

Page 2

Rev. 12/2016

RECOMMENDATION OF THREE REAL ESTATE OWNERS
(Must be in addition to references listed on preceding page)

The following recommendation must be signed by three citizens, real estate owners, not related to the applicant, who own real estate. **(DO NOT USE THE SAME INDIVIDUALS AS USED IN ITEM 12.)**

I certify that I own real estate and I have known the applicant for at least 1 month, and that the applicant named herein, is a resident of Mississippi, bears a good reputation for honesty, competency, and fair dealings. I recommend that a license be granted to applicant to engage in the business of real estate as stated in the business of real estate as stated in the foregoing application.

Signature_____ Address_____
                                                        (Street and Number)   (City) (State)

Print Name _____

Signature_____ Address_____
                                                        (Street and Number)   (City) (State)

Print Name _____

Signature_____ Address_____
                                                        (Street and Number)   (City) (State)

Print Name _____

TO BE COMPLETED BY RESPONSIBLE (SPONSORING) BROKER **IF APPLICABLE.**

Responsible Broker's comments regarding applicant's qualifications, integrity and character. _____

_____

_____

_____

_____

_____

AFFIDAVIT OF SPONSORING BROKER
(Read Carefully)

The undersigned hereby swears (or affirms) that I am the sponsoring broker of the applicant, that , in my opinion, the applicant is honest and trustworthy, that I have thoroughly discussed with the applicant the conditions under which the applicant's license may be revoked or suspended under the provisions of Section 73-35-21, Mississippi Code of 1972, as amended, as well as the Rules and Regulations of the Mississippi Real Estate Commission and am convinced that the applicant understands said provisions and Rules and Regulations, and hereby recommend that a license be granted to the applicant.

_____
Signature of Sponsoring Broker

Subscribed and sworn to before me, this _____ day of _____ 20_____

My Commission expires_____

_____
Notary Public   County   State

Page 3

Rev. 12/2016

REAL ESTATE EDUCATION

List below courses you have completed to satisfy the educational requirements. The original certificate, grade form or transcript, certified copy thereof, must be attached (Copies unless certified can not be accepted.)

Course	Provider/Institution	No. of Hours
_____	_____	_____
_____	_____	_____

ATTACH PHOTOS BELOW

**Full Face
View**

**Profile Face
View**

Application **MUST** be accompanied by the following items:

1. College transcripts or Certificates of Completion from Mississippi Approved Pre-Licensing Education Provider

2. Proper Fee of $120.00

3. Photos – Full Face and Profile Views

4. Make sure signatures are **NOTARIZED** with seal where required.

5. **ALL** questions must be answered to ensure prompt processing **if applicable**.

6. If you have held or hold a Real Estate License in any other state, you **MUST** enclose a *Certification of Licensure* **(NOT A COPY OF ANY REAL ESTATE LICENSE).**

Rev. 12/2016

Broker's Application

INSTRUCTIONS FOR COMPLETING THE RESIDENT BROKER LICENSE APPLICATION

NOTE: This form is ONLY to be used by MISSISSIPPI residents. To qualify for broker, the applicant must be licensed as a Mississippi salesperson on ACTIVE status for a minimum of twelve (12) months immediately prior to applying for a broker license. If the applicant is not currently licensed as a salesperson, college real estate education is required to qualify for a broker license.

Questions 1 – 2: This is the applicant's personal information. All correspondence from MREC is sent to the applicant's home address until they become licensed. If you cannot receive mail at your residence, you **must** provide your mailing address IN ADDITION TO your residential address. We must also have your email address. Be sure to provide a valid email address you have access to and regularly check in the event MREC should need to contact you.

Question 3: This is the address where the applicant will be conducting business. It must be a physical address. Post office boxes are not allowed.

Questions 4 – 5: Should be self-explanatory.

Question 6: If you have ONLY been licensed in Mississippi, **DO NOT** request a certificate of licensure. **ONLY** send a certificate of licensure if you are or were licensed in another state! All certificates of licensure submitted to MREC must be received by MREC within 60 days of the notary date.

Question 7: Should be self-explanatory.

Questions 8 – 9: If you have applied before, and were not licensed because your application expired or you failed the state exam, that does NOT constitute being denied a license or a license being revoked.

Questions 10 – 11: Should be self-explanatory. If you plan to have a job in addition to real estate, you must list it on question 11.

Questions 12 – 13: If you answer 'yes' to any of these questions, you **MUST** provide a SEPARATE statement regarding why you answered 'yes.'
  Regarding arrests and judgments, "all facts" include:
  - The date of arrest and result. Any jail time and/or probation should be listed with dates of when it was or will be completed. Both **misdemeanors** and **felonies** should be disclosed.
  - The date of the judgment, the amount, and when it was or will be paid in full.
  - If you are currently in bankruptcy, you must send a copy of your petition/schedule. If you have been discharged, you ONLY need to send a copy of the discharge paper.

Questions 14 - 21: Note that some questions have multiple parts. Be sure to answer all questions fully.

Question 22: This is for your PERSONAL bank accounts.

Recommendation of Three Real Estate Owners: Should be self-explanatory.

Photos of applicant: You MUST include a full face and a profile (side view) face photo with your application. The photos are not required to be any certain size, but the MUST be clear.

Rev. 12/2016

BEFORE MAILING, BE SURE THE FOLLOWING HAVE BEEN ADDRESSED:

- Application **MUST** be typed or printed. If it is printed, be sure handwriting is VERY CLEAR. MREC is not responsible for any misprints due to illegible handwriting.

- **ALL** questions have been answered in their entirety.

- The application fee is included.

- Your qualifying education certificates are attached. It is not necessary to send your sales pre- or post-license certificates again or a copy of your sales license. Your broker pre-licensing education certificates are all that is needed. If you are not currently licensed as a salesperson and are qualifying by college education, you must include an original transcript.

- If you are currently licensed as a broker/salesperson under another responsible broker, you must include a letter of recommendation from your current broker. The letter should be less than 60 days old when received by MREC. Send the original letter.

- The letter from your bank should be in reference to your personal banking accounts (not business accounts), confirm the banking relationship, and verify that the applicant is in good standing with the bank. The letter should be less than 60 days old when received by MREC. Send the original letter.

- The application must be notarized and must be received by MREC within 60 days of the notary date.

- You **MUST** send the **ORIGINAL** application. A copy or scan (even in color) will NOT be accepted. Also, all signatures must be the **ORIGINAL** signatures. Digital signatures are NOT acceptable.

Rev. 12/2016

Mississippi Real Estate Commission
LeFleur's Bluff Tower, Suite 300
4780 I-55 North, Jackson, MS 39211
OR
Post Office Box 12685
Jackson, MS 39236-2685
(601) 321-6970 – Telephone * (601) 321-6955 – Fax
www.mrec.ms.gov

$150.00 FEE

APPLICATION FOR RESIDENT BROKER'S LICENSE
(TYPE OR PRINT CLEARLY)

1. Legal name of Applicant _____ Age _____ Sex _____

    Name as you want to appear on your license _____

    Marital Status _____ Spouse's Name _____

2. Residence Address of Applicant _____
                     (Number/Street)   *(City)*   *(State)*

    _____ _____   _____ _____
       (County)   *(Zip)*   *(Home Phone)*   *(Other Phone)*

3. Physical Business Address of Applicant _____
                         (Street/Bldg/Suite Number)   *(City)*   *(County)*

    _____ _____ _____ _____ _____ _____
       (PO Box)   *(City)*   *(State)*   *(Zip)*   *(Office Phone)*   *(Office Fax)*

    Email address _____

4. Do you understand the requirements of the real estate license laws as to maintaining a definite place of business within Mississippi and prominent display of your Mississippi Real Estate license? _____

5. Do you certify that if granted a license, you will comply with the requirements in item # 4? _____ Yes _____ No

6. Have you ever held a real estate license as a:

    BROKER _____ Where? _____
                             (Street/Bldg/Suite Number)   *(City)*   *(County)*   *(State)*   *(From)*   *(To)*
    SALESPERSON _____ Where? _____
                             (Street/Bldg/Suite Number)   *(City)*   *(County)*   *(State)*   *(From)*   *(To)*
    (Please attach certification of licensure.)

7. Have you ever applied for a real estate license in the state of Mississippi? _____ Yes _____ No

8. Have you ever been denied a real estate license in this or any other state? _____ Yes _____ No
    (If Yes, furnish a statement of details)

9. Has ANY license ever held by you been revoked or suspended in this or any other state? _____ Yes _____ No
    (This refers to any license for any business or profession regulated by law in this or any other state, district or possession of the United States. If YES, furnish a statement of details)

10. a. What has been your business or occupation for the past five (5) years? Give places where employed for sixty (60) days or more and account for entire time. If self-employed, list nature of your business and address.

    _____ From _____ To _____
    (Employer) *(Street & Number)* *(City)* *(State)*   *(Month/Year)*   *(Month/Year)*

    _____ From _____ To _____
    (Employer) *(Street & Number)* *(City)* *(State)*   *(Month/Year)*   *(Month/Year)*

    _____ From _____ To _____

Rev. 12/2016

37

10.b. Give complete summary of real estate experience, advise whether or not you have operated under a City or County Real Estate Privilege Licensure, where obtained and the date or dates of purchase. Disclose all states in which you have held or currently hold a real estate license and furnish a Certification of Licensure from the state or states.

_____
_____
_____

11. What business, other than real estate, do you expect to engage in and what is the address thereof? _____

12. State if you have ever been convicted of any criminal offense. _____ Yes _____ No *(If Yes, furnish details)* ___ Misdemeanor ___ Felony

13.a. Has anyone ever obtained a judgment against you in any court involving real estate? _____ Yes _____ No *(If Yes, furnish details)*

13.b. Taken bankruptcy? _____ Yes _____ No *(If Yes, furnish petition for voluntary bankruptcy, schedules and discharge)*

14. Are you an American Citizen? _____ Yes _____ No If not, how long have you lived in the United States? _____

15. When were you born? _____ Where _____
     (Mo. Day Yr.) *(City)* *(State)* *(County)*

16. How long, immediately prior to date of execution of this application, have you been a resident of Mississippi? _____

17. Give the name of the city, county and state where you are registered to vote. _____
     (City) *(State)* *(County)*

18. Social Security Number _____

19. Do you have a Mississippi Driver's license? _____ Yes _____ No If Yes, furnish number _____
     If No, please explain _____

20. Have you ever purchases a Mississippi Car Tag? _____ Yes _____ No If Yes, furnish number _____

21. Did you file a Mississippi Income Tax Return last year? _____ Yes _____ No
     If No, please explain _____

22. Give the name and addresses of the banks you have accounts with.

_____
(Bank) *(Street & Number)* *(City)* *(State)* *(Zip)*

( ) Checking ( ) Savings ( ) Loans ( ) Credit Cards

_____
(Bank) *(Street & Number)* *(City)* *(State)* *(Zip)*

( ) Checking ( ) Savings ( ) Loans ( ) Credit Cards

_____
(Bank) *(Street & Number)* *(City)* *(State)* *(Zip)*

( ) Checking ( ) Savings ( ) Loans ( ) Credit Cards

AFFIDAVIT
(READ CAREFULLY)

The undersigned, in making this application to the Mississippi Real Estate Commission for license to carry on the business of real estate Broker under the provisions of the Mississippi Real Estate Broker's License Act of 1954, as Amended, swears (or affirms) that he/she has read and is thoroughly familiar with the provisions of the aforementioned Act, and Rules and Regulations issued by the Commission, and agrees to comply fully with them. The undersigned further swears (or affirms) that all of the information given in this application is true and correct to the best of his/her knowledge and belief. Under Section 73-35-5 (3) his/her application and other information submitted to this Commission may be reviewed by members of the general public under reasonable rule and regulations shall be prescribed by the Commission. I hereby authorize any financial institution, educational institution, or any other agency, public or private, federal or state, to release any information contained in their files to the Mississippi Real Estate Commission.

Signature of Applicant _____

Subscribed and sworn to before me, this _____ day of _____ 20_____.

My Commission expires _____
     Notary Public County State

Rev. 12/2016 **Page 2**

RECOMMENDATION OF THREE REAL ESTATE OWNERS

The following recommendations must be signed by three (3) citizens who have been property owners for at least three (3) years and who have known the applicant for at least three (3) years.

"I certify that I am a citizen of Mississippi, have been a property owner for at least three (3) years, and I am not related to the applicant. The applicant bears a good reputation for honesty and trustworthiness, therefore, I recommend that a real estate license be granted to the applicant."

Signature _____ Address _____
(Street & Number)   *(City)*   *(State)*   *(Zip)*

Print Name _____

Signature _____ Address _____
(Street & Number)   *(City)*   *(State)*   *(Zip)*

Print Name _____

Signature _____ Address _____
(Street & Number)   *(City)*   *(State)*   *(Zip)*

Print Name _____

REAL ESTATE EDUCATION

List below courses you have completed to satisfy the education requirements. The original certificate, grade form or transcript, certified copy thereof, must be attached.

COURSE	PROVIDER/INSTITUTION	NUMBER OF HOURS

Page 3

Rev. 12/2016

ATTACH PHOTOS BELOW

**Full Face
View**

**Profile Face
View**

Application **MUST** be accompanied by the following items:

1. College transcripts or Certificates of Completion from Mississippi Approved Pre-Licensing Education Provider

2. Proper Fee of $150.00

3. Photos – Full Face and Profile Views

4. Make sure signatures are **NOTARIZED** with seal where required.

5. **ALL** questions must be answered to ensure prompt processing.

6. If you have held or hold a Real Estate License in any other state, you **MUST** enclose a *Certification of Licensure* **(NOT A COPY OF ANY REAL ESTATE LICENSE).**

7. Letter from Broker (if presently employed as a salesperson)

8. Letter from bank regarding your handling of financial obligations with that institution.

Rev. 12/2016

§73-35-11. Nonresident may not act except in cooperation with licensed broker of state

Nonresident May Not Act...

Cooperating Broker Agreement

Two Copies have to be delivered to MREC within 10 days.

It shall be unlawful for any licensed broker, salesperson or other person who is not licensed as a Mississippi resident or nonresident broker or salesperson and a licensed broker or licensed salesperson in this state to perform any of the acts regulated by MREC, except that a licensed broker of another state who does not hold a Mississippi real estate license may *cooperate* with a licensed broker of this state provided that any commission or fee resulting from such cooperative negotiation shall be stated on a form filed with the commission *reflecting the compensation to be paid to the Mississippi broker.*

Whenever a Mississippi broker enters into a cooperative agreement, the Mississippi broker shall file within **ten (10) days** with the commission a copy of each such written agreement.

10

By signing the agreement, the nonresident broker who is not licensed in this state agrees to abide by Mississippi law, and the rules and regulations of the commission; and further agrees that civil actions may be commenced against him in any court of competent jurisdiction in any county of this state in which a claim may arise.

The Mississippi broker shall require a listing or joint listing of the property involved.

The written cooperative agreements shall specify all material terms of each agreement, including but not limited to its financial terms.

The showing of property located in Mississippi and negotiations pertaining thereto shall be supervised by the Mississippi broker.

In all advertising of real estate located in Mississippi, **the name and telephone number of the Mississippi broker shall appear and shall be given equal prominence with the name of the nonresident broker who is not licensed in this state.**

The Mississippi broker shall be liable for all acts of the above cooperating broker, as well as for his own acts, arising from the execution of any cooperative agreement.

The Mississippi broker shall **determine that the cooperating broker is licensed** as a broker in another state.

All earnest money pertaining to a cooperative agreement must be held in escrow by the Mississippi broker unless both the buyer and seller agree in writing to relieve the Mississippi broker of this responsibility.

INSTRUCTIONS FOR COMPLETING THE COOPERATING AGREEMENT

NOTE: This form is used when a Mississippi broker is paying any portion of a commission to a non-resident broker not licensed in Mississippi. The Mississippi broker is responsible for filing the agreement with MREC.

- If **LISTING** REFERRAL is checked, the **LOCATION/LEGAL DESCRIPTION OF LISTED PROPERTY MUST** be completed.

- The Non-Resident Broker's Name **MUST** be printed. Do not include the company name.

BEFORE MAILING, BE SURE THE FOLLOWING HAVE BEEN ADDRESSED:

- Application **MUST** be typed or printed. If it is printed, be sure handwriting is VERY CLEAR. MREC is not responsible for any misprints due to illegible handwriting.

- **ALL** questions have been answered in their entirety.

COOPERATING AGREEMENT WITH NON-RESIDENT PRINCIPAL BROKER   (EFFECTIVE-JULY 1, 2004)

Date Agreement Executed: _____ Agreement Expiration Date: _____

Owner/Client/Customer's Name_____ Telephone # _____

Owner/Client/Customer's Address _____

Location/Legal Description of Listed Property (if applicable) _____

AGREEMENT TO BE FINALIZED "PRIOR" TO ANY LICENSABLE REAL ESTATE ACTIVITY:

It is understood and agreed that this Agreement covers: **(Please check ONLY one <1> box)**

[ ] 1. A Joint or Cross Listing with participation by a Non-resident Principal Broker
[ ] 2. A Listing Referral from a Non-resident Principal Broker
[ ] 3. A Client or Customer Referral from a Non-resident Principal Broker
[ ] 4. A Purchase or Sales Contract procured by a Non-resident Principal Broker
[ ] 5. An Auction Agreement with a Non-resident Principal Broker
[ ] 6. Any Other activity for which a real estate license is required

In order to comply with the Mississippi Real Estate Brokers License Act of 1954, as Amended, and the Rules and Regulations of the Mississippi Real Estate Commission (MREC), the Mississippi Principal Broker and the Non-resident Principal Broker agree to the following:

All negotiations, including the showing, listing, and advertising of real property located within the state of Mississippi shall be handled under the direct supervision of the Mississippi Principal Broker, with the Mississippi Principal Broker taking full responsibility. **The Non-resident Principal Broker MUST be present at all times if one of his/her real estate agents, who is NOT licensed by the state of Mississippi, has a physical presence in Mississippi in connection with any real property transaction.** The Non-resident Principal Broker agrees to abide by Mississippi Law and the Rules and Regulations of the MREC and further agrees that civil actions may be commenced against him/her in any court of competent jurisdiction in any county of this state in which a claim may arise.

The Mississippi Principal Broker **MUST** confirm that the Non-resident Principal Broker is licensed as an **"ACTIVE PRINCIPAL BROKER"** in another state. This may be accomplished by direct contact with the Real Estate Licensing authority or by receiving a copy of a current real estate broker license. The Mississippi Principal Broker further agrees to notify the MREC immediately if the Non-resident Principal Broker violates any part of this Cooperative Agreement.

The Non-resident Principal Broker agrees not to place any sign on real property located within the state of Mississippi without the express written permission of the cooperating Mississippi Principal Broker. If such authority is granted, both Principal Brokers agree their signs will be placed in close proximity to one another and in a prominent place on the property. All listing or property management agreements shall be in the name of the Mississippi Principal Broker or they shall require a cross listing or joint listing of such property with the Non-resident Principal Broker.

The Non-resident Principal Broker agrees to not advertise the property in any manner unless the Mississippi Principal Broker is included in the advertising and such advertising shall be with the full knowledge of and under the direct supervision of the Mississippi Principal Broker. The name and phone number of the Mississippi Principal Broker shall be given equal prominence with the Non-resident Principal Broker. If this cooperative agreement involves a listing agreement concerning real property, the Non-resident Principal Broker affirms that the solicitation of the listing of the Mississippi property was conducted in the presence of the Mississippi Principal Broker.

The commissions, fees, or other compensations (considerations) earned during the period this Cooperative Agreement is in force shall be divided between the Mississippi Principal Broker and the Non-resident Principal Broker on a negotiable basis that is agreeable to the two brokers. The Mississippi Principal Broker shall either receive $_____ or_____ % of the compensation and the Non-resident Principal Broker shall either receive $_____ or_____ % of the compensation. All earnest monies or deposits shall be placed in the escrow account of the Mississippi Principal Broker unless both the buyer and the seller agree in writing to relieve the Mississippi Principal Broker of this responsibility.

No licensee shall knowingly pay a commission or a fee to a licensed person knowing that licensee will, in turn, pay any portion of the fee to an individual who does not hold a real estate license.

Mississippi Broker's Name (Print)	Non-resident Principal Broker's Name (Print)
Mississippi Broker's Signature	Non-resident Principal Broker's Signature
Mailing Address	Mailing Address
City, State & Zip Code	City, State & Zip Code
Business Telephone #	Business Telephone #

For a **JOINT LISTING**: I hereby agree to allow the Non-resident Principal Broker to place their sign in close proximity to my sign on the above-referenced listed property during the term of this contract.

_____
Mississippi Principal Broker's Signature

Four copies of the Agreement have been executed. The Non-resident Principal Broker and the Mississippi Principal Broker have each received one copy. It is the duty of the Mississippi Principal Broker to **confirm that the other two copies are filed with the Mississippi Real Estate Commission** at Post Office Box 12685, Jackson, MS 39236-2685, within 10 days after entering into the agreement.

73-35-13. Written examination requirement; exemption for licensee of another state; reciprocity

(1)   In addition to proof of his honesty, trustworthiness and good reputation, the applicant shall take a written examination which shall be held **at least four (4) times each year** at regular intervals and on stated times by the commission and shall test reading, writing, spelling, elementary arithmetic and his general knowledge of the statutes of this state relating to real property, deeds, mortgages, agreements of sale, agency, contract, leases, ethics, appraisals, the provisions of this chapter and such other matters the commission certifies as necessary to the practice of real estate brokerage in the State of Mississippi.

The examination for a broker's license shall differ from the examination for a salesperson's license, in that it shall be of a more exacting nature and require higher standards of knowledge of real estate.

The commission shall cause examinations to be conducted at such times and places as it shall determine.

(2)   In event the license of any real estate broker or salesperson is revoked by the commission subsequent to the enactment of this chapter, no new license shall be issued to such person unless he complies with the provisions of this chapter.

(3)   No person shall be permitted or authorized to act as a real estate broker or salesperson until he has qualified by examination, except as hereinbefore provided.

Any individual who fails to pass the examination for salesperson upon two (2) occasions, shall be ineligible for a similar examination, until after the expiration of three (3) months from the time such individual last took the examination.

Any individual who fails to pass the broker's examination upon two (2) occasions, shall be ineligible for a similar examination until after the expiration of six (6) months from the time such individual last took the examination, and then only upon making application as in the first instance.

(4)   If the applicant is a partnership, association, or corporation, said examination shall be taken on behalf of said partnership, association or corporation by the member or officer thereof who is designated in the application as the person to receive a license by virtue of the issuing of a license to such partnership, association or corporation.

(5)   Upon satisfactorily passing such examination and upon complying with all other provisions of law and conditions of this chapter, a license shall thereupon be issued to the successful applicant who, upon receiving such license, is authorized to conduct the business of a real estate broker or real estate salesperson in this state.

(6)   The commission is authorized to exempt from such examination, in whole or in part, a real estate licensee of another state who desires to obtain a license under this chapter; provided, however, that the examination administered in the other state is determined by the commission to be equivalent to such examination given in this state and provided that such other state extends this same privilege or exemption to Mississippi real estate licensees.

The issuance of a license by reciprocity to a military-trained applicant or military spouse shall most likely be approved. *changed by author

§73-35-14. Real estate schools; regulation by commission

A pre-license course must meet any standards that the Association of Real Estate Licensing Law Officials (ARELLO), or its successor(s), may have for pre-license courses, including, without limitation, standards for content, form, examination, facilities, and instructors.

If ARELLO or its successor(s) operate a certification program for prelicense courses, a pre-license course must be certified by ARELLO or its successor(s) before the commission may approve the course.

The commission may establish by rule such other standards for prelicense education course content as the commission may deem necessary.

No more than eight (8) pre-license hours may be earned in a single day.

Courses covering the general content that are acceptable for credit toward a degree at a college or university as approved by the Southern Association of Colleges and Schools or the comparable regional accrediting authority shall qualify for the minimum standards for pre-license education by virtue of that accreditation.

§73-35-14.4. Distance learning courses

Any distance learning course must meet any standards that the Association of Real Estate Licensing Law Officials (ARELLO), or its successor(s), may have for such courses, including, without limitation, standards for content, form, examination, facilities, and instructors.

If ARELLO or its successor(s) operate a certification program for distance learning courses, a distance learning course must be certified by ARELLO or its successor(s) before the commission may approve the course. **§73-35-14.5 Temporary licenses; post-license education**

Upon passing the Mississippi broker's or salesperson's examination and complying with all other conditions for licensure, a temporary license shall be issued to the applicant. The fee for the temporary license shall also be the same for the permanent license. A temporary license shall be valid for a period of **one (1) year following the first day of the month after its issuance.** 	**Temporary License** **Within One Year of getting your license there is a mandatory 30 hours Post License Course.**

(2) All Mississippi residents who apply for and receive a nonresident Mississippi broker's or salesperson's license shall be subject to the requirements, including temporary licensure and completion of a **thirty-hour post-license course**.

(3) The holder of a temporary license shall not be issued a permanent license until he has satisfactorily completed a thirty-hour post-license course.

The holder of a temporary license shall complete the 30 entire thirty-hour course within twelve (12) months of issuance of his temporary license; otherwise this temporary license shall automatically be placed on inactive status by the Mississippi Real Estate Commission. If the holder of the temporary license does not complete the course and have his permanent license issued within one (1) year following the first day of the month after its issuance, the temporary license shall automatically expire and lapse.

A temporary license is not subject to renewal.

(5) The holder of an active license who has satisfactorily completed the post-license course and whose permanent license has been issued shall not be subject to the sixteen-hour continuing education requirement for the first renewal of his permanent license.

NOTE: The first renewal period is in two years. You do not have to do CE until two years after that. (four years)

§73-35-15. Location of business and responsible broker to be designated

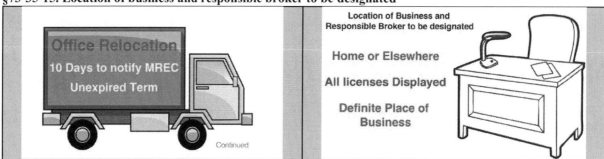

Every person, partnership, association, or corporation licensed as a real estate broker shall be required to have and maintain a definite place of business, which shall be a room either in his home or an office elsewhere, to be used for the transaction of real estate business, or such business and any allied business.

The certificate of registration as broker and the certificate of each real estate salesperson employed by such broker shall be prominently displayed in said office.

The said place of business shall be designated in the license. In case of removal from the designated address, the licensee shall make application to the commission before removal, or within ten (10) days after removal, designating the new location of such office, whereupon the commission shall forthwith issue a new license for the new location for the unexpired period.

(2) All licenses issued to a real estate salesperson or broker-salesperson shall designate the responsible broker of such salesperson or broker salesperson.

Prompt notice in writing, within **three (3) days**, shall be given to the commission by any real estate salesperson of a change of responsible broker, and of the name of the principal broker into whose agency the salesperson is about to enter; and a new license shall thereupon be issued by the commission to such salesperson for the unexpired term of the original license upon the return to the commission of the license previously issued.

The change of responsible broker or employment by any licensed real estate salesperson without notice to the commission as required shall automatically cancel his license.

Upon termination of a salesperson's agency, the responsible broker shall **within three (3) days** return the salesperson's license to the commission for cancellation.

It shall be unlawful for any real estate salesperson to perform any of the acts either directly or indirectly after his agency has been terminated and his license has been returned for cancellation until his license has been reissued by the commission.

§73-35-16. Real estate licensees required to obtain errors and omissions insurance coverage; persons required to submit proof of errors and omissions insurance; minimum requirements of group policy issued to commission; public bid for group insurance contract; requirements for independent coverage; rules and regulations

(1) The following words and phrases shall have the meanings ascribed herein unless the context clearly indicates otherwise:

(a)	"Aggregate limit" means a provision in an insurance contract limiting the maximum liability of an insurer for a series of losses in a given time period such as the policy term.

(b)	"Claims-made" means policies written under a claims-made basis which shall cover claims made (reported or filed) during the year the policy is in force for incidents which occur that year or during any previous period the policyholder was insured under the claims-made contract.

This form of coverage is in contrast to the occurrence policy which covers today's incident regardless of when a claim is filed even if it is one or more years later.

(c)	"Extended reporting period" means a designated period of time after a claims-made policy has expired during which a claim may be made, and coverage triggered as if the claim had been made during the policy period. (d) "Licensee" means any active individual broker, broker salesperson or salesperson, any partnership, or any corporation.

(e) "Per-claim limit" means the maximum limit payable, per licensee, for damages arising out of the same error, omission, or wrongful act.

(f) "Prior acts coverage" applies to policies on a claims-made versus occurrence basis.

Prior acts coverage responds to claims that are made during a current policy period, but the act or acts causing the claim or injuries for which the claim is made occurred prior to the inception of the current policy period.

(g) "Proof of coverage" means a copy of the actual policy of insurance, a certificate of insurance or a binder of insurance.

(h) "Retroactive date" means a provision, found in many claims made policies, that the policy shall not cover claims for injuries or damages that occurred before the retroactive date even if the claim is first made during the policy period.

(2) The following persons shall submit proof of insurance:

(a) Any active individual broker, active broker-salesperson or active salesperson; (b) Any partnership (optional); or (c) Any corporation (optional).

(3) Individuals whose licenses are on inactive status are not required to carry errors and omissions insurance.

(4) All Mississippi licensees shall be covered for activities contemplated under this chapter.

(5) Licensees may obtain errors and omissions coverage through the insurance carrier approved by the Mississippi Real Estate Commission and provided on a group policy basis.

Errors and omissions Insurance

Per-claim not less than $100,000

Annual aggregate not less than $100,000

Maximum deductible per license/claim $2500

Max deductible $1000 for defense per claim

Continue

The following are minimum requirements of the group policy to be issued to the commission, including, as named insureds, all licensees who have paid their required premium:

(a)	All activities contemplated under this chapter are included as covered activities;

(b)	A per-claim limit is not less than One Hundred Thousand Dollars ($100,000.00);

(c)	An annual aggregate limit is not less than One Hundred Thousand Dollars ($100,000.00);

(d) Limits apply per licensee per claim;

(e) Maximum deductible is Two Thousand Five Hundred Dollars ($2,500.00) per licensee per claim for damages; (f) Maximum deductible is One Thousand Dollars ($1,000.00) per licensee per claim for defense costs; and (g) The contract of insurance pays, on behalf of the injured person(s), liabilities owed.

(6)(a) The maximum contract period between the insurance carrier and the commission is to be five (5) consecutive policy terms, after which time period the commission shall place the insurance out for competitive bid.

The commission shall reserve the right to place the contract out for bid at the end of any policy period.

(b) The policy period shall be a twelve-month policy term.

(c) The retroactive date for the master policy shall not be before July 1, 1994.

(i)   The licensee may purchase full prior acts coverage on July 1, 1994, if the licensee can show proof of errors and omissions coverage that has been in effect since at least March 15, 1994.

(ii)   If the licensee purchases full prior acts coverage on July 1, 1994, that licensee shall continue to be guaranteed full prior acts coverage if the insurance carriers are changed in the future.

(iii)   If the licensee was not carrying errors and omissions insurance on July 1, 1994, the individual certificate shall be issued with a retroactive date of July 1, 1994.

This date shall not be advanced if the insurance carriers are changed in the future.

(iv)   For any new licensee who first obtains a license after July 1, 1994, the retroactive date shall be the effective date of licensure.

(v)   For any licensee who changes status of license from inactive to active, the retroactive date shall be the effective date of change to "active" licensure.

(d) Each licensee shall be notified of the required terms and conditions of coverage for the policy at least thirty (30) days before the renewal date of the policy.

A certificate of coverage, showing compliance with the required terms and conditions of coverage, shall be filed with the commission by the renewal date of the policy by each licensee who elects not to participate in the insurance program administered by the commission.

(e) If the commission is unable to obtain errors and omissions insurance coverage to insure all licensees who choose to participate in the insurance program at a premium of no more than Two Hundred Fifty Dollars ($250.00) per twelve (12) months' policy period, the requirement of insurance coverage under this section shall be void during the applicable contract period.

(7) Licensees may obtain errors and omissions coverage independently if the coverage contained in the policy complies with the following minimum requirements:

(a) All activities contemplated under this chapter are included as covered activities;

(b) A per-claim limit is not less than One Hundred Thousand Dollars ($100,000.00);

(c) The deductible is not more than Two Thousand Five Hundred Dollars ($2,500.00) per licensee per claim for damages and the deductible is not more than One Thousand Dollars ($1,000.00) per licensee per claim for defense costs; and

(d) If other insurance is provided as proof of errors and omissions coverage, the other insurance carrier shall agree to a noncancelable policy or to provide a letter of commitment to notify the commission thirty (30) days before the intention to cancel.

(8) The following provisions apply to individual licensees:

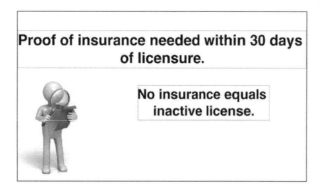

Proof of insurance needed within 30 days of licensure.

No insurance equals inactive license.

(a) The commission shall require receipt of proof of errors and omissions insurance from new licensees within thirty (30) days of licensure.

Any licenses issued at any time other than policy renewal time shall be subject to a pro rata premium. (b) For licensees not submitting proof of insurance necessary to continue active licensure, the commission shall be responsible for sending notice of deficiency to those licensees.

Licensees who do not correct the deficiency within thirty (30) days shall have their licenses placed on inactive status.

The commission shall assess fees for inactive status and for return to active status when errors and omissions insurance has been obtained.

(c) Any licensee insured in the state program whose license becomes inactive shall not be charged an additional premium if the license is reactivated during the policy period.

(9) The commission is authorized to adopt such rules and regulations as it deems appropriate to handle administrative duties relating to operation of the program, including billing and premium collection. §73-35-17.

Fees

(1) A fee not to exceed One Hundred Fifty Dollars ($150.00) shall accompany an application for a real estate broker's license, and in the event that the applicant successfully passes the examination, no additional fee shall be required for the issuance of a license for a one year period; provided, that if an applicant fails to pass the examination, he may be eligible to take the next or succeeding examination without the payment of an additional fee.

Fees

Broker's Application: $150

Salesperson's Application: $120

Partnership or Corporation: $75

(2) For each license as a real estate broker issued to a member of a partnership, association, or officer of a corporation other than the member or officer named in the license issued to such partnership, association or corporation, a fee not to exceed Seventy-five Dollars ($75.00) shall be charged.

(3) A fee not to exceed One Hundred Twenty Dollars ($120.00) shall accompany an application for a real estate salesperson's license, and in the event that the applicant successfully passes the examination, no additional fee shall be required for the issuance of a license for a one year period; provided, that if an applicant fails to pass the examination, he may be eligible to take the next or succeeding examination without the payment of an additional fee.

In the event a contract testing service is utilized, the fee associated with administering the test shall be collected by the testing provider and the application fee for any real estate license shall be collected by the commission.

(4) Except as provided in Section 33-1-39, it shall be the duty of all persons, partnerships, associations, companies, or corporations licensed to practice as a real estate broker or salesperson to register with the commission annually or biennially, in the discretion of the commission, according to rules promulgated by it and to pay the proper registration fee.

An application for renewal of license shall be made to the commission annually no later than December 31 of each year, or biennially on a date set by the commission. A licensee failing to pay his renewal fee after the same becomes due and after two (2) months' written notice of his delinquency mailed to him by United States certified mail addressed to his address of record with the commission shall thereby have his license automatically cancelled. Any licensee renewing in this grace period shall pay a penalty in the amount of one hundred percent (100%) of the renewal fee.	**More Fees** **Broker and Partnership: $75 per year** **Salesperson $60 per year** **Grace Period Renewal: 100% penalty** The renewal fee shall not exceed Seventy-five Dollars ($75.00) per year for real estate brokers, partnerships, associations, and corporations.

The renewal fee for a real estate salesperson's license shall not exceed Sixty Dollars ($60.00) per year.

(5) For each additional office or place of business, an annual fee not to exceed Fifty Dollars ($50.00) shall be charged.

(6) For each change of office or place of business, a fee not to exceed Fifty Dollars ($50.00) shall be charged.

(7) For each duplicate or transfer of salesperson's license, a fee not to exceed Fifty Dollars ($50.00) shall be charged.

(8) For each duplicate license, where the original license is lost or destroyed, and affidavit made thereof, a fee not to exceed Fifty Dollars ($50.00) shall be charged.

(9) To change status as a licensee from active to inactive status, a fee not to exceed Twenty-five Dollars ($25.00) shall be charged. To change status as a licensee from inactive to active status, a fee not to exceed Fifty Dollars ($50.00) shall be charged.

(10)   For each bad check received by the commission, a fee not to exceed Twenty-five Dollars ($25.00) shall be charged.

(11)   A fee not to exceed Five Dollars ($5.00) per hour of instruction may be charged to allay costs of seminars for educational purposes provided by the commission.

(12)   A fee not to exceed Twenty-five Dollars ($25.00) may be charged for furnishing any person a copy of a real estate license, a notarized certificate of licensure or other official record of the commission.

(14) Fees, up to the limits shall be established by the Mississippi Real Estate Commission.

§73-35-18. License renewal; continuing education requirements; exemptions; rules and regulations; reinstatement of expired license.

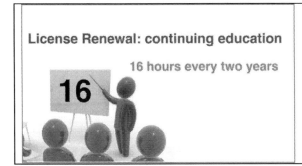

License Renewal: continuing education

16 hours every two years

16

Each individual applicant for renewal of a license issued by the Mississippi Real Estate Commission shall, on or before the expiration date of his license, or at a time directed by the commission, submit proof of completion of not less than **sixteen (16) clock hours** of approved course work to the commission, in addition to any other requirements for renewal.

The sixteen (16) clock hours' course work requirement shall apply to each two-year license renewal, and hours in excess thereof shall not be cumulated or credited for the purposes of subsequent license renewals except as provided in this subsection

(1). The commission shall develop standards for approval of courses and shall require certification of such course work of the applicant.

The commission may determine any required subject matter within the mandated sixteen (16) hours; provided that the required subjects shall not exceed eight (8) hours of the total sixteen (16) hours.

Approved continuing education hours earned in the final three (3) months of a licensee's renewal period, if in excess of the required minimum sixteen (16) hours, may be carried over and credited to the next renewal period.

However, no more than six (6) hours may be carried over in this manner.

Any member of the Mississippi Legislature who has a real estate license shall be credited with eight (8) hours of credit for the attendance of each year of a legislative session.

No person may receive continuing education credit for pre-license education courses taken, except as follows: a licensee whose license is on inactive status and whose continuing education credits are at least thirty (30) hours in arrears may, at the discretion of the commission, receive continuing education credit for retaking pre-license coursework, provided the entire pre-license course is retaken.

(2)   This section shall apply to renewals of licenses which expire on and after July 1, 1994; however, an applicant for first renewal who has been licensed for not more than one (1) year shall not be required to comply with this section for the first renewal of the applicant's license.

The provisions of this section shall not apply to persons who have held a broker's or salesperson's license in this state for at least twenty-five (25) years and who are older than seventy (70) years of age. Inactive licensees are not required to meet the real estate continuing education requirements specified in this section; however, such inactive licensees, before activating their license to active status, must cumulatively meet requirements missed during the period their license was inactive.

(3)   A renewal of a license issued by the commission which expires after June 30, 2019, must include a current email address for the applicant.

Any email address previously provided by an applicant to the commission which is no longer valid, or the primary email address of the applicant must be updated when a renewal application is submitted under this section.

(4)   The commission shall promulgate rules and regulations as necessary to accomplish the purposes of this section in accordance with the Mississippi Administrative Procedures Law.

§73-35-19. Real estate license fund

All fees charged and collected under this chapter shall be paid by the administrator at least once a week, accompanied by a detailed statement thereof, into the treasury of the state to credit of a fund to be known as the "Real Estate License Fund," which fund is hereby created.

All monies which shall be paid into the State Treasury and credited to the "Real Estate License Fund" are hereby appropriated to the use of the commission in carrying out the provisions of this chapter including the payment of salaries and expenses, printing an annual directory of licensees, and for educational purposes.
Maintenance of a searchable, internet-based web site shall satisfy the requirement for publication of a directory of licensees under this section.

§73-35-21. Grounds for refusing to issue or suspending or revoking license; hearing

(1) The commission may, upon its own motion and shall upon the verified complaint in writing of any person, hold a hearing for the refusal of license or for the suspension or revocation of a license previously issued, or for such other action as the commission deems appropriate.

The commission shall have full power to refuse a license for cause or to revoke or suspend a license where it has been obtained by false or fraudulent representation, or where the licensee in performing or attempting to perform any of the acts mentioned herein, is deemed to be guilty of:
(a) Making any substantial misrepresentation in connection with a real estate transaction

	(1) The commission may, upon its own motion and shall upon the verified complaint in writing of any person, hold a hearing for the refusal of license or for the suspension or revocation of a license previously issued, or for such other action as the commission deems appropriate. The commission shall have full power to refuse a license for
Grounds for refusing to issue or suspend or revoking license **False or fraudulent representation** **Substantial misrepresentation** **False promises**	cause or to revoke or suspend a license where it has been obtained by false or fraudulent representation, or where the licensee in performing or attempting to perform any of the acts mentioned herein, is deemed to be guilty of: (a) Making any substantial misrepresentation in connection with a real estate transaction;

(b) Making any false promises of a character likely to influence, persuade or induce;

(c) Pursuing a continued and flagrant course of misrepresentation or making false promises through agents or salespersons or any medium of advertising or otherwise;

(d) Any misleading or untruthful advertising;

(e) Acting for more than one (1) party in a transaction or receiving compensation from more than one (1) party in a transaction, or both, without the knowledge of all parties for whom he acts;

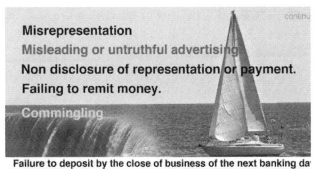

Misrepresentation
Misleading or untruthful advertising
Non disclosure of representation or payment.
Failing to remit money.
Commingling
Failure to deposit by the close of business of the next banking da

---

continued
Failure to deliver copies immediately.

Putting a sign on property you have no listing on.

Substitution of parties for personal gain.

Accepting money from someone other than your broker.

(f) Failing, within a reasonable time, to account for or to remit any monies coming into his possession which belong to others or commingling of monies belonging to others with his own funds.

Every responsible broker procuring the execution of an earnest money contract or option or other contract who shall take or receive any cash or checks shall deposit, within a reasonable period of time, the sum or sums so received in a trust or escrow account in a bank or trust company pending the consummation or termination of the transaction.

"Reasonable time" in this context means by the close of business of the next banking day;

(g) Entering a guilty plea or conviction in a court of competent jurisdiction of this state, or any other state or the United States of any felony;

(h) Displaying a "for sale" or "for rent" sign on any property without the owner's consent;

(i) Failing to furnish voluntarily, at the time of signing, copies of all listings, contracts and agreements to all parties executing the same;

Bad faith, incompetency, untrustworthiness, dishonesty, fraudulent or improper dealing.

Practising law or conveyancer activities.

Being out of compliance with an order for support.

(j) Paying any rebate, profit or commission to any person other than a real estate broker or salesperson licensed under the provisions of this chapter;

(k) Inducing any party to a contract, sale or lease to break such contract for the purpose of substituting in lieu thereof a new contract, where such substitution is motivated by the personal gain of the licensee;

(l) Accepting a commission or valuable consideration as a real estate salesperson for the performance of any of the acts specified in this chapter from any person, except his employer who must be a licensed real estate broker; or

(m) Failing to successfully pass the commission's background investigation for licensure or renewal.

(n) Any act or conduct, whether of the same or a different character than hereinabove specified, which constitutes or demonstrates bad faith, incompetency or untrustworthiness, or dishonest, fraudulent or improper dealing.

However, simple contact and/or communication with any mortgage broker or lender by a real estate licensee about any professional, including, but not limited to, an appraiser, home inspector, contractor, and/or attorney regarding a listing and/or a prospective or pending contract for the lease, sale and/or purchase of real estate shall not constitute conduct in violation.

(2) **No real estate broker shall practice law or give legal advice** directly or indirectly unless said broker be a duly licensed attorney under the laws of this state.

He shall **not act as a public conveyancer** nor give advice or opinions as to the legal effect of instruments nor give opinions concerning the validity of title to real estate; nor shall he prevent or discourage any party to a real estate transaction from employing the services of an attorney; nor shall a broker undertake to prepare documents fixing and defining the legal rights of parties to a transaction.

However, when acting as a broker, he may use an earnest money contract form.

A real estate broker shall not participate in attorney's fees, unless the broker is a duly licensed attorney under the laws of this state and performs legal services in addition to brokerage services.

(3)   It is expressly provided that it is not the intent and purpose of the Mississippi Legislature to prevent a license from being issued to any person who is found to be of good reputation, is able to give bond, and who has lived in the State of Mississippi for the required period or is otherwise qualified.

(4)   **The commission shall be authorized to suspend the license of any licensee for being out of compliance with an order for support.**

(5)   Nothing in this chapter shall prevent an associate broker or salesperson from owning any lawfully constituted business organization, including, but not limited to, a corporation, limited liability company or limited liability partnership, for the purpose of receiving payments.

The business organization shall not be required to be licensed and shall not engage in any other activity requiring a real estate license.

§73-35-23. Powers of commission as to violations; hearings upon revocation; subpoena

(1) The commission is hereby authorized and directed to take legal action against any violator of this chapter.

Upon complaint initiated by the commission or filed with it, the licensee or any other person charged with a violation of this chapter shall be given **fifteen (15) days' notice** of the hearing upon the charges filed, together with a copy of the complaint.

The applicant or licensee or other violator shall have an opportunity to be heard in person or by counsel, to offer testimony, and to examine witnesses appearing in connection with the complaint. Hearings shall be held at the offices of the Mississippi Real Estate Commission, or at the commission's sole discretion, at a place determined by the commission.

At such hearings, all witnesses shall be sworn, and stenographic notes of the proceedings shall be taken and filed as a part of the record in the case.

Power of Commission

Can issue subpoenas for attendance of witness or the production of books and papers.

Any party to the proceedings shall be furnished with a copy of such stenographic notes upon payment to the commission of such fees as it shall prescribe, not exceeding, however, the actual cost to the commission.

The commission shall render a decision on any complaint and shall immediately notify the parties to the proceedings in writing of its ruling, order or decision.

(2) In addition to the authority granted to the commission as hereinabove set forth, the commission is hereby vested with the authority to bring injunctive proceedings in any appropriate forum against any violator or violators of this chapter, and all judges or courts now having the power to grant injunctions are specifically granted the power and jurisdiction to hear and dispose of such proceedings.

(3) The commission is hereby authorized and empowered to issue subpoenas for the attendance of witnesses and the production of books and papers.

The process issued by the commission shall extend to all parts of the state, and such process shall be served by any person designated by the commission for such service.

The person serving such process receive such compensation as may be allowed by the commission, not to exceed the fee prescribed by law for similar services.

All witnesses who are subpoenaed and who appear in any proceedings before the commission receive the same fees and mileage as allowed by law, and all such fees shall be taxed as part of the costs in the case.

(4) Where in any proceeding before the commission any witness shall fail or refuse to attend upon subpoena issued by the commission, shall refuse to testify, or shall refuse to produce any books and papers the production of which is called for by the subpoena, the attendance of such witness and the giving of his testimony and the production of the books and papers shall be enforced by any court of competent jurisdiction of this state in the same manner as the attendance and testimony of witnesses in civil cases are enforced in the courts of this state.

(5) The commission may obtain legal counsel privately to represent it in proceedings when legal counsel is required.

§73-35-25. Appeals

Any applicant or licensee or person aggrieved shall have the right of appeal from any adverse ruling or order or decision of the commission to the circuit court of the county of residence of the applicant, licensee or person, or of the First Judicial District of Hinds County, **within thirty (30) days** from the service of notice of the action of the commission upon the parties in interest.

(2) Notice of appeals shall be filed in the office of the clerk of the court who shall issue a writ of certiorari directed to the commission commanding it, within thirty (30) days after service thereof, to certify to such court its entire record in the matter in which the appeal has been taken.

The appeal shall thereupon be heard in due course by said court, without a jury, which shall review the record and make its determination of the cause between the parties.

(3) Any order, rule or decision of the commission shall not take effect until after the time for appeal to said court shall have expired. In the event an appeal is taken by a defendant, such appeal may act, in the discretion of the court, as a supersedeas and the court shall dispose of said appeal and enter its decision promptly.

(4) Any person taking an appeal shall post a satisfactory bond in the amount of Five Hundred Dollars ($500.00) for the payment of any costs which may be adjudged against him.

(5) Actions taken by the commission in suspending a license when required are not actions from which an appeal may be taken under this section.

Any appeal of a license suspension that is required shall be taken in accordance with the appeal procedure as the case may be, rather than the procedure.

§73-35-27. Duties of commission

The commission is hereby authorized to assist in conducting or holding real estate courses or institutes, and to incur and pay the necessary expenses in connection therewith, which courses or institutes shall be open to any licensee or other interested parties.

(2) The commission is hereby authorized to assist libraries, real estate institutes, and foundations with financial aid, or otherwise, in providing texts, sponsoring studies, surveys and educational programs for the benefit of real estate and the elevation of the real estate business.

§73-35-29. Administrator to give bond

The administrator, appointed by the commission, in the discretion of the commission, shall give bond in such sum and with such surety as the commission may direct and approve, and the premium thereon shall be paid by the commission.

§73-35-31. Penalties for violations of chapter

(1) Any person violating a provision of this chapter shall, upon conviction of a first violation thereof, if a person, be punished by a fine or not less than Five Hundred Dollars ($500.00) nor more than One Thousand Dollars ($1,000.00), or by imprisonment for a term not to exceed ninety (90) days, or both; and if a corporation, be punished by a fine of not more than Two Thousand Dollars ($2,000.00).	**Penalties for Violations** First violation up to $1000 and 90 days. Double for the second violation.

Upon conviction of a second or subsequent violation, if a person, shall be punished by a fine of not less than One Thousand Dollars ($1,000.00) nor more than Two Thousand Dollars ($2,000.00), or by imprisonment for a term not to exceed six (6) months, or both; and if a corporation, be punished by a fine of not less than Two Thousand Dollars ($2,000.00) nor more than Five Thousand Dollars ($5,000.00).

Any officer or agent of a corporation, or any member or agent of a partnership or association, who shall personally participate in or be accessory to any violation of this chapter by such corporation, partnership or association, shall be subject to the penalties herein prescribed for individuals.

(2)   In case any person, partnership, association or corporation shall have received any sum of money, or the equivalent thereto, as commission, compensation or profit by or in consequence of his violation of any provision of this chapter, such person, partnership, association or corporation shall also be liable to a penalty of not less than the amount of the sum of money so received and not more than four (4) times the sum so received, as may be determined by the court, which penalty may be sued for and recovered by any person aggrieved and for his use and benefit, in any court of competent jurisdiction.

(3)   No fee, commission or other valuable consideration may be paid to a person for real estate brokerage activities as unless the person provides evidence of licensure or provides evidence of a cooperative agreement.

§73-35-33. License required to sue for compensation; suit by salesperson in own name

No person, partnership, association or corporation shall bring or maintain an action in any court of this state for the recovery of a commission, fee or compensation for any act done or services rendered, the doing or rendering of which is prohibited under the provisions of this chapter for persons other than licensed real estate brokers, unless such person was duly licensed hereunder as a real estate broker at the time of the doing of such act or the rendering of such service.

(2) No real estate salesperson shall have the right to institute suits in his own name for the recovery of a fee, commission or compensation for services as a real estate salesperson, but any such action shall be instituted and brought by the broker employing such salesperson.

However, any real estate salesperson shall have the right to bring an action in his own name if the action is against the broker employing such salesperson for the recovery of any fees owed to him.

§73-35-35. Commission to adopt rules and regulations

(1)   The commission may act by a majority of the members thereof, and authority is hereby given to the commission to adopt, fix and establish all rules and regulations in its opinion necessary for the conduct of its business, the holdings of hearings before it, and otherwise generally for the enforcement and administration of the provisions of this chapter.

Further, the commission is empowered with the authority to adopt such rules and regulations as it deems appropriate to regulate the sale of timesharing and condominium properties within the state of Mississippi and the sale of timesharing and condominium properties in other states to residents of Mississippi.

(2)   Beginning on July 1, 2019, the commission shall provide notice by email to each real estate broker and real estate salesperson who has provided an email address to the commission.

The notice required under this subsection must be given on no less than three (3) separate occasions during

the notice period prescribed under the Mississippi Administrative Procedures Law. **Chapter 43, Title 25,**

Mississippi Code of (1972). 51 §73-35-101. (IREBEA)

Short title Sections 73-35-101 through 73-35-105 shall be known and may be cited as the "**Interest on Real Estate Brokers' Escrow Account**s Act." §73-35-103.

IREBEA **Interest on Real Estate Broker Escrow Account** **A voluntary program.** 	**Definitions** (a) "Real estate broker" or "broker" means an individual, partnership or corporation licensed.
(b) "IREBEA" means the program created and governed by Sections 73-35-101 through 73-35-105. (c) "Interest earnings" means the total interest earnings generated by the IREBEA at each individual financial institution. (d) "Local affiliate of Habitat for Humanity International, Inc.," means an independently run 501(c)(3) organization that acts in partnership with and on behalf of Habitat for Humanity International, Inc., to coordinate all aspects of Habitat home building in a specific geographical area.	**IREBEA** **Interest collected is paid quarterly to the** **Mississippi Housing Opportunity Fund**  AFFORDABLE HOUSING (e) Local affiliate of Fuller Center for Housing, Inc., means an independently run 501(c)(3) organization that acts in partnership with and on behalf of Fuller
IREBEA	Center for Housing, Inc., to coordinate all aspects of home building on behalf of the Fuller Center in a specific geographical area. (f) "Chair of real estate" means the endowment fund held and administered by any Mississippi university. For those universities which do not designate, or which do not have a "chair of real estate," the term "chair of real estate" includes a professorship of real estate.

73-35-105. Interest on Real Estate Brokers' Escrow Accounts (IREBEA) program

The IREBEA program shall be a voluntary program based upon willing participation by real estate brokers, whether proprietorships, partnerships or professional corporations.

(2)   IREBEA shall apply to all clients or customers of the participating brokers whose funds on deposit are either nominal in amount or to be held for a short period of time.

(3)   The following principles shall apply to clients' or customers' funds which are held by brokers who elect to participate in IREBEA:

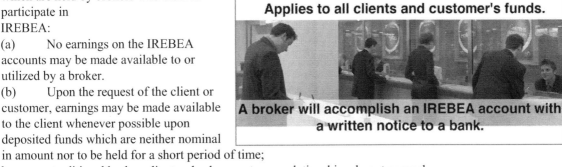

IREBEA

Applies to all clients and customer's funds.

A broker will accomplish an IREBEA account with a written notice to a bank.

(a)   No earnings on the IREBEA accounts may be made available to or utilized by a broker.

(b)   Upon the request of the client or customer, earnings may be made available to the client whenever possible upon deposited funds which are neither nominal in amount nor to be held for a short period of time; however, traditional broker-client or broker customer relationships do not compel brokers either to invest clients' or customers' funds or to advise clients or customers to make their funds productive.

(c)   Clients' or customers' funds which are nominal in amount or to be held for a short period of time shall be retained in an interest bearing checking or savings trust account with the interest, less any service charge or fees, made payable at least quarterly to any chair of real estate, local affiliate of Habitat for Humanity International, Inc., or local affiliate of Fuller Center for Housing, Inc.

A separate accounting shall be made annually for all funds received.

(d) The broker shall select in writing that the chair of real estate, local affiliate of Habitat for Humanity International, Inc., or local affiliate of Fuller Center for Housing, Inc., shall be the beneficiary of such funds for the interest earnings on such funds.
The interest earnings shall not be divided between one or more beneficiaries.

(e) The determination of whether clients' or customers' funds are nominal in amount or to be held for a short period of time rests in the sound judgment of each broker, and no charge of ethical impropriety or other breach of professional conduct shall attend a broker's exercise of judgment in that regard.

(f) Notification to clients or customers whose funds are nominal in amount or to be held for a short period of time is unnecessary for those brokers who choose to participate in the program.

Participation in the IREBEA program is accomplished by the broker's written notification to an authorized financial institution.

That communication shall contain an expression of the broker's desire to participate in the program and, if the institution has not already received appropriate notification, advice regarding the Internal Revenue Service's approval of the taxability of earned interest or dividends to a chair of real estate, or a local affiliate of Habitat for Humanity International, Inc., or local affiliate of Fuller Center for Housing, Inc.

(4) The following principles shall apply to those clients' or customers' funds held in trust accounts by brokers who elect not to participate in IREBEA:

(a) No earnings from the funds may be made available to any broker.

(b) Upon the request of a client or customer, earnings may be made available to the client or customer whenever possible upon deposited funds which are neither nominal in amount nor to be held for a short period of time;

however, traditional broker-client or broker-customer relationships do not compel brokers either to invest clients' or customers' funds or to advise clients or customers to make their funds productive.

(c) Clients' or customers' funds which are nominal in amount or to be held for short periods of time, and for which individual income generation allocation is not arranged with a financial institution, shall be retained in a noninterestbearing demand trust account.

(d) The determination of whether clients' or customers' funds are nominal in amount or to be held for a short period of time rests in the sound judgment of each broker, and no charge of ethical impropriety or other breach of professional conduct shall attend a broker's exercise of judgment in that regard.

(5) The Mississippi Real Estate Commission shall adopt appropriate and necessary rules in compliance with the provisions of Sections 73-35- 101 through 73-35-105.

§89-1-501. Applicability of real estate transfer disclosure requirement provisions

The provisions apply only with respect to transfers by sale, exchange, installment land sale contract, lease with an option to purchase, any other option to purchase or ground lease coupled with improvements, of real property on which a dwelling unit is located, or residential stock cooperative improved with or consisting of not less than one **(1) nor more than four (4) dwelling** units, when the execution of such transfers is by, or with the aid of, a duly licensed real estate broker or salesperson.

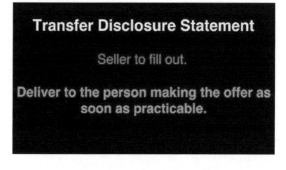

TO

PROPERTY CONDITION DISCLOSURE STATEMENT (PCDS)

THIS FORM MAY BE DUPLICATED BUT IT MAY NOT BE ALTERED OR PERSONALIZED BY THE SELLER(S), ANY BROKERAGE FIRM OR LICENSEE.

The following is a Property Condition Disclosure Statement (PCDS) required by §89-1-507 through §89-1-527 of the Mississippi Real Estate Brokers Act of 1954, as Amended, and made by the **SELLER(S)** concerning the condition of the **RESIDENTIAL PROPERTY (1 TO 4 UNITS)** located at: _____.

SELLER(S): _____ Approximate Age of the Residence_____

This document is a disclosure of the condition of real property known by the SELLER on the date that this statement is signed and it is based on their actual knowledge of the property. It is **NOT a warranty of any kind** by the Seller or any Real Estate Licensee representing a principal in this transaction and this PCDS is not a substitute for any home inspection(s) or warranties the purchaser(s) may wish to obtain. However, the purchaser(s) may rely on the information contained herein when deciding to negotiate the terms for the purchase of the residential real property. This statement may be made available to other parties and **is to be attached to the Listing Agreement and signed by the SELLER(S).** This statement is **NOT** intended to be part of any contract between the seller and the purchaser.

IF THE RESIDENCE IS NEW (NEVER OCCUPIED) OR PROPOSED RESIDENTIAL CONSTRUCTION and a real estate licensee is involved in the transaction, the **BUILDER/OWNER/SELLER** must complete the PCDS in its entirety and should reference specific plans/specifications, building material lists and/or change orders.

DO NOT LEAVE ANY QUESTIONS UNANSWERED AND DO NOT LEAVE BLANK SPACES. THE SELLER(S) MAY ATTACH ADDITIONAL PAGES IF NECESSARY TO FULLY EXPLAIN A PROPERTY'S CONDITION. THE ACRONYM "N/A" MAY BE USED FOR "NOT APPLICABLE" AND "UNK" MAY BE USED FOR "UNKNOWN".

A. GENERAL INFORMATION:

1. Does the Transferor/Seller currently have a deeded title to the residence? Yes _____ No _____. If "YES", when did the current Seller receive the title to the property? _____.
2. Does the Transferor/Seller currently occupy the residence? Yes _____ No _____. If "NO", has the current seller ever occupied the residence? Yes _____ No _____. If "YES", what were the dates of Occupancy? _____.
3. Is the site improved with a Factory Built (Manufactured Housing Unit) or a Modular Home constructed on a permanent foundation? Yes _____ No _____. If "YES", indicate the Home Identification number on the Data Plate _____.
4. Was the residence built in conformity with an approved building code? Yes _____ No _____ Unknown _____. If "YES", was a PERMIT secured from the City/County Building Authority? Yes _____ No _____ Unknown _____.
5. Do you have a Home Inspection Report which was completed for you? Yes _____ No _____. If "YES", is the report available for review by a prospective purchaser? Yes _____ No _____.

B. STRUCTURAL ITEMS & SOILS:

1. Are you aware of any settlement/heaving of soils, any collapsible or expansive soils or poorly compacted fill on the Property? Yes _____ No _____ Unknown _____. If "YES", please describe, to your knowledge, the nature and location of any settlement or heaving _____
2. Are you aware of any past or present movement, shifting, deterioration or other problems with the walls (interior or exterior) or the foundation of the Property? Yes _____ No _____ Unknown _____. If "YES", please describe, to your knowledge, the nature and location of any such problems _____
3. Are you aware of any tests to determine the composition/compaction of the soil or the presence of any "expandable soils" being present on the Property? Yes _____ No _____. If "YES", please provide copies of the results if they are available.
4. Are you aware of any foundation repairs made in the past? Yes _____ No _____. If "Yes", is there a written report which will indicate the foundation repairs? Explain _____
5. If foundation repairs were completed is there a Warranty which can be transferred to a new owner? Yes _____ No _____.
6. To your knowledge, are any foundation repairs currently needed? Yes _____ No _____ Unknown _____. If "YES", please explain in detail _____
7. Except for "Cosmetic Upgrades" (carpet, paint, wallpaper, etc) have you remodeled, made any room additions, made structural modifications or other alterations or improvements to the Property? If "YES", please describe, to your knowledge, the nature of all such remodels/alterations_____
8. To your knowledge, were all necessary work PERMITS and approvals secured in compliance with local/city/county building codes? Yes _____ No _____ Unknown _____. If "YES", please indicate the name of the Licensed Contractor who completed the work and the dates of the work _____

C. ROOF:

1. Has all or any portion of the roof been repaired or replaced during your ownership? Yes _____ No _____. If "YES", please indicate the dates of the roof work (if known) and describe, to the best of your knowledge, the nature of any roof repairs or replacements. _____ .
2. To your knowledge, are there any written warranties presently in place for the roof? Yes _____ No _____. If "YES", please attach copies of any warranties in your possession.
3. Are you aware of any current leaks or defects with the roof such as structural issues, dry rot, water backups, moisture issues, wind damage or hail damage? Yes _____ No _____. If "YES", please describe, to your knowledge, the nature of the defects and their location_____ .
4. How long have you known about the current problems with the roof? _____
5. The roof is _____ years old.

D. HISTORY OF INFESTATION: TERMITES, CARPENTER ANTS, ETC:

1. Are you aware of any ongoing, recurring or habitual problems with termites, dry rot, mildew, vermin, rodents or other pests which affect the Property? Yes _____ No _____. If "YES", please describe, to your knowledge, the nature of the problem and the location of the problem _____
2. Are you aware of any DAMAGE to the Property which was caused by termites, dry rot, mildew, vermin, rodents or other pests? Yes _____ No _____. If "YES", please describe, to your knowledge, the location of such damage and what efforts were taken to mitigate and/or repair the damage _____
3. If a Wood Destroying Insect Treatment was required for the residence, which Pest Control Company treated the Property for the problem? _____
4. If DAMAGE to the residence was actually mitigated/repaired, who was the contractor who repaired the DAMAGE to the Property? _____
5. To your knowledge, are there any written warranties or other termite or pest control coverage(s) presently in place for the Property? Yes _____ No _____. If "YES", please attach copies of such warranties in your possession.

E. STRUCTURE/FLOOR/WALLS/CEILINGS/WINDOWS/FEATURES:

1. During your ownership, has there been DAMAGE to any portion of the physical structure resulting from fire, windstorm, hail, tornados, hurricane or any other natural disaster? Yes _____ No _____ If "YES", please describe, to your best knowledge, the cause of the damage, in detail, and supply the dates of the losses _____
2. Are you aware of any past or present problems, malfunctions or defects with the windows (including storm windows and screens), the flooring (hardwood, marble, stone, tile or carpeting), fireplace/chimneys, ceilings, walls (interior), jetted bathtub, hot tub, sauna, skylights, shower or wet bar; including any modifications to them? Yes _____ No _____. If "YES", please describe, to your knowledge, the nature of any such problem; for example, the skylight leaked or the motor which operates the jetted bathtub had to be replaced, etc. _____
3. Are you aware of any past or present problems, malfunctions or defects with the lawn sprinkler system, swimming pool, hot tub, rain gutters, tile drains (French drains), driveway, patio, storage building, gazebo, outdoor fireplace, or outdoor kitchen appliances (which are remaining with the property)? Yes _____ No _____. If "YES", please describe, to your knowledge, the nature of such problems; for example, the French drains are clogged and do not remove rain water or the timer for the sprinkler system is not functioning properly, etc. _____
4. During your ownership, have there been any notices concerning safety issues with a swimming pool or other improvements to the property? Yes _____ No _____. If "YES". Please describe, to the best of your knowledge, those safety issue in detail. _____
5. Except for regular maintenance of the exterior surfaces of the Property (painting, staining, etc) are you aware of any past or present problems, malfunctions or defects with any portion of the exterior walls, fascias, soffits, stucco, windows, doors or trim? Yes _____ No _____. If "YES", please describe, to your knowledge, the nature of the problems. (for example, there is moisture damage behind the stucco) _____

F. LAND AND SITE DATA:

1. Is there an engineer's survey or a recorded plat of the Property available? Yes _____ No _____. If "YES", please attach a copy of the survey (if available). If "YES", please indicate by whom the survey was completed _____ and the Date the survey was completed_____.
2. Are you aware of the existence of any of the following, to wit:

Encroachments:	Yes ___ No ___ Unknown ___		Boundary Dispute:	Yes ___ No ___ Unknown ___	
Easements:	Yes ___ No ___ Unknown ___		Soil/Erosion:	Yes ___ No ___ Unknown ___	
Soil Problems:	Yes ___ No ___ Unknown ___		Standing Water:	Yes ___ No ___ Unknown ___	
Land Fill:	Yes ___ No ___ Unknown ___		Drainage Problems:	Yes ___ No ___ Unknown ___	

3. Are you aware of any current pending litigation, foreclosure, zoning regulations, restrictive covenants, building code violations, mechanics liens, judgments, special assessments or any other type of restriction which could negatively affect your Property? Yes ____ No ____ If "YES", please explain _____
4. Other than the utility easements, are you aware of any easement which impacts the residence? Yes _____ No _____.
5. Are there any rights-of-way, easements, eminent domain proceedings or similar matters which may negatively impact your ownership interest in the Property? Yes _____ No _____ If "YES", please explain _____
6. Are you aware if any portion of the Property (including a part of the site) is currently located in or near a FEMA Designated Flood Hazard Zone? Yes _____ No _____ Unknown _____. If "YES", please indicate the source of your information and the current Map Number used to determine the Flood Zone _____
7. Is Flood Insurance currently required on the Property? Yes _____ No _____. If "YES", please indicate the amount of the premium currently being paid and when the premium was last adjusted _____
8. Are you aware if any portion of the Property (Site) is currently designated as being located within a WETLANDS area and is subject to specific restrictive uses? Yes _____ No _____. If "YES", please explain in detail _____
9. Are you aware if the Property has ever had standing water in the front, rear or side yards for more than forty-eight (48) hours following a heavy rain? Yes _____ No _____. If "YES", please describe, to your knowledge, any unusual circumstances causing the problem _____

10. Are you aware, **FOR ANY REASON,** in the past or present of water penetration problems in the walls, windows, doors, crawl space, basement or attic? Yes _____ No _____. If "YES", please describe, to your knowledge, the nature of the problem and what steps were taken to remedy the problem _____ .

11. **FOR ANY REASON,** past or present, has any portion of the interior of the Property ever suffered water damage or moisture related damage which was caused by flooding, lot drainage, moisture seepage, condensation, sewer overflow, sewer backup, leaking or broken water pipes (during or after construction) pipe fittings, plumbing fixtures, leaking appliances, fixtures or equipment? Yes _____ No _____. If "YES", please describe, to your knowledge, the nature of the problems and what steps were taken to remedy the problems _____ .

12. Are you aware, **FOR ANY REASON,** of any leaks, back-ups, or other problems relating to any of the plumbing, water, sewage, or related items during your ownership? Yes _____ No _____. If "YES", please describe, to your best knowledge, the problem you experienced and how it was mitigated _____ .

G. APPLIANCES/MECHANICAL EQUIPMENT:

Following is a list of appliances and mechanical systems which may or may not be present in the residence. Please complete the information to the best of your knowledge. You may use the "Item Blanks" at the bottom of the page for additional items.

APPLIANCES/ITEMS/SYSTEMS <u>REMAINING</u> WITH THE PROPERTY:

ITEMS	YES/ #ITEMS	NO N/A	GAS/ ELECTRIC	REPAIRS COMPLETED IN LAST TWO YEARS	AGE
BUILT-IN COOKTOP					
BUILT-IN OVEN(S)					
BUILT-IN DISHWASHER					
GARBAGE DISPOSAL					
ICE-MAKER (STAND ALONE)					
MICROWAVE OVEN					
TRASH COMPACTOR					
KITCHEN VENT FAN(S)					
CENTRAL AIR SYSTEM(S)					
CENTRAL HEATING SYSTEM(S)					
HUMIDIFIERS OR EVAPORATORS					
AIR PURIFIERS					
WATER HEATER(S)					
TANKLESS WATER HEATER(S)					
CEILING FAN(S)					
ATTIC FANS					
BATHROOM VENT FAN(S)					
GARAGE DOOR OPENER(S)					
SMOKE/MONOXIDE DETECTORS					
SECURITY SYSTEM					
INTERCOM/SOUND SYSTEM					
REFRIGERATOR					
FREE STANDING STOVE					

H. OTHER:

1. Are you aware of any past or present hazardous conditions, substances or materials on the Property such as asbestos or asbestos components, lead-based paint, urea-formaldehyde insulation, the presence of Chinese dry-wall, methane gas, radon gas, underground storage tanks and lines or any past industrial uses occurring on the premises? Yes _____ No _____ If "YES", please describe, to your best knowledge, the nature of any such hazardous conditions and any attempts to mitigate any such hazardous condition(s) _____

2. Are you aware of any past or present contaminations which have resulted from the storing or the manufacturing of methamphetamines? Yes _____ No _____. If "YES", please describe _____

3. Are you aware if there are currently, or have previously been, any inspections by qualified experts or orders issued on the property by any governmental authority requiring the remediation of MOLD or any other public health nuisance on the Property? Yes _____ No _____. If "YES", please describe, to your best knowledge, any attempts to mitigate such condition(s) _____

4. Are you aware of any problems or conditions that affect the desirability or functionality of the Heating, Cooling, Electrical, Plumbing, or Mechanical Systems? Yes _____ No _____. If "YES", please described, to your best knowledge, all known problems in complete detail _____

5. The water supply is: Public _____ Private _____ On-site Well _____ Neighbor's Well _____ Community _____

6. If your drinking water is from a well, when was the water quality last checked for safety, what were the results of the test and who was the qualified entity who conducted the test? _____

7. Is the water supply equipped with a water softener? Yes _____ No _____ Unknown _____

8. The Sewage System is: Public _____ Private _____ Septic _____ Cesspool _____ Treatment Plant _____ Other _____

9. If the sewer service is by an individual system, has it been inspected by the proper state/county Health Department officials? Yes _____ No _____. If "YES", please give complete details _____

10. How many bedrooms are allowed by the Individual Waste Water Permit? _____

11. Is there a sewage pump installed? Yes _____ No _____ Date of the last Septic Inspection _____

I. MISCELLANEOUS:

1. Is the residence situated on Leasehold or Sixteenth Section land? Yes _____ No _____ Unknown _____ If "YES", please indicate the terms of the lease including payments and expiration date _____

2. Are you aware of any hidden defects or needed repairs about which the purchaser should be informed **PRIOR** to their purchase? Yes _____ No _____. If "YES", please describe, to your best knowledge, the problem(s) which need to be disclosed _____

3. What is the **APPROXIMATE SQUARE FOOTAGE** of the Heated and Cooled Living Area? _____

4. How was the approximation of the Gross Living Area (square footage) determined? _____

5. Are there any finished hardwood floors beneath the floor coverings? Yes _____ No _____ Unknown _____. If "YES", please indicate, to your best knowledge, the condition and the location of the hardwood floors _____

6. Are there Homeowner's Association Fees associated with ownership? Yes _____ No _____ Amount _____ (Yr/Mth/Quarter)

7. Does the HOA levy dues or assessments for maintenance of common areas and/or other common expenses? _____

8. Are you aware of any HOA, Public (municipal) special improvement district (**PID**) or other assessments that are presently owing or that have been approved but not yet levied against the Property? Yes _____ No _____. If "YES", please indicate the tax (assessing) entity and the amount of the taxes/assessments _____

9. Please indicate the contact information for the HOA _____

10. What is the **YEARLY** Real Estate Tax Bill? County Taxes _____ City Taxes _____ Special District Taxes _____

11. Has Homestead Exemption been filed for the **current** year? Yes _____ No _____ Unknown _____.

12. Are you aware of any additional tax exemptions which accrue to the Property? Yes _____ No _____ Unknown _____. If "YES", please describe the exemptions and the amount of the tax _____

13. What is the average **YEARLY** Electric Bill? $_____ What is the average **YEARLY** Gas Bill? $_____

14. Is the residence serviced by Propane (LP) Gas? If "YES", what is the average **YEARLY** Propane Bill? $_____

15. The Propane Tank is: Owned _____ Leased _____ If Leased, how much is the lease payment? $_____

16. Is Cable Television Service available at the site? Yes _____ No _____ Service Provider _____

17. Is Fiber Optic Cable (Internet) available at the site? Yes _____ No _____ Service Provider _____

18. List any item remaining with the Property which is financed separately from the mortgages _____

MECHANICAL EQUIPMENT WHICH IS CONSIDERED _PERSONAL PROPERTY_ AND IS NOT CONVEYED BY DEED AS PART OF THE REAL PROPERTY SHOULD BE NEGOTIATED IN THE CONTRACT OF SALE OR OTHER SUCH INSTRUMENT IF THE ITEMS ARE TO REMAIN WITH THE RESIDENCE.

To the extent of the Seller's knowledge as a property owner, the Seller(s) acknowledges that the information contained above is true and accurate for those areas of the property listed. The owner(s) agree to save and hold the Broker harmless from all claims, disputes, litigation and/or judgments arising from any incorrect information supplied by the owner(s) or from any material fact known by the owner(s) which owner(s) fail to disclose except the Broker is not held harmless to the owner(s) in claims, disputes, litigation, or judgments arising from conditions of which the Broker had actual knowledge.

_____ _____
SELLER (UPON LISTING)   DATE   SELLER (UPON LISTING)   DATE

_____ _____
SELLER (AT CLOSING)   DATE   SELLER (AT CLOSING)   DATE

PROSPECTIVE PURCHASER'S SIGNATURE _____

PURCHASER(S) ACKNOWLEDGE RECEIPT OF REPORT   DATE

FORM #0100   EFFECTIVE DATE: April 1, 2017

§89-1-501. Applicability of real estate transfer disclosure requirement provisions Excluded from Property Condition Disclosure

Transfers pursuant to court order, including	Transfers ordered by a probate court in administration of an estate, transfers pursuant to a writ of execution	Transfers by any foreclosure sale	Sale, transfers by a trustee in bankruptcy
Transfers by eminent domain	Transfers resulting from a decree for specific performance	Transfers to a mortgagee by a mortgagor or successor in interest who is in default	Transfers to a beneficiary of a deed of trust
Transfers by any foreclosure sale after default	Transfers made to a spouse, or to a person or persons in the lineal line of consanguinity of one or more of the transferors	Transfers from one coowner to one or more other co-owners.	Transfers made to a spouse, or to a person or persons in the lineal line of consanguinity
Transfers or exchanges to or from any governmental entity.	Transfers of real property on which no dwelling is located.	Transfers between spouses	Transfers by deed in lieu of foreclosure or decree of foreclosure

Transfers by a mortgagee or a beneficiary under a deed of trust who has acquired the real property at a sale conducted pursuant to a power of sale under a mortgage or deed of trust.

89-1-527. §89-1-503. Delivery of written statement required; indication of compliance; right of transferee to terminate for late deliver;

The transferor of any real property shall deliver to the prospective transferee the written property condition disclosure statement.
(a) In the case of a sale, as **soon as practicable** before transfer of title.
(b) **In the case of transfer by a real property sales contract, or by a lease together with an option to purchase, or a ground lease coupled with improvements, as soon as practicable before execution of the contract.**

Execution means the making or acceptance of an offer.

With respect to any transfer, the transferor shall indicate compliance either on the receipt for deposit, the real property sales contract, the lease, or any addendum attached thereto or on a separate document.

If any disclosure, or any material amendment of any disclosure, required to be made is delivered after the execution of an offer to purchase, the transferee shall have three (3) days after delivery in person or five (5) days after delivery by deposit in the mail, to terminate his or her offer by delivery of a written notice of termination to the transferor or the transferor's agent.

Transfer Disclosure Statement

If the offeror does not receive the disclosure, they shall have 3 days in person or 5 days by mail to cancel the offer.

Limit on duties and liabilities with respect to information required or delivered.

(1)   **Neither the transferor nor any listing or selling agent shall be liable for any error, inaccuracy or omission of any information delivered if the error, inaccuracy or omission was not within the personal knowledge of the transferor or that listing or selling agent, was based on information timely provided by public agencies or by other persons providing information that is required to be disclosed and ordinary care was exercised in obtaining and transmitting it.**

(2)   The delivery of any information required to be disclosed to a prospective transferee by a public agency or other person providing information required to be disclosed shall be deemed to comply with the requirements and shall relieve the transferor or any listing or selling agent of any further duty with respect to that item of information.

(3)   The delivery of a report or opinion prepared by a licensed engineer, land surveyor, geologist, structural pest control operator, contractor or other expert, dealing with matters within the scope of the professional's license or expertise, shall be sufficient compliance for application of the exemption if the information is provided to the prospective transferee pursuant to a request therefor, **whether written or oral.**

In responding to such a request, an expert may indicate, in writing, an understanding that the information provided will be used in fulfilling the requirements MREC and, if so, shall indicate the required disclosures, or parts thereof, to which the information being furnished is applicable.

Where such a statement is furnished, the expert shall not be responsible for any items of information, or parts thereof, other than those expressly set forth in the statement.

§89-1-507. Approximation of certain information required to be disclosed; information subsequently rendered inaccurate

If information disclosed is subsequently rendered inaccurate as a result of any act, occurrence or agreement subsequent to the delivery of the required disclosures, the inaccuracy resulting therefrom does not constitute a violation.

If at the time the disclosures are required to be made, an item of information required to be disclosed is unknown or not available to the transferor, and the transferor or his agent has made a **reasonable effort** to ascertain it, the transferor may use an approximation of the information, provided the approximation is clearly identified as such, is reasonable, is based on the best information available to the transferor or his agent, and is not used for the purpose of circumventing or evading.

§89-1-509. Form of seller's disclosure statement

The disclosures required pertaining to the property proposed to be transferred shall be set forth in and shall be made on a copy of a disclosure form, the structure and composition of which shall be determined by the Mississippi Real Estate Commission.

§89-1-511.Disclosures to be made in good faith

Each disclosure required and each act which may be performed in making the disclosure, shall be **made in good faith.**

§89-1-513. Provisions not exhaustive of items to be disclosed

The specification of items for disclosure does not limit or abridge any obligation for disclosure created by any other provision of law or which may exist in order to avoid fraud, misrepresentation or deceit in the transfer transaction.

§89-1-515. Amendment of disclosure

Any disclosure made may be amended in writing by the transferor or his agent, but the amendment shall be subject to MREC.

§89-1-517. Delivery of disclosure

Delivery of disclosure required shall be by personal delivery to the transferee or by mail to the prospective transferee. For the purposes **delivery to the spouse of a transferee shall be deemed delivery to the transferee**, unless provided otherwise by contract.

§89-1-519. Agent; extent of agency

Any person or entity, other than a duly licensed real estate broker or salesperson acting in the capacity of an escrow agent for the transfer of real property shall not be deemed the agent of the transferor or transferee for purposes of the disclosure requirements, unless the person or entity is empowered to so act by an express written agreement to that effect.

The extent of such an agency shall be governed by the written agreement.

§89-1-521. Delivery of disclosure where more than one agent; inability of delivering broker to obtain disclosure document; notification to transferee of right to disclosure

If more than one (1) licensed real estate broker is acting as an agent in a transaction, the broker who has obtained the offer made by the transferee shall, except as otherwise provided, deliver the disclosure to the transferee, unless the transferor has given other written instructions for delivery.

(2) If a licensed real estate broker responsible for delivering the disclosures under this section cannot obtain the disclosure document required and does not have written assurance from the transferee that the disclosure has been received, the broker shall advise the transferee in writing of his rights to the disclosure.

A licensed real estate broker responsible for delivering disclosures under this section shall maintain a record of the action taken to effect compliance.

§89-1-523. Noncompliance with disclosure requirements not to invalidate transfer; liability for actual damages

Transfer Disclosure Statement

The agent responsible for not getting the Property Transfer Disclosure statement to the buyer shall be responsible for any Actual Damages suffered by the Buyer.

Actual Damages

No transfer shall be invalidated solely because of the failure of any person to comply disclosure law.

However, any person who willfully or negligently violates or fails to perform any duty shall be liable in the amount of **actual damages** suffered by a transferee.

§89-1-525. Enforcement by Mississippi Real Estate Commission

The Mississippi Real Estate Commission is authorized to enforce violations.

Any violation shall be treated in the same manner as a violation of the Real Estate Broker License Law of 1954, and shall be subject to same penalties as provided in that chapter.

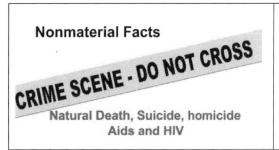 **Nonmaterial Facts** Natural Death, Suicide, homicide Aids and HIV	Failure to disclose nonmaterial fact regarding property as site of death or felony crime, as site of act or occurrence having no effect on physical condition of property, or as being owned or occupied by persons affected or exposed to certain diseases; failure to disclose information provided or maintained on registration of sex offenders.

The fact or suspicion that real property is or was:

The site of a natural death, suicide, homicide or felony crime (except for illegal drug activity that affects the physical condition of the property, its physical environment or the improvements located thereon);

(b)   The site of an act or occurrence that had no effect on the physical condition of the property, its physical environment or the improvements located thereon;

(c)   Owned or occupied by a person affected or exposed to any disease not known to be transmitted through common occupancy of real estate including, but not limited to, the human immunodeficiency virus (HIV) and the acquired immune deficiency syndrome (AIDS); does not constitute a material fact that must be disclosed in a real estate transaction.

A failure to disclose such nonmaterial facts or suspicions shall not give rise to a criminal, civil or administrative action against the owner of such real property, a licensed real estate broker or any affiliated licensee of the broker.

(2)   A failure to disclose in any real estate transaction any information that is provided or maintained, or is required to be provided or maintained, shall not give rise to a cause of action against an owner of real property, a licensed real estate broker or any affiliated licensee of the broker.

Likewise, no cause of action shall arise against any licensed real estate broker or affiliated licensee of the broker for revealing information to a seller or buyer of real estate.

Any factors, if known to a property owner or licensee shall be disclosed if requested by a consumer.

(3)   Failure to disclose any of the facts or suspicions of nonmaterial facts shall not be grounds for the termination or rescission of any transaction in which real property has been or will be transferred or leased.

This provision does not preclude an action against an owner of real estate who makes intentional or fraudulent misrepresentations in response to a direct inquiry from a purchaser or prospective purchaser regarding facts or suspicions that are not material to the physical condition of the property including, but not limited to nonmaterial facts.

REAL ESTATE BROKER'S LICENSE Miss. Code Ann. §73-5-7 (Amended, Effective July 1, 2020)

Broker's License Shall be age twenty- one (21) years or over.

Have his legal domicile in the State of Mississippi at the time he applies.

Be subject to the jurisdiction of this state, subject to the income tax laws and other excise laws thereof, subject to the road and bridge privilege tax laws.

Not be an elector in any other state.

Have held a license as an active real estate salesperson for **twelve (12) months** prior to making application for the broker's examination.

Have successfully completed a minimum of one hundred twenty (120) hours of courses in real estate.

Successfully completed the real estate broker's examination.

Have successfully been cleared for licensure by the commission's background investigation.

Sign a form under penalty of perjury stating that the applicant will not hire any real estate salespersons for thirtysix (36) months from the date of approval of his or her active real estate salesperson's license.

Application Fee

A fee not to exceed **One Hundred Fifty Dollars ($150.00)** shall accompany an application for a real estate broker's license, and in the event that the applicant successfully passes the examination, no additional fee shall be required for the issuance of a license for a one year period; provided, that if an applicant fails to pass the examination, he may be eligible to take the next or succeeding examination without the payment of an additional fee.

In the event a contract testing service is utilized, the fee associated with administering the test shall be collected by the testing provider and the application fee for any real estate license shall be collected by the commission. (Right now it is $75.
An application fee must accompany the application and will not be refunded after the applicant is scheduled for the examination.

36 Month Rule for Brokers

Any person who desires to hire a real estate salesperson in less than thirty-six (36) months from the date of approval of his or her active real estate salesperson's license shall:
be age twenty-one (21) years or over, and have his or her legal domicile in the State of Mississippi at the time he or she applies;

(b) be subject to the jurisdiction of this state, subject to the income tax laws and other excise laws thereof, subject to the road and bridge privilege tax laws thereof;
(c) not be an elector in any other state;
(d) **have held a license as an active real estate salesperson for thirty-six (36) months prior to making application for the broker's examination hereafter specified**; (e) have successfully completed a minimum of one hundred twenty **(120) hours** of courses in real estate as hereafter specified; (f) have successfully completed the real estate broker's examination as hereafter specified; and (g) have 15 successfully been cleared for licensure by the commission's background investigation.

REAL ESTATE BROKER'S LICENSE Miss. Code Ann. §73-5-7 (Amended, Effective July 1, 2020)

In its 2020 Regular Session, the Mississippi Legislature enacted an amendment to Miss. Code Ann. §73-5-7 which made changes to the experience requirements for persons seeking to be licensed as a real estate broker in

Mississippi, including certain restrictions on new broker licensee employment of real estate salespersons.

The legislation was approved by Governor Tate Reeves and became effective July 1, 2020.

> As amended, the relevant statutory provisions for obtaining a real estate broker's license now include: 12 months licensure as Salesperson prior to application for Broker's license and month restriction on employment of Salespersons

An applicant for a broker's license must have held an active license as a real estate salesperson for a minimum of twelve (12) months prior to making application. The required period of active licensure as a real estate salesperson may be satisfied by evidence of cumulative period(s) of active licensure as a real estate salesperson totaling a minimum of twelve (12) months prior to application for licensure as a real estate broker.

> **Broker Certification Form**
>
> Applicant must execute the Broker Certification Form (available on Commission website) and swear/affirm, under penalty of perjury, the broker will not hire any real estate salespersons for a period of thirty-six (36) months following the date of approval of the broker's original (active) salesperson's license.

Exclusions

The thirty-six (36) month restriction on employment of real estate salespersons shall not apply to brokers who have held a license as an active real estate salesperson for a **cumulative period** of thirty-six (36) months prior to making application for the broker's license examination.

The thirty-six (36) month restriction on employment of real estate salespersons shall not apply to brokers who have completed a minimum of **one hundred fifty (150) classroom hours of real estate courses**, which courses are acceptable for credit toward a degree at a college or university as approved by the Southern Association of Colleges and Schools.

RULES AND REGULATIONS PART 1601 – MISSISSIPPI REAL ESTATE COMMISSION

Chapter 1 – Licensing Rule

1.1 Applying for a license
Rule 1.2 Changing the state of a license
Miss. Code Ann. §73-35-35

Chapter 2 – Fees Rule 2.1 Fees

Rule 2.2 All fees are the same for both resident and nonresident licenses
Miss. Code Ann. §73-35-35

Chapter 3 – Administration/Conducting Business Rule

3.1 General Rules Rule
3.2 Documents Rule
3.3 Advertising Rule
3.4 Earnest Money
Miss. Code Ann. §73-35-35
Rule 3.5 Real Estate Teams or Groups
Miss. Code Ann. §73-35-3(4); §73-35-18(3); §73-35-21(d)

Chapter 4 – Agency Relationship Disclosure

Rule 4.1 Purpose
Rule 4.2 Definitions Rule
4.3 Disclosure Requirements Rule
4.4 Disclosure Exception
Miss. Code Ann. §73-35-35

Chapter 5 – Complaint Procedure

Rule 5.1 Notifications of complaints to the Commission
Miss. Code Ann. §73-35-35 2

Chapter 6 – Continuing Education

Rule 6.1 Approved Courses
Rule 6.2 Procedures and criteria for approval of courses
Rule 6.3 Qualifications of instructors
Rule 6.4 Administrative requirements
Rule 6.5 Advertising and solicitation
Rule 6.6 Relationship with providers
Rule 6.7 Suspension or revocation of approval
Miss. Code Ann. §73-35-35

Chapter 7 – Inspection of Offering from Out-of-State

Rule 7.1 Out-of-state developers

Miss. Code Ann. §73-35-35

Chapter 8 – Time Share Rule 8.1 Licensing

Rule 8.2 Definitions Rule 8.3 Registration
Rule 8.4 Public offering statement
Rule 8.5 Amendment to registration information/public offering statement
Rule 8.6 Registration review time frame
Rule 8.7 Purchase contracts
Rule 8.8 Exchange program
Rule 8.9 Escrows and alternatives assurances
Rule 8.10 Insurance
Rule 8.11 Advertising and marketing
Rule 8.12 Management
Rule 8.13 Liens
Rule 8.14 Owner referrals
Miss. Code Ann. §73-35-35

Chapter 9 – Errors and Omissions Insurance Coverage

Rule 9.1 Administration
Rule 9.2 Licensee status
Rule 9.3 Independent coverage
Miss. Code Ann. §73-35-35 3

PART 1602 – ORAL PROCEEDING AND DECLARATORY OPINIONS

Chapter 1 – Oral Proceedings

Rule 1.1 Scope
Rule 1.2 When oral proceedings will be scheduled on proposed rules
Rule 1.3 Request format
Rule 1.4 Notifications of oral proceedings
Rule 1.5 Presiding officer
Rule 1.6 Public presentation and participation
Rule 1.7 Conduct of oral proceeding
Miss. Code Ann. §25-43-3-104 (Rev. 2010)

PART 1503 – DECLARATORY OPINIONS

Chapter 2 – Declaratory Opinions Rule 2.1 Scope
Rule 2.2 Persons who may request declaratory opinions
Rule 2.3 Subjects which may be addressed in declaratory opinions
Rule 2.4 Circumstances in which declaratory opinions will not be issued
Rule 2.5 Written request required
Rule 2.6 Where to send requests
Rule 2.7 Name, address, and signature of requestor
Rule 2.8 Question presented
Rule 2.9 Time for board response
Rule 2.10 Opinion not final for sixty (60) days
Rule 2.11 Notice by board to third parties
Rule 2.12 Public availability of requests and declaratory opinions

Rule 2.13 Effect of a declaratory opinion
Miss. Code Ann. §25-43-2-103 (Rev. 2010)

PART 1603 – BOARD ORGANIZATION

Chapter 1 – Board Members Rule 1.1 Members
Miss. Code Ann. §73-35-5 4

MISSISSIPPI REAL ESTATE COMMISSION RULES AND REGULATIONS TITLE 30

Professions and Occupations PART 1601:

Chapter 1: Licensing Rule

Applying for a License

A.   An applicant for a broker's license must pass the National Portion of the broker's examination with a grade of at least 75% and must pass the State Specific Portion of the examination with a grade of at least 80%.

B.   An applicant for a salesperson's license must pass the National Portion of the salesperson's examination with a grade of at least 70% and must pass the State Specific Portion of the examination with a grade of at least 75%.

C.   An application fee must accompany the application and will not be refunded after the applicant is scheduled for the examination.

D.   The approved Examination Testing Provider will administer examination in various locations in and near the State of Mississippi. Applicants will arrange the time and place of their examination with the Testing Provider.

E.   When an applicant is approved for either examination, applicant has two months in which to take and pass both exams.

Months to take and pass the exam

State Specific Portion	National Portion

If the applicant fails to appear for the examination within the two months allowed, applicant's fee will be forfeited, and their file closed.

If the applicant fails to pass the first examination, applicant will be allowed to take the next examination with the payment of an additional fee to the Testing Provider. If the applicant fails to appear for the second examination, fees will be forfeited, and their file closed.

F.   If a corporation has been chartered by the state of Mississippi, the license will be issued in the corporate name except that no license will be issued for a corporation, company, or trade name where there exists in that county or trade area a real estate broker or real estate agency having a substantially similar name.

Reciprocal License

G.   A real estate licensee of another state who desires to obtain a license under this chapter shall be exempt from the examination provided the examination administered in the other state is determined by the Commission to be equivalent to such examination given in this state and provided that such other state extends this same privilege or exemption to Mississippi real estate licensees.

Real estate education courses obtained through sources (providers) which are accepted in the state where the applicant is licensed, may be accepted by the Commission provided the state where the applicant is licensed has entered into a reciprocal agreement with this state.

Rule 1.2 Changing the Status of a License

A. To change a license from active to inactive status, licensee shall notify the Commission in writing, shall insure that the license is returned to the Commission and shall pay the appropriate fee.

A licensee who is on inactive status at time of renewal may renew the license on inactive status by filing a renewal application and paying the renewal fee. A broker who terminates a real estate business may place the business license on inactive status.

To return to active status, a salesperson or broker/salesperson must file a transfer application.

A broker and/or a business license may be activated by notifying the Commission by letter or transfer application including required fee.

B.   When a licensee wishes to transfer from one broker to another, the transferring licensee must file a transfer application signed by the new broker accompanied by the transfer fee and must furnish a statement that the licensee is not carrying any listings or pertinent information belonging to the former broker unless that broker so consents.

C.   Any licensee who has entered active duty military service due to draft laws or national emergency shall, upon his return to civilian life and within twelve (12) months after honorable discharge, be considered, so far as this Commission is concerned, to have been continuously engaged in the real estate business in the same capacity as when the licensee entered military service.

Chapter 2: Fees Rule 2.1

The following fees are set by the Commission in accordance with Section 73-35-17:

A. Application and one year's use of license: (1) Broker..................................$150.00 (2) Salesperson.....................$120.00

B. Application for license as a real estate broker issued for partnership, association, or corporation and one year's use of license:

Partnership, association or corporation..........................$75.00

(2) Branch Office $50.00

7 C. Renewal fees for two-year period (Maximum):

(1) Broker individual)……………………………………………..$150.00

(2) Broker (partnership, association, corporation) …………$150.00

(3) Salesperson…………………………………………………………….$120.00

(4) Branch Office ………………………………………………………

$100.00 Penalty for late renewal within grace period – 100%

D. Changes:

(1) Place of business change (active license only)…………..$50.00

(2) Each duplicate license …………………………………………$50.00 (3) Each transfer of license ……………………………………..$50.00

(4) Status change from active to inactive status………………$25.00

(5) Status change from inactive to active status………………$50.00 E. Check charge:

(1) Each check returned not paid to the Commission ………$25.00

Rule 2.2 All fees are the same for both Resident and Nonresident Licenses.

Fees and monies payable to the Mississippi Real Estate Commission may be by personal check, cash, cashier's check or money order.

All personal checks shall be made payable to the Mississippi Real Estate Commission.
☞☞ Any personal checks returned not paid or for any other reason shall constitute justifiable grounds for refusing, suspending or revoking a license.

Non-sufficient fund (NSF) checks, if not made good by renewal deadline, will cause the licensee to be in nonrenewal status and necessitates the payment of a penalty (100%) by licensee.

Chapter 3: Administration/Conducting Business Rule

Rule 3.1 General Rules A.

☞☞ It shall be the duty of the responsible broker to instruct the licensees licensed under that broker in the fundamentals of
real estate practice, ethics of the profession and the Mississippi Real Estate License Law and to exercise supervision of their real estate activities for which a license is required.

Responsible Broker

Responsible for; Fundamentals, Ethics, License Law and Supervision

It is not the responsibility to make an agents educational requirements are complete.

👏👏 A real estate broker who operates under the supervision of a responsible broker must not at any time act independently as a broker.

👏👏 The responsible broker shall at all times be responsible for the action of the affiliated broker to the same extent as though that licensee were a salesperson and that affiliated broker shall not perform any real estate service without the full consent and knowledge of his employing or supervising broker.

Affiliate Brokers must not act independtly Of their responsible broker unless mutually agreed upon. and they Inform MREC.

👏👏 However, should the responsible broker agree that a broker under his supervision may perform certain real estate services outside the responsible broker's supervision or direction the responsible broker shall notify the Commission in writing as to the exact nature of such relationship and the names of the broker or brokers involved.

👏👏 The responsible broker shall immediately notify the Commission in writing upon the termination of such relationship.

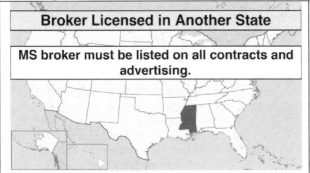

Broker Licensed in Another State

MS broker must be listed on all contracts and advertising.

The commissions or other compensation resulting from the sale/rent/lease/property management or auction of the Mississippi real property and which are earned during the period the cooperative agreement is in force shall be divided on a negotiable basis between the Mississippi broker and the nonresident broker.

👏👏 **COOPERATING BROKER**

A licensed Mississippi broker may cooperate with a broker licensed in another state who does not hold a Mississippi license through the use of a cooperative agreement.

A separate cooperative agreement must be filed for each property, prospective user or transaction with said writing reflecting the compensation to be paid to the Mississippi licensed broker.

The listing or property management agreement for the Mississippi real property shall in such cases remain in the name of the Mississippi licensed broker.

A responsible (principal) nonresident broker described herein is defined as an active, licensed responsible real estate broker of another state who does not possess an active responsible nonresident real estate broker's license issued by the Mississippi Real Estate Commission (MREC).

A Mississippi broker described herein is a responsible (principal) real estate broker whose license is on active status and whose license was issued by MREC either as a responsible resident Mississippi broker or as a responsible nonresident Mississippi broker.

The responsible nonresident broker cannot place any sign on real property located in the state of Mississippi without the written consent of the cooperating responsible Mississippi broker.

When the consent is obtained, the sign of the responsible Mississippi broker must be placed in a prominent place and in close proximity to the responsible nonresident broker's sign.

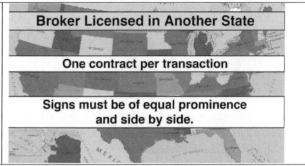

Broker Licensed in Another State

One contract per transaction

Signs must be of equal prominence and side by side.

Any licensed responsible Mississippi broker assisting or cooperating in the sale, lease, property management, rental or auction of real property within the state of Mississippi with a responsible nonresident broker who fails or refuses to list his or her name in such advertisement, or fails or refuses to cross-list such property with him or her, in writing, shall be deemed in violation of Section 73-35-11 of the Real Estate Broker's License Act, and shall be subject to a revocation or suspension of his or her license.

Broker Licensed in Another State

MS Broker Responsibilities

Verify license is active.

Responsible for their own acts and the acts of the other broker.

In such instance herein where a responsible Mississippi broker enters into a cooperative agreement with a responsible nonresident broker pertaining to the sale of real property within the state of Mississippi, the responsible Mississippi broker must file two copies of the cooperating agreement with the Mississippi Real Estate Commission.

Broker Office

A responsible broker must maintain an office and display the license therein. If the broker has more than one office, the broker shall display a branch office license in each branch office. The broker is responsible for the real estate practices of those licensees.

Licenses must be displayed in main office.

Branch office license needed in branch office.

Broker is responsible for the real estate practices of his agents.

Compensation

No licensee shall pay any part of a fee, commission, or other compensation received by such licensee in buying, selling, exchanging, leasing, auctioning or renting any real estate except to another licensee through the licensee's responsible broker.

No licensee shall knowingly pay a commission, or other compensation to a licensed person knowing that licensee will in turn pay a portion or all of that which is received to a person who does not hold a real estate license

Broker always receives the compensation.

Person must have a license or a cooperating agreement to be paid a referral fee.

No referral fees to unlicensed persons.

Compensation from previous broker

If a listing or transaction was done under the employment contract of the broker you left, you can receive money directly from that broker.

COMPENSATION FROM PREVIOUS BROKER

A licensee who has changed to inactive status or who has transferred to another responsible broker may receive compensation from the previous responsible broker if the commission was generated from activity during the time that the licensee was under the supervision of that responsible broker.

PRIMA FACIE GUILTY OF IMPROPER DEALINGS

Any licensee who fails in a timely manner to respond to official Mississippi Real Estate Commission written communication or who fails or neglects to abide by Mississippi Real Estate Commission's Rules and Regulations shall be deemed, prima facie, to be guilty of

If you do not respond to MREC in a timely manner, you will be found Prima Facie, guilty of improper dealing.

improper dealing. ### BPO – BROKER PRICE OPINION

A real estate broker or salesperson in the ordinary course of business may give an opinion as to the sales price of real estate for the purpose of a prospective listing or sale; however, this opinion as to the listing price or the sale price shall not be referred to as an appraisal and must be completed in compliance with Section 73-35- 4 of the Real Estate Broker's License Act and must conform to the Standards established by the National Association of Broker Price Opinion

Standards used are from the National Association of Broker Price Opinion Professionals.

BPO

Not an Appraisal and can be paid.

Professionals (NABPOP).

BPO's are never used for the origination of a loan.

☞☞ DOCUMENT AND DATE THE

SELLER'S ACCEPTANCE OR REJECTION

When an offer is made on property owned by a party with whom a broker has entered into a listing agreement, such broker shall document and date the seller's personal acceptance or rejection of the offer and upon written request, shall provide a copy of such document to the person making the offer.

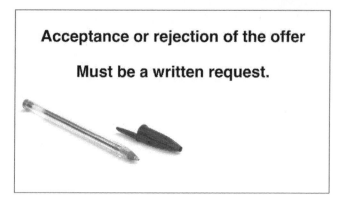

Acceptance or rejection of the offer

Must be a written request.

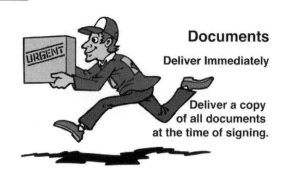

When selling own property, you must indicate that you are licensed in all advertising and contracts (involving real estate).

☞ SELLING OWN PROPERTY

A real estate licensee shall not be exempt from disciplinary actions by the commission when selling property owned by the licensee.

Rule 3.2 Documents

A real estate licensee shall immediately ☞ **(at the time of signing)** deliver a true and correct copy of any instrument to any party or parties executing the same.

Documents

Deliver Immediately

Deliver a copy of all documents at the time of signing.

NEW LISTING

Exclusive Listing Agreements
Must be in writing.
Identify all the terms and conditions.
Must clearly identify the type of listing.

☞☞ All exclusive listing agreements shall be in writing, properly identify the property to be sold, and contain all of the terms and conditions under which the transaction is to be consummated; including the sales price, the considerations to be paid, the signatures of all parties to the agreement, and a **definite date of expiration.**

☞☞ No listing agreement shall contain any provision requiring the listing party to notify the broker of their intention to cancel the listing after such definite expiration date.

☞☞ An **"Exclusive Agency"** listing or **"Exclusive Right to Sell"** listing shall clearly indicate in the listing agreement that it is such an agreement.

All **exclusive buyer representation agreements** shall be in writing and properly identify the terms and conditions under which the buyer will rely on the broker for the purchase of real estate; including the sales price, the considerations to be paid, the signatures of all parties to the agreement, and a definite date of expiration. The buyer may terminate the agreement upon **fifteen (15) calendar days written notice to the buyer's exclusive agent.**

An Exclusive Buyer Representation agreement shall clearly indicate in the body of the document that it is such an agreement.

In the event that more than one written offer is made before the owner has accepted an offer, any other written offer received by the listing broker, whether from a prospective purchaser or from another licensee cooperating in a sale, shall be presented to the owner unless the listing broker has specific, written instructions from the owner to postpone the presentation of other offers.

Broker should caution the seller against countering on more than one offer at the same time.

Every real estate contract must reflect whom the broker represents by a statement over the signatures of the parties to the contract.

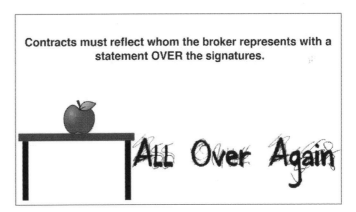

83

No false sales contracts to lenders.

The True and actual selling price must be used.

☞☞ No licensee shall represent to a lender or any other interested party, either verbally or through the preparation of a false sales contract, an amount in excess of the true and actual selling price.

Keep records three years.

They can be kept electronically.

☞☞ A real estate broker must keep on file for three years following its consummation, complete records relating to any real estate transaction.
This includes, but is not limited to: listings, options, leases, offers to purchase, contracts of sale, escrow records, agency agreements and copies of all closing statements.

☞☞ **Documents that need to be kept**

listings	options	leases	offers to purchase
contracts of sale	escrow records	agency agreements	copies of all closing statements

No Substantial Misrepresentation.

No Blind Ads.

Rule 3.3 Advertising

"Advertising" means the use of any oral, written, visual, printed or electronically generated advertisement by a real estate licensee or other person on behalf of a real estate licensee.

"Advertisement" means any oral, written, visual, printed or electronic media advertisement and encompasses any correspondence, mailing, newsletter, brochure, business card, for sale or for lease signage or sign rider, promotional items, automobile signage, telephone directory listing, radio and television broadcasts, telephone solicitation and electronic media to include e-mails, text messaging, public blogs, social media networking websites, and/or internet displays.

👍👎 A broker shall advertise in the name in which the license is issued.

👍👎 A broker may use a descriptive term after the broker's name to indicate the occupation in which engaged, for example, "realty", "real estate" or "property management".

If advertising in any other form, a partnership, trade name, association, company or corporation license must be obtained prior to advertising in that manner.

👍👎 All advertising must be under the direct supervision and in the name of the Principal Broker or in the name of the real estate Brokerage Firm and must prominently display the name of the Principal Broker or the name of the Brokerage Firm in such a manner that it is conspicuous, discernible and easily identifiable by a member of the public.

Principal Brokers are required to verify and determine that their name or the name of the Brokerage Firm is prominently displayed on all advertising and that the name of any real estate licensee or any approved real estate Team or Group is situated near the name of the Brokerage Firm.

👍👎 The Broker or the Brokerage Firm must be identified by using the same size or larger print as that of a Licensee or a **Team** in all advertising.

👍👎 All advertising must include the telephone number of the Principal Broker or the Brokerage Firm.

👍👎 No Principal Broker or licensee sponsored by said broker shall in any way advertise property or place a sign on any such property offering the property for sale or rent without first obtaining the written authorization to do so by all owners of the property or by any appointed person or entity who also has full authority to convey the property.

Licensee Selling Own Property

You can sell "by owner".
You don't have to use your broker.
If you do something wrong, your broker is still responsible.

👍👎 When a licensee is advertising their own property for sale, purchase or exchange which is not listed with a broker, the licensee must indicate that he or she is licensed.

The disclosure of licensee's status must be made in all forms of advertising enumerated in Rule 3.3 (A), including the "for sale" sign.

In addition to disclosing their licensed status in all advertisements, licensees are required to disclose their licensed status on all real estate contracts in which they have an ownership interest.

A licensee shall not advertise to sell, buy, exchange, auction, rent or lease property in a manner indicating that the offer to sell, buy, exchange, auction, rent, or lease such property is being made by a private party who is not engaged in the real estate business.

No advertisement shall be inserted by a licensee in any publication where only a post office box number, telephone number, e-mail address or street address appears.

Every licensee, when advertising real estate in any publication, shall indicate that the party advertising is licensed in real estate; whether on active or inactive status.

Rule 3.4 Earnest Money

The responsible broker is responsible at all times for earnest money deposits.

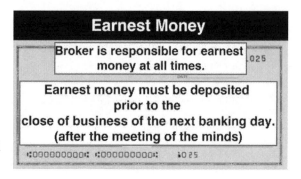

Earnest money accepted by the broker or any licensee for which the broker is responsible and upon acceptance of a mutually agreeable contract is required to deposit the money into a trust account prior to the close of business of the next banking day.

The responsible broker is required to promptly account for and remit the full amount of the deposit or earnest money at the consummation or termination of transaction.

A licensee is required to pay over to the responsible broker all deposits and earnest money immediately upon receipt thereof.

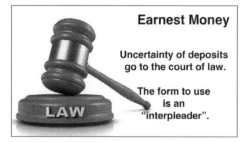

Earnest money must be returned promptly when the purchaser is rightfully entitled to same allowing reasonable time for clearance of the earnest money check.

In the event of uncertainty as to the proper disposition of earnest money, the broker may turn earnest money over to a court of law for disposition.

Failure to comply with this regulation shall constitute grounds for revocation or suspension of license.

If the Seller is unable to consummate the transaction,
the earnest money
gets returned to the buyer even
If your commission was earned.

You should look to the seller for compensation.

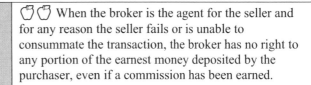 When the broker is the agent for the seller and for any reason the seller fails or is unable to consummate the transaction, the broker has no right to any portion of the earnest money deposited by the purchaser, even if a commission has been earned.

 The entire amount of the earnest money deposit must be returned to the purchaser and the broker should look to the seller for compensation.

Accurate records shall be kept on escrow accounts of all monies received, disbursed, or on hand.

All monies shall be individually identified as to a particular transaction.

Trust / Escrow Accounts

Accurate Records for deposits must be kept by the broker.

Standard Accounting Practices must be used.

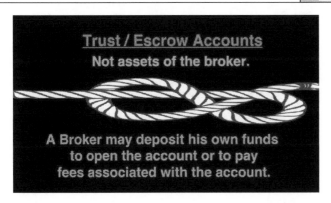

Trust / Escrow Accounts
Not assets of the broker.

A Broker may deposit his own funds to open the account or to pay fees associated with the account.

Escrow records shall be kept in accordance with standard accounting practices and shall be subject to inspection at all times by the Commission. Monies received in a trust account on behalf of clients or customers are not assets of the broker; however, a broker may deposit and keep in each escrow account or rental account some personal funds for the express purpose of covering service charges and other bank debits related to each account.

If a broker, as escrow agent, accepts a check and later finds that such check has not been honored by the bank on which it was drawn, the broker shall immediately notify all parties involved in the transaction.

Checks not honored!

Notify all parties immediately.

Rule 3.5 Real Estate Teams or Groups

A "Team or Group" shall mean a collective name used by two or more active real estate licensees who represent themselves to the public as being part of a single entity which is organized with the written approval of a Principal Broker to perform licensable real estate activity. To qualify as a **"Real Estate Team or Group"** the active real estate licensees must be working together and each must

(a) work under the direct supervision of the same Principal Broker,

(b) work together on real estate transactions to provide real estate brokerage services,

(c) must represent themselves to the public as being part of a Team or Group,

(d) must be designated by a specific team or group name, and

(e) must conduct all real estate activity from the primary office or branch office where their individual licenses are displayed.

B.   All Principal Brokers must have specific information on each Team operating within their Brokerage and must register each Team with the Real Estate Commission on forms provided for that purpose; to include a detailed list indicating all approved Team names, the name of the Team Leader, the name of the individual Team members and the name of any unlicensed employee(s) of the Team.

The working list(s) should indicate the dates that Team members are added to or deleted from any Team and should enable the Principal Broker and/or the Real Estate Commission to determine Team membership at any point in time.

Adjustments to a Team should be filed with the Real Estate Commission within ten (10) working day of any change and should be on forms provided by the Commission.

C.   All teams must appoint a Team Leader, who will be a Broker Associate with a minimum of one years' real estate experience and will have supervisory responsibility (under the supervision of the Principal Broker) over the Team

members.

The Team Leader may be subject to disciplinary action for violations of the Mississippi Real Estate Brokers Act by Team members under their supervision.

D.   A Team Name may, with the written approval of the Principal Broker and the Team Leader, be used in any type of advertising. Any individual whose name is displayed in any advertisement must be an active licensee who is sponsored by the Principal Broker.

All advertising must fully comply with the guidelines established in MREC Administrative Rule 3.3.

Principal Brokers and Team Leaders must confirm that the name of the Principal Broker or the Brokerage Firm and their telephone number is prominently displayed on all advertising.

The name of the Team must be situated near the name of the Brokerage Firm and shall be identified with the same sized or smaller print as that of the Brokerage.

E.   Neither team names nor team advertising should suggest that the team is an independent real estate brokerage. Team names must not include terms such as

(a) real estate brokerage,

(b) realty,

(c) real estate, or

(d) company.

Chapter 4: Agency Relationship Disclosure

Rule 4.1 Purpose

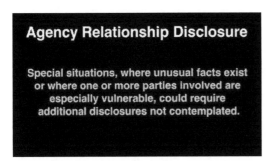

Consumers shall be fully informed of the agency relationships in real estate transactions identified in Section 73-353.

This rule places specific requirements on Brokers to disclose their agency relationship.

This does not abrogate the laws of agency as recognized under common law and compliance with the prescribed disclosures will not always guarantee that a Broker has fulfilled all of his responsibilities under the common law of agency.

 Compliance will be necessary in order to protect licensees from impositions of sanctions against their license by the Mississippi Real Estate Commission.

Special situations, where unusual facts exist or where one or more parties involved are especially vulnerable, could require additional disclosures not contemplated by this rule.

In such cases, Brokers should seek legal advice prior to entering into an agency relationship.

WORKING WITH A REAL ESTATE BROKER

Approved 01/2003 By
MS Real Estate Commission
P. O. Box 12685
Jackson, MS 39232

THIS IS NOT A LEGALLY BINDING CONTRACT

GENERAL

Before you begin working with any real estate agent, you should know whom the agent represents in the transaction. Mississippi real estate licensees are required to disclose which party they represent in a transaction and to allow a party the right to choose or refuse among the various agency relationships.

There are several types of relationships that are possible and you should understand these at the time a broker or salesperson provides specific assistance to you in a real estate transaction.

The purpose of the Agency Disclosure is to document an acknowledgement that the consumer has been informed of various agency relationships, which are available in a real estate transaction.

For the purpose of this disclosure, the term seller and/or buyer will also include those other acts specified in Section 73-35-3

(1), of the Miss. Code, "...list, sell, purchase, exchange, rent, lease, manage, or auction any real estate, or the improvements thereon including options."

INSTRUCTIONS FOR COMPLETING THE WORKING WITH A REAL ESTATE BROKER FORM

NOTE: This form **MUST** be completed at the **FIRST** meeting a real estate licensee has with a prospective client. It MUST be signed by all parties, MUST be in the licensee's files for that client or property, and the customer or client MUST receive a copy IMMEDIATELY!

■ One of the four boxes **MUST** be checked.

■ **DO NOT** check both the client AND customer boxes.

A seller or buyer can only be a client OR a customer.

The seller or buyer should sign on the line that corresponds with the box checked.

For example, if the box is checked for client (Seller's or Landlords Agent), the client signs directly below, and NOT on the "customer" line.

Rule 4.2 Definitions

"Agency" shall mean the relationship created when one person, the Principal (client), delegates to another, the agent, the right to act on his behalf in a real estate transaction and to exercise some degree of discretion while so acting.

Agency may be entered into by expressed agreement, implied through the actions of the agent and or ratified after the fact by the principal accepting the benefits of an agent's previously unauthorized act.

An agency gives rise to a fiduciary relationship and imposes on the agent, as the fiduciary of the principal, certain duties, obligations, and high standards of good faith and loyalty.

"Agent" shall mean one who is authorized to act on behalf of and represent another.

A real estate broker is the agent of the principal (client) to whom a fiduciary obligation is owed.

(State and National Contradict here) Salespersons licensed under the broker are sub-agents of the Broker, regardless of the location of the office in which the salesperson works.

"Agent" shall mean one who is authorized to act on behalf of and represent another.

A real estate broker is the agent of the principal (client) to whom a fiduciary obligation is owed.

Salespersons licensed under the broker are sub-agents of the Broker, regardless of the location of the office in which the salesperson works.

"Client" shall mean the person to whom the agent owes a fiduciary duty.

It can be a seller, buyer, landlord, tenant or both.

"Compensation" is that fee paid to a broker for the rendering of services. Compensation, when considered alone, is not the determining factor in an agency relationship.
The relationship can be created regardless of whether the seller pays the fee, the buyer pays the fee, both pay the fee or neither pays a fee.

WORKING WITH A REAL ESTATE BROKER

Approved 01/2003 By
MS Real Estate Commission
P. O. Box 12685
Jackson, MS 39232

THIS IS NOT A LEGALLY BINDING CONTRACT

GENERAL

Before you begin working with any real estate agent, you should know whom the agent represents in the transaction. Mississippi real estate licensees are required to disclose which party they represent in a transaction and to allow a party the right to choose or refuse among the various agency relationships.

There are several types of relationships that are possible and you should understand these at the time a broker or salesperson provides specific assistance to you in a real estate transaction.

The purpose of the Agency Disclosure is to document an acknowledgement that the consumer has been informed of various agency relationships, which are available in a real estate transaction.

For the purpose of this disclosure, the term seller and/or buyer will also include those other acts specified in Section 73-35-3 (1), of the Miss. Code, "...list, sell, purchase, exchange, rent, lease, manage, or auction any real estate, or the improvements thereon including options."

SELLER'S AGENT

A seller can enter into a "listing agreement" with a real estate firm authorizing the firm and its agent(s) to represent the seller in finding a buyer for his property. A licensee who is engaged by and acts as the agent of the Seller only is known as a Seller's Agent. A Seller's agent has the following duties and obligations:

To the Seller:

*The fiduciary duties of loyalty, confidentiality, obedience, disclosure, full accounting and the duty to use skill, care and diligence.

To the Buyer and Seller:

*A duty of honesty and fair dealing.

*A duty to disclose all facts known to the Seller's agent materially affecting the value of the property, which are not known to, or readily observable by, the parties in a transaction.

BUYER'S AGENT

A buyer may contract with an agent or firm to represent him/her. A licensee who is engaged by and acts as the agent of the Buyer only is known as the Buyer's Agent.

If a Buyer wants an agent to represent him in purchasing a property, the buyer can enter into a Buyer's Agency Agreement with the agent. A Buyer's Agent has the following duties and obligations:

To the Buyer:

* The fiduciary duties of loyalty, confidentiality, obedience, disclosure, full accounting and the duty to use skill, care and diligence.

To the Seller and Buyer:

* A duty of honesty and fair dealing.

DISCLOSED DUAL AGENT

A real estate agent or firm may represent more than one party in the same transaction. A Disclosed Dual Agent is a licensee who, with the informed written consent of the Seller and Buyer, is engaged as an agent for both Seller and Buyer.

As a disclosed dual agent, the licensee shall not represent the interests of one party to the exclusion or detriment of the interests of the other party. A disclosed dual agent has all the fiduciary duties to the Seller and Buyer that a Seller's or Buyer's agent has except the duties of full disclosure and undivided loyalty.

A Disclosed Dual Agent may not disclose:

(a) To the Buyer that the Seller will accept less than the asking or listed price, unless otherwise instructed in writing by the Seller.

(b) To the Seller that the Buyer will pay a price greater than the price submitted in a written offer to the Seller, unless otherwise instructed in writing by the Buyer.

(e) The motivation of any party for selling, buying, or leasing a property, unless otherwise instructed in writing by the respective party, or

(d) That a Seller or Buyer will agree to financing terms other than those offered, unless otherwise instructed in writing by the respective party.

IMPORTANT NOTICE!

"Customer" shall mean that person not represented in a real estate transaction. It may be the buyer, seller, landlord or tenant.

A Buyer may decide to work with a firm that is acting as agent for the Seller (a Seller's Agent or subagent). If a Buyer does not enter into a Buyer Agency Agreement with the firm that shows him properties, that firm and its agents may show the buyer properties as an agent or subagent working on the seller's behalf. Such a firm represents the Seller (not the Buyer) and must disclose that fact to the Buyer.

When it comes to the price and terms of an offer, the Seller's Agent will ask you to decide how much to offer for any property and upon what terms and conditions. They can explain your options to you, but the final decision is yours, as they cannot give you legal or financial advice. They will attempt to show you property in the price range and category that you desire so that you will have information on which to base your decision.

The Seller's Agent will present to the Seller any written offer that you ask them to present. You should keep to yourself any information that you do not want the Seller to know (i.e. the price you are willing to pay, other terms you are willing to accept, and your motivation for buying). The Seller's agent is required to tell all such information to the Seller. You should not furnish the Seller's agent anything you do not want the Seller to know. If you desire, you may obtain the representation of an attorney or another real estate agent, or both.

THIS IS NOT A CONTRACT. THIS IS AN ACKNOWLEDGEMENT OF DISCLOSURE

The below named Licensee has informed me that brokerage services are being provided me as a:

☐ Client   (Seller's or Landlord's Agent)

☐ Client   (Buyer's or Tenant's Agent)   ☐ Customer   (Not as my Agent)

☐ Client   (Disclosed Dual Agent)

By signing below, I acknowledge that I received this informative document and explanation prior to the exchange of confidential information which might affect the bargaining position in a real estate transaction involving me.

_____

(Date)

_____   _____   _____
(Client)   (Licensee)   (Customer)

_____   _____   _____
(Client)   (Company)   (Customer)

LICENSEE -Provide a copy of disclosure acknowledgement to all parties and retain signed original for your files.

SPC 01/2003   MREC Rev 91/2003

🍎🍎 "Customer" shall mean that person not represented in a real estate transaction.

It may be the buyer, seller, landlord or tenant.

"Disclosed Dual Agent" shall mean that agent representing both parties to a real estate transaction with the informed consent of both parties, with written understanding of specific duties and representation to be afforded each party.

There may be situations where disclosed dual agency presents conflicts of interest that cannot be resolved without breach of duty to one party or another.

Brokers who practice disclosed dual agency should do so with the utmost caution to protect consumers and themselves from inadvertent violation of demanding common law standards of disclosed dual agency.

"Fiduciary Responsibilities" are those duties due the principal (client) in a real estate transaction are:

(1) 'Loyalty' – the agent must put the interests of the principal above the interests of the agent or any third party.

(2) 'Obedience' – the agent agrees to obey any lawful instruction from the principal in the execution of the transaction that is the subject of the agency.

(3) 'Disclosure' – the agent must disclose to the principal any information the agent becomes aware of in connection with the agency.

(4) 'Confidentiality' – the agent must keep private information provided by the principal and information which would give a customer an advantage over the principal strictly confidential, unless the agent has the principal's permission to disclose the information.

This duty lives on after the agency relationship is terminated.

(5) 'Reasonable skill, care and diligence' – the agent must perform all duties with the care and diligence which may be reasonably expected of someone undertaking such duties.

(6) 'Full accounting' – the agent must provide a full accounting of any money or goods coming into the agent's possession which belong to the principal or other parties.

H. "First Substantive Meeting" shall be: (1) In a real estate transaction in which the Broker is the agent for the seller, first substantive meeting shall be before or just immediately prior to the first of any of the following: (a) Showing the property to a prospective buyer. (b) Eliciting confidential information from a buyer concerning the buyers' real estate needs, motivation, or financial qualifications. (c) The execution of any agreements governed by Section 73-35-3 of the Mississippi Code of 1972 Annotated.	(2) For the seller's agent, the definition shall not include: (a) A bona fide "open house" or model home showing which encompasses (1)(a) above only; however, whenever an event described in (1)(b) or (1)(c) occurs, disclosure must be made. (b) Preliminary conversations or "small talk" concerning price range, location and property styles. (c) Responding to general factual questions from a prospective buyer concerning properties that have been advertised for sale or lease.
(3) In a real estate transaction in which the Broker is the agent for the buyer, first substantive meeting shall be at the initial contact with a seller or a seller's agent or before or just immediately prior to the first of any of the following: (a) Showing the property of a seller to a represented buyer. (b) Eliciting any confidential information from a seller concerning their real estate needs, motivation, or financial qualifications. (c) The execution of any agreements governed by Section 73-35-3 of the MS Code.	(4) For the buyer's agent, the definition shall not include: (a) A bona fide "open House" or model home showing which encompasses (3)(a) above only; however, whenever an event described in (3)(b) or (3)(c) occurs, disclosure must be made. (b) Preliminary conversations or "small talk" concerning price range, location and property styles. (c) Responding to general factual questions from a prospective buyer concerning properties that have been advertised for sale or lease.

Rule 4.3 Disclosure Requirements

"Single Agency" shall mean a broker who has chosen to represent only one party to a real estate

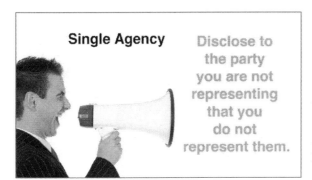

In a single agency, a broker is required to disclose, transaction.

It may be either the buyer, seller, lessor or lessee or any party in a transaction governed by Section 73-35-3.

in writing, to the party for whom the broker is an agent in a real estate transaction that the broker is the agent of the party.

The written disclosure must be made 👏👏 **before the time an agreement for representation** is entered into between the broker and the party.

This shall be on an MREC Agency Disclosure Form.

👏👏 In a single agency, a real estate broker is required to disclose, in writing, to the party for whom the broker is not an agent, that the broker is an agent of another party in the transaction.

The written disclosure shall be made at the time of the first substantive meeting with the party for whom the broker is not an agent. This shall be on an MREC Agency Disclosure Form.

👏👏 **DUAL AGENCY**

Brokers operating in the capacity of disclosed dual agents must obtain the informed written consent of all parties prior to or at the time of formalization of the dual agency.

Informed written consent to disclosed dual agency shall
be deemed to have been timely obtained if all of the following occur:

Dual Agency
1 + 1 = 2
MREC Disclosed Dual Agency Form
Must have informed written consent by both parties.

This Dual Agency Confirmation is an addendum to and made part of the Offer to Purchase dated _____, 20____, between the above-captioned Seller and Buyer for the purchase of the specifically identified property.

The undersigned acknowledges that the licensee has explained dual agency representation to them and they have received the following information regarding disclosed dual agency:

1. A disclosed dual agent is a licensee who, with the informed written consent of Seller and Buyer, is engaged as an agent for both Seller and buyer.
2. As a disclosed dual agent the licensee shall not represent the interests of one party to the exclusion or detriment of the interests of the other party. A disclosed dual agent has all the fiduciary duties to the Seller and Buyer that a Seller's or Buyer's agent has except the duties of full disclosure and undivided loyalty.
3. A disclosed dual agent may NOT disclose:
   (a) To the Buyer that the Seller will accept less than the asking or listed price, unless otherwise instructed in writing by the Seller;
   (b) To the Seller that the Buyer will pay a price greater than the price submitted in a written offer to the Seller, unless otherwise instructed in writing by the Buyer;
   (c) The motivation of the Seller or Buyer for selling, buying or leasing a property, unless otherwise instructed in writing by the respective party or
   (d) That a Seller or Buyer will agree to financing terms other than those offered unless instructed in writing by the respective party.

The buyer shall give his/her consent by signing the MREC Dual Agency Confirmation Form which shall be attached to the offer to purchase.

The Broker must confirm that the seller(s) also understands and consents to the consensual dual agency relationship prior to presenting the offer to purchase.

The seller shall give his/her consent by signing the MREC Dual Agency Confirmation Form attached to the buyer's offer.

The form shall remain attached to the offer to purchase regardless of the outcome of the offer to purchase.

☞☞ AGENCY CHANGES

In the event the agency relationship changes between the parties to a real estate transaction, new disclosure forms will be acknowledged by all parties involved.

☞☞ In the event the agency relationship changes between the parties to a real estate transaction, new disclosure forms will be acknowledged by all parties involved.

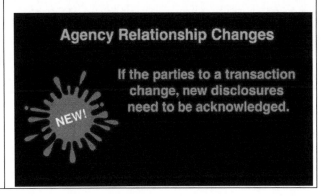

Agency Relationship Changes

If the parties to a transaction change, new disclosures need to be acknowledged.

NEW!

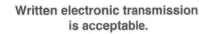

If Parties are unavailable, disclosure can be made orally.

The Broker must note the forms.

The forms are to be forwarded.

☞☞ In the event one or more parties are not available to sign one or more of the Disclosure Forms, the disclosure will be accomplished orally.

The applicable form will be so noted by the Broker and said forms will be forwarded for signature(s) as soon as possible. Written electronic transmission will fulfill this requirement.

☞☞ In the event any party receiving a disclosure form requests not to sign that form acknowledging receipt, the Broker shall annotate the form with the following statement:

Written electronic transmission is acceptable.

If a party is unwilling to acknowledge a document, note it on the form.

A copy of this form was delivered to _____ Date _____ .

Recipient declined to acknowledge receipt of this form

"A COPY OF THIS FORM WAS DELIVERED TO DATE . RECIPIENT DECLINED TO ACKNOWLEDGE RECEIPT OF THIS FORM."

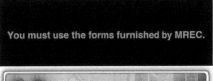

You must use the forms furnished by MREC.

Mississippi Real Estate Commission

👐 The terms of the agency relationship shall be ratified on all contracts pertaining to real estate transactions.

👐 The Commission mandated disclosure form may be duplicated in content and size but not altered.

Agency relationships must be ratified on all contracts pertaining to real estate transactions.

Disclosures may be duplicated in content and size but not altered.

Font sizes may be enlarged for the Americans With Disabilities Act (ADA).

ADA25
AMERICANS WITH
DISABILITIES ACT
1990-2015

Maintain disclosures according to MREC license law.

Three Years

Completed Agency Disclosure Forms shall be maintained in accordance with Rules and Regulations IV.

Rule 4.4 Disclosure Exception

Disclosure Exceptions

Agency Disclosures

Corporation, non profit corporation, professional corporation, professional association, limited liability company, partnership, REIT, business trust, charitable trust, family trust, or any governmental entity.

A licensee shall not be required to comply with the provisions when engaged in transactions with any;

corporation	non-profit corporation	professional corporation	professional association	limited liability company

partnership	real estate investment trust	business trust	charitable trust	family trust

or any governmental entity in transactions involving real estate.

Operating under this exception in no way circumvents the common law of agency.

Chapter 5: Complaint Procedure

Complaint Procedure Rule 5.1. Notifications of Complaints to the Commission

All complaints submitted to the Commission shall be properly certified on forms furnished by the Commission.

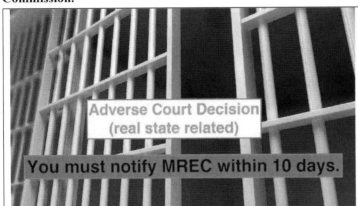

Every licensee shall, within ten days, notify the Real Estate Commission of any adverse court decisions in which the licensee appeared as a defendant.

Adverse Court Decision (real state related)
You must notify MREC within 10 days.

It shall be mandatory for a responsible broker to notify the Commission if the responsible broker has reason to believe that a licensee for whom the broker is responsible has violated the Real Estate License Law or Rules and Regulations of the Commission.

If the responsible broker finds a broker salesperson is acting independently, he must forward the Broker salesperson's license to MREC.

FORWARD

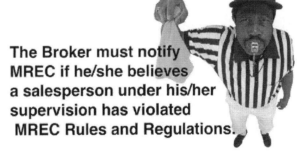

The Broker must notify MREC if he/she believes a salesperson under his/her supervision has violated MREC Rules and Regulations.

If a broker finds that a licensee licensed under that broker has been operating independently or through some other broker, the broker shall notify the Commission immediately and forward said individual's license to the Commission.

A Real Estate Commissioner shall avoid private interviews, arguments, briefs or communication that may influence said Commissioner's decision on any pending complaints or hearings.

**Expiration, suspension or revocation of a responsible broker's license.** **Licensees may transfer to another responsible broker.**	The expiration, suspension or revocation of a responsible broker's license shall automatically suspend the license of every real estate licensee currently under the supervision of that broker. In such cases, a licensee may transfer to another responsible broker.

Part 1601 Chapter 7: Inspection of Offerings from Out-of-State

Rule 7.1 Out-of-state Developers

Out-of-state land developers who desire to advertise out-of-state property in Mississippi (except in national publications) shall first contact the Mississippi Real Estate Commission to have the property approved for advertising.

The Mississippi Real Estate Commission may in its discretion conduct an on-site inspection of the property at the cost of the developer.

The developer shall, upon request from the Mississippi Real Estate Commission, provide such documentation which will establish the truth and accuracy of the proposed advertisements. A Mississippi broker who becomes the agent or representative of the out-of-state developer, shall be responsible for the truth and accuracy of representation, offerings and advertising of such properties in the State of Mississippi.

Chapter 8: Time Shares

Rule 8.1 Licensing

Any seller, other than the developer and its regular employees, of a timeshare plan within the State of Mississippi must be a licensed Real Estate Broker or Real Estate Salesperson pursuant to and subject to Mississippi Law and the Rules and Regulations of the Mississippi Real Estate Commission.

Any seller, other than the developer and her/his regular employees must be licensed.

Rule 8.2 Definitions

A. "Accommodations" means any structure, service improvement, facility, apartment, condominium or cooperative unit, cabin, lodge, hotel or motel room, or any other private or commercial structure, which is situated on real property and designed for occupancy by one or more individuals.

B. "Advertising" or "Advertisement" means any written, oral, or electronic communication which contains a promotion, inducement, or offer to sell a timeshare plan, including, but not limited to, brochures, pamphlets, radio and television scripts, electronic media, telephone and direct mail solicitations, and other means of promotion.

C. "Assessment" means the share of funds required for the payment of common expenses that are assessed from time to time against each timeshare interest owner by the managing entity.

D. "Association" means the organized body consisting of the owners of timeshare interests in a timeshare plan.

E. "Common Expenses" means taxes, casualty and liability insurance, and those expenses properly incurred for the maintenance, operation, and repair of all accommodations constituting the timeshare plan and any other expenses designated as common expenses by the timeshare instrument.

F. "Developer" means and includes any person who creates a timeshare plan or is in the business of selling timeshare interests, or employs agents to do the same, or any person who succeeds to the interest of a developer by sale, lease, assignment, mortgage, or other transfer, but the term includes only those persons who offer timeshare interests for disposition in the ordinary course of business and does not include those sellers who sell timeshare interests on the developer's behalf.

G. "Managing entity" means the natural person or other entity that undertakes the duties, responsibilities, and obligations of the management of a timeshare plan.

H. "Exchange program" means any method, arrangement, or procedure for the voluntary exchange of timeshare interests or other property interests.

The term does not include the assignment of the right to use and occupy accommodations to owners of timeshare interests within a timeshare plan.

Any method, arrangement, or procedure that otherwise meets this definition in which the purchaser's total contractual financial obligation exceeds three thousand dollars ($3,000) per any individual, recurring timeshare period, shall be regulated as a timeshare plan in accordance with these rules.

For purposes of determining the purchaser's total contractual financial obligation, amounts to be paid as a result of renewals and options to renew shall be included except for the following:

(1)   the amounts to be paid as a result of any optional renewal that a purchaser, in his or her sole discretion may elect to exercise or

(2)   the amounts to be paid as a result of any automatic renewal in which the purchaser has a right to terminate during the renewal period at any time and receive a pro rata refund for the remaining unexpired renewal term or

(3)   amounts to be paid as a result of an automatic renewal wherein the purchaser receives a written notice no less than 30 nor more than 90 days prior to the date of renewal informing the purchaser of the right to terminate prior to the date of renewal.

Notwithstanding these exceptions, if the contractual financial obligation exceeds three thousand dollars ($3,000) for any three-year period of any renewal term, amounts to be paid as a result of that renewal shall be included in determining the purchaser's total contractual financial obligation.

I. "Offer to sell", "offer for sale," "offered for sale," or "offer" means solicitation of purchasers, the taking of reservations, or any other method whereby a purchaser is offered the opportunity to participate in a timeshare plan.

J. "Purchaser" means any person, other than a developer, who by means of a voluntary transfer for consideration acquires a legal or equitable interest in a timeshare plan other than as security for an obligation.

K. "Reservation system" means the method or arrangement which purchasers are required to utilize in order to reserve the use and occupancy of accommodations in a timeshare plan.

L. "Seller" means any developer or any other person, or agent or employee thereof: who offers timeshare periods for sale to the public in the ordinary course of business, except a person who has acquired a timeshare period for the person's own use and occupancy and who later offers it for resale.

M. "Timeshare instrument" means one or more documents, by whatever name denominated, creating or governing the operation of a timeshare plan and includes the declaration or other legal instrument dedicating the accommodations to the timeshare plan.

N. "Timeshare interest" means and includes either of the following:

(1)   A "timeshare estate," which is the right to occupy a timeshare property, coupled with a freehold estate or an estate for years with a future interest in a timeshare property or a specified portion thereof.

(2)   A "timeshare plan" which is the right to occupy a timeshare property, which right is neither coupled with a freehold interest, nor coupled with an estate for years with a future interest, in a timeshare property.

O. "Timeshare plan" means any arrangement, plan, scheme, or similar device, other than an exchange program, whether by membership agreement, sale, lease, deed, license, right to use agreement, or by any other means, whereby a purchaser, in exchange for consideration, receives ownership rights in or the right to use accommodations for a period of time less than a full year during any given year, on a recurring basis for more than one year, but not necessarily for consecutive years.

A timeshare plan may be either of the following:
(1) A "single-site timeshare plan" which is the right to use accommodations at a single timeshare property; or

(2) A "multi-site timeshare plan" that includes either of the following:

(a)   A "specific timeshare interest" which is the right to use accommodations at a specific timeshare property, together with use rights in accommodations at one or more other component sites created by or acquired through the timeshare plan's reservation system; or

(b)   A "non-specific timeshare interest" which is the right to use accommodations at more than one component site created by or acquired through the timeshare plan's reservation system but including no right to use any specific accommodation.

P.   "Timeshare property" means one or more accommodations subject to the same timeshare instrument, together with any other property or rights to property appurtenant to those accommodations.

Q.   "Mississippi Real Estate Commission," or "Commission" means the agency of the State of Mississippi created by §73-35-1, et seq.

To regulate the licensing of real estate brokers and salespersons and by §73-35-35 directed to regulate the sale of timeshare and condominium properties. Miss. Code Ann. §73-35-35

Rule 8.3 Registration

A. Developer registration; offer or disposal of interest. – A developer, or any of its agents, shall not sell, offer or dispose of a timeshare interest in the state unless all necessary registration requirements are completed and approved by the Mississippi Real Estate Commission, or the sale, offer, or disposition is otherwise permitted by or exempt from these rules.

A developer, or any of its agents, shall not sell, offer or dispose of a timeshare interest in the state while an order revoking or suspending a registration is in effect.

B. Exemptions from developer registration

(1) A person is exempt from the registration requirements under the following circumstances.

(a)   An owner of a timeshare interest who has acquired the timeshare interest from another for the owner's own use and occupancy and who later offers it for resale; or

(b)   A managing entity or an association that is offering to sell one or more timeshare interests acquired through foreclosure, deed in lieu of foreclosure or gratuitous transfer, if such acts are performed in the regular course of or as incident to the management of the association for its own account in the timeshare plan; or

(c)   The person offers a timeshare plan located outside of Mississippi in a national publication or by electronic media, which is not directed to or targeted to any individual located in Mississippi and contains appropriate disclaimers; or

(d)   The person is conveyed, assigned, or transferred more than seven timeshare interests from a developer in a single voluntary or involuntary transaction arid subsequently conveys, assigns, or transfers all of the timeshare interests received from the developer to a single purchaser in a single transaction.

(e)(i) The developer is offering a timeshare interest to a purchaser who has previously acquired a timeshare interest from the same developer if the developer has a timeshare plan registered with the Commission, which was originally approved by the Commission within the preceding seven (7) years and, further, provides the purchaser:

(A) a cancellation period of at least seven (7) calendar days;

(B) all the timeshare disclosure documents that are required to be provided to purchasers
    as if the sale occurred in the state or jurisdiction where the timeshare property is
    located; and

(ii) By making such an offering or disposition, the person is deemed to consent to the jurisdiction of the Commission in the event of a dispute with the purchaser in connection with the offering or disposition.

(f) An offering of any plan in which the purchaser's total financial obligation is $3,000 or less during the term of
    the plan; for purposes of determining the purchaser's total financial obligation, all amounts to be paid during
    any renewal or periods of optional renewal shall be included.

(g) Hotels including any hotel, inn, motel, tourist court, apartment house, rooming house, or other place where
    sleeping accommodations are furnished or offered for pay if four (4) or more rooms are available therein for
    transient guests as defined in Miss. Code Ann. §41-49-3.

(h) Campground, which is located on real property, made available to persons for camping, whether by tent,
    trailer, camper, cabin, recreational vehicle or similar device and shall include the outdoor recreational facilities
    located on the real property;

(i) Hunting camp which means land or facilities located on real property which is established for the principal
    purpose of hunting or fishing activities which are subject to licensing by the State of Mississippi pursuant to
    Miss. Code Ann. §49-7-1, et seq.

(j) Owner referrals as described in Section N of these rules.

C. Developer Registration Requirements

(1)   Any person who, to any individual in Mississippi, sells, offers to sell, or attempts to solicit prospective purchasers to purchase a timeshare interest, or any person who creates a timeshare plan with an accommodation in Mississippi must register the timeshare plan with the Commission unless the timeshare plan is otherwise exempt from this Chapter.

(2)   The developer shall have the duty to supervise and control all aspects of the offering of a timeshare plan including, but not limited to the promotion, advertising, contracting and closing.

(3)   The developer must provide proof as part of the registration that he will comply with escrow, bonding, or other financial assurance requirements for purchaser funds, including escrow during the rescission period, escrow funds until substantial completion, or bonding, letter of credit or other financial assurances acceptable to the Commission.

(4)   All timeshare plans shall maintain a one-to-one purchaser to accommodation ratio, which is the ratio of the number of purchasers eligible to use the accommodations of a timeshare plan on a given day to the number of

accommodations available for use within the plan on that day, such that the total number of purchasers eligible to use the accommodations of the timeshare plan during a given calendar year never exceeds the total number of accommodations available for use in the timeshare plan during that year.

For purposes of calculation under this subsection, each purchaser must be counted at least once, and no individual timeshare unit may be counted more than 365 times per calendar year (or more than 366 times per leap year).

A purchaser who is delinquent in the payment of timeshare plan assessments shall continue to be considered eligible to use the accommodations of the timeshare plan.

D. Comprehensive registration

(1) In registering a timeshare plan, the developer shall provide all of the following information:

(a) The developer's legal name, any assumed names used by the developer, principal office, street address, mailing address, primary contact person, telephone, electronic mail and facsimile numbers;

(b) The name of the developer's authorized or registered agent in Mississippi upon whom claims may be served or service of process be had, the agent's street address in Mississippi and telephone number;

(c) The name, street address, mailing address, primary contact person and telephone, electronic mail and facsimile numbers of any timeshare plans being registered;

(d) The name, street address, mailing address and telephone, electronic mail and facsimile numbers of any managing entity of the timeshare plan if other than the developer;

(e) Current status of title by a title insurance company qualified and registered to do business in Mississippi, or in the jurisdiction where the timeshare plan is located;

(f) A copy of the proposed or existing covenants, conditions and restrictions applicable to the timeshare plan;

(g) Exemplars of all contracts, deeds, fact sheets and other instruments to be used in marketing, financing and conveying the timeshare interests;

(h) A copy of the management agreement for the timeshare plan;

(i) A detailed description of the furnishing(s) and other personal property to be included in the timeshare plans;

(j) Agreement of the developer to subsidize maintenance and operation of the timeshare plan, if any;

(k) Description of other services and amenities advertised with the timesharing plan;

(l) Evidence of financial assurances, if any;

(m) Evidence of compliance with escrow or other financial assurance requirements for protection of purchaser funds pursuant to these rules.

(n) Where the timeshare plan uses a reservation system, the developer shall provide evidence that provisions are in place to assure that, in the event of termination of the operator of the reservation system, an adequate period of continued operation exists to assure a transition to a substitute operator or mechanism for the operation of the reservation system.

In addition, there shall be a requirement to transfer all relevant data contained in the reservation system to the successor operator of the system.

(o) A description of the inventory control system that will ensure compliance with subsection 3.c. of this section.

(p) A public offering statement which complies with the requirements set forth below; and

(q) Any other information regarding the developer, timeshare plan, or managing entities, as reasonably required by the Commission for the protection of the purchasers.

E. Abbreviated Registration

(1) The Commission may accept an abbreviated application from a developer of a timeshare plan in which all accommodations are located outside of the state.

A developer of a timeshare plan with any accommodation located in Mississippi may not file an abbreviated filing, with the exception of a succeeding developer after a merger or acquisition when the developer's timeshare plan was registered in the state immediately preceding the merger or acquisition.

(2) As a part of any application for an abbreviated registration, the developer must provide a certificate of registration or other evidence of registration from the appropriate regulatory agency in the jurisdiction in which the accommodations offered in Mississippi are located, or other evidence of compliance by the timeshare plan with the laws of the jurisdiction where the accommodations are located.

Such other jurisdiction must have disclosure requirements that are substantially equivalent or greater than the information required to be disclosed to purchasers by these rules.

A developer filing an abbreviated registration application must also provide the following:

(a)   The developer's name, any assumed names used by the developer, the developer's principal office location, mailing address, primary contact person and telephone, electronic mail and facsimile numbers;

(b)   The name, location, mailing address, primary contact person and the telephone, electronic mail and facsimile numbers of the timeshare plan, if different from the developer;

(c)   The name of the authorized agent or registered agent in Mississippi upon whom claims can be served or service of process can be had, and the address in Mississippi of the authorized agent or registered agent;

(d)   The names of any sales entity if other than the developer and the managing' entity and their principal office locations, mailing address and telephone, electronic mail and facsimile numbers;

(e)   A statement as to whether the timeshare plan is a single site timeshare plan or a multi-site timeshare plan and, if a multi-site timeshare plan, whether it consists of specific timeshare interests or non-specific timeshare interests;

(f)   Disclosure of each jurisdiction in which the developer has applied for registration of the timeshare plan and whether the timeshare plan, its developer or any of its sales agents or managing entities utilized were denied registration or were the subject of any disciplinary proceedings;

(g)   Copies of any disclosure documents required to be given to purchasers or required to be filed with the jurisdiction in which the timeshare plan is approved or accepted as may be requested by the Commission; (h) The appropriate fees, if any, and

(a) Other information reasonably required by the Commission or established by rule.

F. Preliminary Permits

(1) The state may grant a preliminary permit allowing the developer to begin offering and selling timeshare interests while the registration is in process.

To obtain a preliminary permit, the developer must do all of the following:
(a) Submit a formal written request to the Mississippi Real Estate Commission for a preliminary permit;

(b) Submit a substantially complete application for registration to the Commission, including any appropriate fees and exhibits;

(c) Provide evidence acceptable to the state agency that all funds received by the developer will be placed into an independent escrow account in accordance with the escrow requirements until a final registration has been granted;

(d) Give to each purchaser a copy of the proposed public offering statement that the developer has submitted to the Commission with the initial application; and

(e) Give to each purchaser the opportunity to cancel the purchase contract during the applicable rescission period.

The purchaser shall have an additional opportunity to cancel upon the issuance of an approved registration if the Commission determines that there is a material and adverse difference in the disclosures contained in the final public offering statement and those given to the purchaser in the proposed public offering statement.

Rule 8.4 Public Offering Statement

A. Public Offering Statement Requirements

(1)   A developer must prepare a public offering statement that shall fully and accurately disclose the facts concerning the timeshare developer and timeshare plan as required by these rules.

The developer shall provide the public offering statement to each purchaser of a timeshare interest in any timeshare plan prior to execution of the purchase contract.

The public offering statement shall be dated and shall require the purchaser to certify in writing the receipt thereof.

Upon approval by the Commission, the developer may also deliver the public offering statement on CD ROM or other electronic media.

(2)   With regard to timeshare interests offered in a single-site timeshare plan or in the specific interest of a multi-site timeshare plan, the public offering statement should fully and accurately disclose the following:

(a) The name of the developer and the principal address of the developer;

(b) Information regarding the developer's business and property management experience;

(c) A description of the type of timeshare interests being offered;

(d) The number of accommodations and timeshare interests, expressed in periods of seven-days use availability or other time increments applicable to the multi-site timeshare plan for each component site committed to the multi-site timeshare plan and available for use by purchasers, purchasers and a representation about the percentage of useable time authorized for sale, and if that percentage is 100 percent, then a statement describing how adequate periods of time for maintenance and repair will be provided.

A general description of the existing and proposed accommodations and amenities of the timeshare plan, including their type and number personal property furnishing the accommodation, any use restrictions, and any required fees for use;

(e) A description of any accommodations and amenities that are committed to be built, including, without limitation: (i) the developer's schedule of commencement and completion of all accommodations and amenities;

(ii) the estimated number of accommodations per site that may become subject to the timeshare plan;

(iii) a brief description of the duration, phases, and operation of the timeshare plan; and

(iv) the extent to which financial arrangements have been provided for completion of all promised improvements.

(f) If the timeshare plan requires the use of a reservation system, include a description of the reservation system which shall include the following:

(i) The entity responsible for operating the reservation system, its relationship to the developer, and the duration of any agreement for operation of the reservation system.

(ii) A summary of the rules and regulations governing access to and use of the reservation system.

(iii)   The existence of an explanation regarding any priority reservation features that affect a purchaser's ability to make reservations for the use of a given accommodation on a first-come, first serve basis.

(iv) An explanation of any demand-balancing standard utilized to assure equitable use of the accommodations among participants.

(g) The current annual budget, if available, or the projected annual budget for the timeshare plan. The budget must include, without limitations:

(i) a statement of the amount included in the budget as a reserve for repairs and replacement;

(ii) the projected common expense liability, if any, by category of expenditures for the timeshare plan; and

(iii) a statement of any services or expenses not reflected in the budget that the developer provides or pays.

(h) Information regarding all fees that the purchaser is required to pay in conjunction with the purchase and ownership including, but not limited to, closing cost and annual assessments;

(i) A description of any liens, defects or encumbrances on or affecting the title to the timeshare interests;

(j) A description of any financing offered by or available through the developer;

(k) A statement that within seven (7) calendar days after receipt of the public offering statement or after execution of the purchase contract, whichever is later, a purchaser may cancel any purchase contract for a timeshare interest from a developer together with a statement providing the name and street address to which the purchaser shall mail any notice of cancellation.

If by agreement of the parties by and through the purchase contract, the purchase contract allows for cancellation of the purchase contract for a period of time exceeding seven (7) calendar days, then the public offering statement shall include a statement that the cancellation of the purchase contract is allowing for that period of time exceeding seven (7) calendar days;

(l) A description of any bankruptcies, pending civil or criminal suits, adjudications, or disciplinary actions of which the developer has knowledge, which would have a material effect on the developer's ability to perform its obligations.

(m) Any restrictions on alienation of any number or portion of any timeshare interests;

(n) A statement describing liability and casualty insurance for the timeshare property;

(o) Any current or expected fees or charges to be paid by timeshare purchasers for the use of any amenities related to the timeshare plan;

(p) A statement disclosing any right of first refusal or other restraint on the transfer of all or any portion of a timeshare interest.

(q) A statement of disclosing that any deposit made in connection which the purchase of a timeshare interest shall be held by an escrow agent until expiration of any right to cancel the contract and that any deposit shall be returned to the purchaser if he or she elects to exercise his or her right of cancellation.

Alternatively, if the Commission has accepted from the developer a surety bond, irrevocable letter of credit, or other financial assurance in lieu of placing deposits in an escrow account, account:

(i) a statement disclosing that the developer has provided a surety bond, irrevocable letter of credit, or other financial assurance in an amount equal to or in excess of the funds that would otherwise be placed in an escrow account and,

(ii) a description of the type of financial assurance that has been arranged,

(iii) a statement that if the purchaser elects to exercise his or her right of cancellation as provided in the contract, the developer shall return the deposit, and

(iv) a description of the person or entity to whom the purchaser shall apply for payment.

(r)   If the timeshare plan provides purchasers with the opportunity to participate in an exchange program, a description of the name and address of the exchange company and the method by which a purchaser accesses the exchange program;

(s)   Such other information reasonable required by the state agency and established by administrative rule necessary for the protection of purchasers of timeshare interests in timeshare plans; and

(t)   Any other information that the developer, with the 50 approval of the Commission, desires to include in the public offering statement.

(3) Public offering statements for specific timeshare interest and multi-site timeshare plans shall include

the following disclosures in addition to those required in (b) above:

(a) A description of each component site, including the name and address of each Component site.

(b) The number of accommodations and timeshare interest, expressed in periods of seven-day use availability or other time increments applicable to each component site of the timeshare plan, committed to the multi-site timeshare plan and available for use by purchasers, and a representation about the percentage of useable time authorized for sale, and if that percentage is 100 percent, then a statement describing how adequate periods of time for maintenance and repair will be provided.

(c) Each type of accommodation in terms of the number of bedrooms, bathrooms, and sleeping capacity, and a statement of whether or not the accommodation contains a full kitchen.
For purposes of this description, a "full kitchen" means a kitchen having a minimum of a dishwasher, range, sink, oven, and refrigerator.

(d) A description of amenities available for use by the purchaser at each component site.

(e) A description of the reservation system, which shall include the following:

(i) The entity responsible for operating the reservation systems, its relationship to the developer, and the duration of any agreement for operation of the reservation system.

(ii) A summary of the rules and regulations governing access to and use of the reservation system.

(iii) The existence of and an explanation regarding any priority reservations for the use of a given accommodation on a first-come, first-served basis.

(iv) An explanation of any demand-balancing standard utilized to assure equitable use of the accommodations among participants.

(v) A description of any method utilized to permit additions, substitutions, or deletions of accommodations.

(vi) A description of any criteria utilized in the use and operation of the reservation system (such as historical occupancy levels by season, location, demand, etc.)

(f) The name and principal address of the managing entity of the multi-site timeshare plan and description of the procedures, if any, for altering the powers and responsibilities of the managing entity and for removing or replacing it.

(g) A description of any right to make any addition, substitutions, or deletion of accommodations, amenities, or component sites, and a description of the basis upon which accommodations, amenities, or component sites may be added to, substituted in, or deleted from the multi-site timeshare plan.

(h) A description of the purchaser's liability for any fees associated with the multi-site timeshare plan.

(i) The location of each component site of the multi-site timeshare plan, the historical occupancy of each component site for the prior 12-month period, if the component site was part of the multi-site timeshare plan during the 12month time period, as well as any periodic adjustment or amendment to the reservation system that may be needed in order to respond to actual purchaser use patterns and changes in purchaser use demand for the accommodations existing at that time within the multisite timeshare plan.

(j) Any other information that the developer, with the approval of the Commission, desires to include in the timeshare disclosure statement.

(4) Public offering statements for nonspecific timeshare multi-site timeshare plans shall include the following:

(a) The name and address of the developer.

(b) A description of the type of interest and usage rights the purchaser will receive.

(c) A description of the duration and operation of the timeshare plan.

(d) A description of the type of insurance coverage provided for each component site.

(e) An explanation of who holds title to the accommodations of each component site.

(f) A description of each component site, including the name and address of each component site.

(g) The number of accommodations and timeshare interest expressed in periods of seven-day use availability or other time increments applicable to the multi-site timeshare plan for each component site committed to the multi-site timeshare plan and available for use by purchasers. purchasers and a representation about the percentage of useable time authorized for sale, and if that percentage is 100 percent, then a statement describing how adequate periods of time for maintenance and repair will be provided.

(h) Each type of accommodation in terms of the number of bedrooms, bathrooms, and sleeping capacity, and a statement of whether or not the accommodation contains a full kitchen.

For purposes of this description, a "full kitchen" means a kitchen having a minimum of a dishwasher, range, sink, oven, and refrigerator.

(i) A description of amenities available for use by the purchaser at each component site.

(j) A description of any incomplete amenities at any of the component sites along with a statement as to any assurance for completion and the estimated date the amenities will be available.

(k) The location of each component site of the multi-site timeshare plan, the historical occupancy of each component site for the prior 12-month period, if the component site was part of the multi-site timeshare plan during such 12month time period, as well as any periodic adjustment or amendments to the reservation system that may be needed in order to respond to actual purchaser use patterns and changes in purchaser use demand for the accommodations existing at that time within the multi-site timeshare plan.

(l) A description of any rights to make any additions, substitutions, or deletions of accommodations, amenities, or component sites, and a description of the basis upon which accommodations, amenities, or component sites may be added to, substituted in, or deleted form the multi-site timeshare plan.

(m) A description of the reservation system that shall include all of the following:

(i) The entity responsible for operating the reservation system, its relationship to the developer, and the duration of any agreement for operation of the reservation system.

(ii) A summary of the rules and regulations governing access to and use of the reservation system.

(iii) The existence of and an explanation regarding any priority reservation features that affect a purchaser's ability to make reservations for the use of a given accommodation on a first-come, first served basis.

(n) The name and principal address of the managing entity for the multi-site timeshare plan and a description of the procedures, if any, for altering the powers and responsibilities of the managing entity and for removing or replacing it, and a description of the relationship between a multi-site timeshare plan managing entity and the managing entity of the component sites of a multisite timeshare plan, if different from the multi-site timeshare plan managing entity.

(o) The current annual budget as provided in Section L. of these rules, along with the projected assessments and a description of the method of calculation and apportioning the assessments among purchasers, all of which shall be attached as an exhibit to the public offering statement.

(p) Any current fees or charges to be paid by timeshare purchasers for the use of any amenities related to the timeshare plan and statement that the fees or charges are subject to change.

(q) Any initial or special fee due from the purchaser at closing, together with a description of the purpose and method of calculating the fee.

(r) A description of any financing offered by or available through the developer.

(s) A description of any bankruptcies, pending civil or criminal suits, adjudications, or disciplinary actions of which the developer has knowledge, which would have a material effect on the developer's ability to perform its obligations.

(t) A statement disclosing any right of first refusal or other restraint on the transfer of all or any portion of a timeshare interest.

(u) A statement disclosing that any deposit made in connection with the purchase of a timeshare interest shall be held by an escrow agent until expiration of any right to cancel the contract and that any deposit shall be returned to the purchaser if he or she elects to exercise his or her right of cancellation.

Alternatively, if the Commission has accepted from the developer a surety bond, irrevocable letter of credit, or other financial assurance in lieu of placing deposits in an escrow account, account:

(i)   a statement disclosing that the developer has provided a surety bond, irrevocable letter of credit, or other financial assurance in an amount equal to or in excess of the funds that would otherwise be placed in an escrow account and,

(ii) a description of the type of financial assurance that has been arranged,

(iii) a statement that if the purchaser elects to exercise his or her right of cancellation as provided in the contract, the developer shall return the deposit, and

(iv) a description of the person or entity to whom the purchaser should apply for payment.

(v)   If the timeshare plan provides purchasers with the opportunity to participate in an exchange program, a description of the name and address of the exchange company and the method by which a purchaser accesses the exchange program.

(w) Any other information that the developer, with the approval of the Commission, desires to include in the timeshare disclosure statement.

Rule 8.5 Amendment to Registration Information and Public Offering Statement

The developer shall amend or supplement its Public Offering Statement and registration information to reflect any material change in any information contained therein.

All such amendments, supplements and changes shall be filed with and approved by the Commission.

Each approved amendment to the Public Offering Statement, other than an amendment made only for the purpose of the addition of a phase or phases to the timeshare plan in the manner described in the timeshare instrument or any amendment that does not materially alter or modify the offering in a manner that is adverse to a purchaser, shall be delivered to a purchaser no later than 10 days prior to closing.

Rule 8.6 Registration Review Time

20-15-20

Every registration required to be filed with the Commission must be reviewed and issued a certificate of registration in accordance with the following schedule: A. Comprehensive registration.

Registration shall be effective only upon the issuance of a certificate of registration issued by the Commission, which, in the ordinary course of business, should occur no more than sixty (60) calendar days after actual receipt by the state agency of the properly completed application.

The Commission must provide a list of deficiencies in the application, if any, and the time for issuance of the certificate of registration by the Commission will be sixty (60) calendar days from receipt by the Commission of the information listed in the deficiencies in the application. B. Abbreviated registration.

Registration shall be effective only upon the issuance of a certificate of registration issued by the Commission, which, in the ordinary course of business, should occur no more than thirty (30) calendar days after receipt by the Commission of the properly completed application.

The Commission must provide a list of deficiencies in the application, if any, and the time for issuance of the certificate of registration by the Commission will occur no more than thirty (30) calendar days from receipt by the Commission of the information listed in the deficiencies in the application. C. Preliminary permit.

A preliminary permit shall be issued within twenty **(20) calendar days** after receipt of a properly completed application, unless the Commission provides to the applicant a list of deficiencies in the application.

A preliminary permit shall be issued within **fifteen (15) calendar** days after receipt by the Commission of the information listed in the deficiencies in the application.

D. The applicant nor a presumption of approval of the application.

The Commission may, for cause, extend the approval periods. Miss. Code Ann.

Rule 8.7 Purchase Contracts

A. Each developer shall furnish each purchaser with a fully completed and executed copy of a contract, which contract shall include the following information:

(1) The actual date the contract is executed by all parties;

(2) The names and addresses of the seller, the developer and the timeshare plan;

(3) The total financial obligation of the purchaser, including the purchase price and any additional charges to which the purchaser may be subject, such as any recurring assessment;

(4) The estimated date of availability of each accommodation, which is not completed;

(5) A description of the nature and duration of the timeshare interest being sold, including whether any interests in real property is being conveyed and the specific number of years or months constituting the term of contract;

(6) Immediately above the signature line of the purchaser(s), the following statement shall be printed in conspicuous type:

(7) These statements in Paragraph f. may not be waived and failure to include them in a timeshare contract shall render the contract void.

Timeshare cancellation period is 7 days.

(8)   Seller shall refund all payments made by the purchaser under the contract and return all negotiable instruments, other than checks, executed by the purchaser in connection with the contract within 30 days from the receipt of the notice of cancellation transmitted to the developer from the purchaser or if the purchaser has received benefits under the contract, refund all payments made less actual cost of benefits actually You may cancel this contract without any penalty or obligation within seven (7) calendar days from the date you sign this contract and seven (7) calendar days after you receive the public offering statement, whichever is later.

Immediately above the signature line of the purchaser(s), the following statement shall be printed in conspicuous type:

> You may cancel this contract without any penalty or obligation within seven (7) calendar days from the date you sign this contract and seven (7) calendar days after you receive the public offering statement, whichever is later. If you decide to cancel this contract, you must notify the developer in writing of your intent to cancel. Your notice of cancellation shall be effective upon the date sent and shall be sent to (name of developer) at (address of developer). If you cancel the contract during a the seven-day cancellation period, the developer shall refund to you all payments made under the contract within thirty (30) days after receipt of your cancellation notice.
>
> No purchaser should rely upon representations other than those included in this contract.

If you decide to cancel this contract, you must notify the developer in writing of your intent to cancel. Your notice of cancellation shall be effective upon the date sent and shall be sent to (name of developer) at (address of developer).

If you cancel the contract during a the seven-day cancellation period, the developer shall refund to you all payments made under the contract within thirty (30) days after receipt of your cancellation notice.

No purchaser should rely upon representations other than those included in this contract. received by the purchaser before the date of cancellation, with an accounting of the actual costs of the benefits deducted from payments refunded.

The developer has 30 days to remit any funds requested.

Rule 8.8 Exchange Program

A. If a purchaser is offered the opportunity to subscribe to an exchange program, the purchaser should receive written information concerning the exchange program prior to or concurrently with the execution of the contract with the exchange company.

Such information should include, without limitation, the following information.

(1) The name and address of the exchange company;

(2) The names of all officers, directors and shareholders of greater that 10% interests of the exchange company;

(3) A description of the purchaser's contractual relationship with the exchange program and the procedure by which changes may be made;

4) A description of the procedure to qualify for and effectuate changes;

(5) A description of the limitations, restrictions or priority employed in the operation of the exchange program;

(6) The fees or range of fees for participation in the exchange program and the circumstances under which the fees may be changed;

(7) The name and address of each timeshare plan participating in the exchange program;

(8) The number of timeshare interests reported in seven (7) day usage periods in each timeshare plan participating in the exchange program; and

(9) The number of purchasers for each timeshare plan participating in the exchange program.

B. The exchange program should report on an annual basis following an audit by an independent certified public accountant the following:

(1) The number of purchasers enrolled in the exchange program;

(2) The number of accommodations that have current affiliation agreements with the exchange program;

(3) The percentage of confirmed reservations;

(4) The number of timeshare periods for which the exchange program has an outstanding obligation to provide an exchange to a purchaser who relinquished a timeshare period during the year; and

(5) The number of exchanges confirmed by the exchange program during the year.

C.   No developer shall have any liability with respect to any violation of these rules arising out of the publication by the developer of information provided to it by an exchange company pursuant to this section.

No exchange company shall have any liability with respect to any violation of these rules arising out of the use by a developer of information relating to an exchange program other than that provided to the developer by the exchange company.

D.   An exchange company may elect to deny exchange privileges to any purchaser whose use of the accommodations of the purchaser's timeshare plan is denied, and no exchange program or exchange company shall be liable to any of its members or any third parties on account of any such denial of exchange privileges.

Rule 8.9 Escrows and Alternatives Assurances

In order to protect the purchaser's right to refund during the rescission period and during any period in which construction of the timeshare property is not complete and available for occupancy by purchasers, the developer shall provide financial assurances as required by this section.

A. A developer of a timeshare plan shall deposit into an escrow account in an acceptable escrow depository all funds that are received in Mississippi during the purchaser's rescission period.
 An acceptable escrow depository includes banks, trust companies, saving and loans associations, real estate broker trust accounts at such an institution, title insurers, and underwritten title companies.

The handling of these funds shall be in accordance with an executed escrow agreement between an escrow agreement between an escrow agent and the developer.

Funds will be handled to assure the following:

(1)   Funds may be disbursed to the developer by the escrow agent from the escrow account or from the broker trust account only after expiration of the purchaser's rescission period and in accordance with the purchase contract, subject to paragraph 2.

(2)   If a prospective purchaser properly cancels the purchase contract following expiration of the cancellation period pursuant to its terms, the funds shall be paid to the prospective purchaser or paid to the developer if the prospective purchaser's funds have been previously refunded by the developer.

B. If a developer contracts to sell a timeshare interest and the construction of the accommodation in which the timeshare interest being conveyed is located has not been completed, the developer, upon expiration of the rescission period, shall continue to maintain in an escrow account all funds received by or on behalf of the developer from the prospective purchaser under his or her purchase contract.

The Commission shall determine the types of documentation which shall be required for evidence of completion, including, but not limited to, a certificate of occupancy, a certificate of substantial completion, or an inspection by the State Fire Marshal or designee or an equivalent public safety inspection by the appropriate agency in the applicable jurisdiction.

Unless the developer submits an alternative financial assurance in accordance with paragraph 3, funds shall not be released from escrow until a certificate of occupancy, or its equivalent, has been obtained and the rescission period has passed, and the timeshare interest can be transferred free and clear of blanket encumbrances, including mechanics' liens. Funds to be released from escrow shall be released as follows:

(1)   If a prospective purchaser properly cancels the purchase contract pursuant to its terms, the funds shall be paid to the prospective purchaser or paid to the developer if the developer has previously refunded the prospective purchaser's funds.

(2)   If a prospective purchaser defaults in the performance of the prospective purchaser's obligations under the purchase contract, the funds shall be paid to the developer.

(3)   If the funds of a prospective purchaser have not been previously disbursed in accordance with the provisions of this paragraph 2., they may be disbursed to the developer by the escrow agent upon the issuance of acceptable evidence of completion of construction and closing.

C In lieu of the provisions in paragraphs 1 and 2, the Commission may accept from the developer a surety bond, escrow bond, irrevocable letter of credit, or other financial assurance or arrangement acceptable to the Commission.

Any acceptable financial assurances shall be in an amount equal to or in excess of the lesser of

(1) the funds that would otherwise be place in escrow, or

(2) in an amount equal to the cost to complete the incomplete property in which the timeshare interest is located.

However, in no event shall the amount be less that the amount of funds that would otherwise be placed in escrow pursuant to subparagraph a. of paragraph 1.

D. The developer shall provide escrow account or broker trust account information to the Commission and shall execute in writing an authorization consenting to an audit or examination of the account by the Commission.

The developer shall make documents related to the escrow or trust account or escrow obligation available to the Commission upon request.

The escrow agent or broker shall maintain any disputed funds in the escrow account until either of the following occurs:

(1) Receipt of written direction agreed to by signature of all parties.

(2) Deposit of the funds with a court of competent jurisdiction in which a civil action regarding the funds has been filed

E. Excluding any encumbrance placed against the purchaser's timeshare interest securing the purchaser's payment of purchase money financing for the purchase, the developer shall not be entitled to the release of any funds escrowed under this section

J. with respect to each timeshare interest and any other property or rights to property appurtenant to the timeshare interest, including any amenities represented to the purchaser as being part of the timeshare plan, until the developer has provided satisfactory evidence to the Commission of one of the following:

(1) The timeshare Interest together with any other property or rights to property appurtenant to the timeshare interest, including any amenities represented to the purchaser as being part of the timeshare plan, are free and clear of any of the claims of the developer, any owner of the underlying fee, a mortgagee, judgment creditor, or other lien holder, or any other person having an interest in or lien or encumbrance against the timeshare interest or appurtenant property or property rights.

The developer, any owner of the underlying fee, a mortgagee, judgment creditor, or other lien holder, or any other person having an interest in or lien or encumbrance against the timeshare interest or appurtenant property or property rights, including any amenities represented to the purchaser as being part of the timeshare plan, has recorded a subordination and notice to creditors document in the appropriate public records of the jurisdiction in which the timeshare interest is located.

The subordination document shall expressly and effectively provide that the interest holder's right, lien or encumbrance shall not adversely affect, and shall be subordinate to, the rights of the owners of the timeshare interests in the timeshare plan regardless of the date of purchase.

(2) The developer, any owner of the underlying fee, a mortgagee, judgment creditor, or other lien holder, or any other person having an interest in or lien or encumbrance against the timeshare interest or appurtenant property or property rights, including any amenities represented to the purchaser as being part of the timeshare plan, has transferred the subject accommodations, amenities, or all use rights in the amenities to a nonprofit organization or owners' association to be held for the use and benefit of the owners of the timeshare plan, which organization or owners association shall act as a fiduciary to the purchasers, and the developer has transferred control of the entity to the owners or does not exercise its voting rights in the entity with respect to the subject accommodations or amenities:

Prior to the transfer, any lien or other encumbrance against the accommodation or facility shall be made subject to a subordination and notice to creditors, instrument pursuant to subparagraph b. or be free and clear of all liens and

encumbrances.

(3)   Alternative arrangements have been made which are adequate to protect the rights of the purchasers of the timeshare interests and approved by the Commission.

F.   Nothing in this section shall prevent a developer from accessing any escrow funds if the developer has complied with paragraph 3 of this section.

G.   The developer shall notify the Commission of the extent to which an accommodation may become subject to a tax or other lien arising out of claims against other purchasers in the same timeshare plan.

H.   Developers, sellers, escrow agents, brokers and their employees and agents have a fiduciary duty to purchasers with respect to funds required to be deposited under these rules.

Any Mississippi broker or salesperson who fails to comply with rules concerning the establishment of an escrow or broker trust account, deposits of funds, and property into escrow or withdrawal there from, shall be in violation of the Mississippi Real Estate Brokers Act of 1954, as amended, and the Rules and Regulations of the Commission.

The failure to establish an escrow or trust account or to place funds therein as required under these rules is prima facie evidence of an intentional and purposeful violation.

Rule 8.10 Insurance

A. For single site timeshare plans and component sites of multi-site timeshare plans located in this state, the timeshare instrument shall require that the following insurance be at all times maintained in force to protect timeshare interest owners in the timeshare plan:

(1)   Insurance against property damage as a result of fire and other hazards commonly insured against, covering all real and personal property comprising the timeshare plan in an amount not less than 80 percent of the full replacement value of the timeshare property.

(2)   Liability insurance against death, bodily injury, and property damage arising out of or in connection with the use, ownership, or maintenance for the accommodations of the timeshare plan.

The amounts of the insurance shall be determined by the association but shall not be less than five hundred thousand dollars ($500,000) to One Million Dollars ($1,000,000) for personal injury and One Hundred Thousand Dollars ($100,000) for property damage.

B.   In a timeshare use offering, the trustee, if one exists, shall be a named coinsured, and if for any reason, title to the accommodation is not held in trust, the association shall be named as a coinsured as the agent for each of the timeshare interest owners.

C.   In a timeshare estate offering, the association shall be named as a coinsured if it has title to the property

or as a coinsured as agent for each of the timeshare interest owners if title is held by the owners as tenants in

common. **Rule 8.11 Advertising and Marketing** A. No advertising shall:

(1) Misrepresent a fact or create a false or misleading impression regarding the timeshare plan.

(2) Make a prediction of increases in the price or value of timeshare periods.

(3) Contain any contradictory statements.

(4) Describe any improvements to the timeshare plan that will not be built or that are described as completed when not completed.

B. No promotional device, sweepstakes, lodging certificate, gift award, premium, discount, drawing, prize or display in connection with an offer to sell a timeshare interest may be utilized without the applicable disclosure as follows:

(1) That the promotional device is being used for the purposes of soliciting sales of timeshare periods;

(2) Of the name and address of each timeshare plan or business entity participating in the program;

(3) Of the date and year when all prizes are to be awarded;

(4) Of the method by which all prizes are to be awarded;

(5) If applicable, a statement that it is a national program with multiple sponsors and the gifts offered are not limited solely 69 to customers of said development but apply also to other developments. C. The following are not considered to be advertising materials:

(1) Any stockholder communication, financial report, prospectus or other material required to be delivered to owners, prospective purchasers or other persons by an agency of any state or the federal government;

(2) Any communication addressed to and relating to the account of any person who has previously executed a contract for the purchase of a timeshare interest in a timeshare plan to which the communication relates;

(3) Any oral or written statement disseminated to the broadcast, print or other news media, other than paid advertising, regarding plans for the acquisition or development of timeshare property.

However, any redistribution of such oral or written statements to a prospective purchaser in any manner would constitute an advertisement;

(4) Any publication or material relating to the promotion of accommodations for transient rental, so long as a mandatory tour of a timeshare plan or attendance at a mandatory sales presentation is not a term or condition of the availability of such accommodations, so long as the failure of the transient renter to take a tour of a timeshare plan or attend a sales presentation does not result in the transient renter receiving less than what was promised in such materials;

(5) Any audio, written or visual publication or material relating to an exchange company or exchange program providing to an existing member of that exchange company or exchange program.

Rule 8.12 Management

A. Before the first sale of a timeshare period, the developer shall create or provide for a managing entity, which may be the developer, a separate management firm, or an owner's association, or some combination thereof.

B. The management entity shall act in the capacity of fiduciary to the purchasers of the timeshare plans.

C. The duties of the management entity shall include, but are not limited to:

(1) Management and maintenance of all accommodations constituting the timeshare plan.

(2) Preparing an itemized annual operating and reserve budget.

(3) The assessment and collection of funds for common expenses.

(4) The assessment and collection of property taxes and casualty insurance and liability insurance against the owners, for which managing entity shall he primarily liable.

(5) Maintenance of all books and records concerning the timeshare plan and making all of them reasonably available for inspection by any purchaser, or the authorized agent of such purchaser.

(6) Arranging for an annual independent audit to be conducted of all the books and financial records of the timeshare plan by a certified public accountant.

A copy of the audit shall be forwarded to the officers of the owner's association; or, if no association exists, the owner of each timeshare period shall be notified in writing that such audit is available upon request.

(7) Scheduling occupancy of the timeshare units so that all purchasers will be provided the use and possession of the accommodations for which they have contracted.

(8) Notifying purchasers of common assessments and the identity of the managing entity.

(9) Performing any other functions and duties that are necessary and proper to maintain the accommodations and operate the owner's association as provided in the contract or the timeshare instruments.

(10) Maintaining appropriate insurance as required by Rule 8.9 of these rules.

D. The managing entity shall not be required to provide a reserve budget for any timeshare plan or accommodation for which a timeshare instrument has been approved prior to adoption of these rules.

Rule 8.13 Liens

A. The management entity has a lien on a timeshare period from the date an assessment becomes due.

B. The management entity may bring an action in its name to foreclose a lien for assessments in the manner a mortgage of real property is foreclosed and may bring an action to recover a money judgment for the unpaid assessments, or, when no interest in real property is conveyed, an action under the Uniform Commercial Code.

C. The lien is effective from the date of recording in the public records of the county or counties in which the accommodations are located, or as otherwise provided by the laws of the jurisdiction in which the accommodations are located.

D. A judgment in any action or suit brought under this section may include costs and reasonable attorney's fees for the prevailing party.

E. Labor or materials furnished to a unit shall not be the basis for the filing of a lien against the timeshare unit of any timeshare interest owner not expressly consenting to or requesting the labor or materials.

8.14 Owner Referrals

A. Referrals of prospective customers to the developer by any existing timeshare owner shall be permitted, without the owner holding a real estate license and compensation may be paid to the referring owner, only under the following circumstances: (1) The existing timeshare owner refers no more than twenty (20) prospective customers in any twelve (12) month period; and (2) The existing timeshare owner limits his or her activities to referring customers to the developer or the developer's employees or agents and does not show, discuss terms or conditions of purchase or otherwise participate in any negotiations with the purchase of a timeshare interest.

Referrals from Current homeowners allowed.

No more than 20 prospective Customers within 12 months.

Chapter 9: Errors and Omissions Insurance Coverage

Rule 9.1 Administration

A. Invitations to bid on the Errors and Omissions coverage shall be by advertisement published in the appropriate newspaper having state- wide coverage.

B. Selection and approval of the Errors and Omissions Insurance carrier shall be by Commissioners utilizing consultants or committees as deemed appropriate by the Commission.

C. Upon approval of the carrier, invoices shall be sent via First Class Mail to all licensees; including companies and corporations; along with the necessary information describing the various available coverages, the period of coverage and the minimum requirements for independent coverage if desired by a licensee.

D. Coverage shall be a twelve (12) month period beginning October 1, 1994 and continuing thereafter on twelve-month basis.

E. Premiums shall be collected by the carrier or the Commission, at the Commission's discretion.

F. The Commission may maintain computer or written records as required for accurate documentation and administration of this program.

Rule 9.2 Licensee Status

A.   Active licensees not submitting the required premium or providing the required proof of acceptable independent coverage within 30 days after the due date of the premium shall be placed automatically on inactive status at the end of the 30-day period.

B.   Inactive licensees will not be required to pay the premium until changing to active status and the premium will be assessed on a pro rata basis.

However, inactive licensees will be invoiced at the beginning of the policy period.

They may pay the full premium at that time if they desire.

C.   New licensees will be given notice when their license is issued to provide proof of coverage within 30 days of the issuance of license or pay the premium specified on a pro rata basis. Failure to do so will result in their license being changed to inactive status.

Rule 9.3 Independent Coverage

A. Licensees having independent coverage shall submit proof of coverage by the beginning of the policy period as set forth above.

Any deficiency in supplying proof of coverage must be corrected within no more than 30 days after the beginning of the policy period. Proof of coverage shall be by a "Certificate of Insurance" provided by the independent insurance carrier.

B. Minimum requirements of independent coverage shall be:

(1) Coverage must be for all activities for which a real estate license is required under this Chapter.

(2) A per claim limit is not less than $100,000.00.

(3) The deductible is not more than $2,500.00 per licensee, per claim, for any damages and the deductible is not more than $1,000.00 per licensee, per claim, for defense costs.

(4) The independent insurance carrier shall agree to a non- cancelable policy or provide a letter of commitment to notify the Commission 30 days prior to intention to cancel.

TITLE 30: Professions and Occupations PART 1602: Oral Proceedings & Declaratory

Opinions Chapter 1: Oral Proceedings Rule Scope.

These rules apply to all oral proceedings held for the purpose of providing the public with an opportunity to make oral presentations on proposed new rules and amendments to rules before the Mississippi Real Estate Commission.

Rule 1.2 When Oral Proceedings will be scheduled on Proposed Rules.

When Oral Proceedings will be scheduled on Proposed Rules.

The Commission will conduct an oral proceeding on a proposed rule or amendment if requested by a political subdivision, an agency or ten (10) persons in writing within twenty (20) days after the filing of the notice of the proposed rule.

Rule 1.3 Request Format

Each request must be printed or typewritten or must be in legible handwriting. Each request must be submitted on standard business letter- 76 size paper (81/2 inches by 11 inches). Requests may be in the form of a letter addressed to the Commission and signed by the requestor(s).

Rule 1.4 Notification of Oral Proceeding

The date, time and place of all oral proceedings shall be filed with the Secretary of State's office and mailed to each requestor.

The oral proceedings will be scheduled no earlier than twenty (20) days from the filing of this information with the Secretary of State.

Rule 1.5 Presiding Officer

The Commission Administrator or his designee, who is familiar with the substance of the proposed rule, shall preside at the oral proceeding on a proposed rule.

Rule 1.6 Public Presentation and Participation

A.   At an oral proceeding on a proposed rule, persons may make oral statements and make documentary and physical submissions, which may include data, views, comments or arguments concerning the proposed rule.

B.   Persons wishing to make oral presentations at such a proceeding shall notify the Board at least one business day prior to the proceeding and indicate the general subject of their presentations.
The presiding officer in his or her discretion may allow individuals to participate that have not previously contacted the Commission.

C.   At the proceeding, those who participate shall indicate their names and addresses, identify any persons or organizations they may represent, and provide any other information relating to their participation deemed appropriate by the presiding officer.

D.   The presiding officer may place time limitations on individual oral presentations when necessary to assure the orderly and expeditious conduct of the oral proceeding.

To encourage joint oral presentations and to avoid repetition, additional time may be provided for persons whose presentations represent the views of other individuals as well as their own views.

E.   Persons making oral presentations are encouraged to avoid restating matters that have already been submitted in writing.

F.   There shall be no interruption of a participant who has been given the floor by the presiding officer, except that the presiding officer may in his or her discretion interrupt or end the participant's time where the orderly conduct of the proceeding so requires.

Part 1503 Chapter 2: Declaratory Opinions Rule

These rules set forth the Mississippi Real Estate Commission's rules governing the form, content and filing of requests for declaratory opinions, and the Commission's procedures regarding the requests. These rules are intended to supplement and be read in conjunction with the provisions of the Mississippi Administrative Procedures Law, which may contain additional information regarding the issuance of declaratory opinions.

In the event of any conflict between these rules and the Mississippi Administrative Procedures Law, the latter shall govern.

Rule 2.2. Persons Who May Request Declaratory Opinions

Any person with a substantial interest in the subject matter may request a declaratory opinion from the Commission by following the specified procedures.

A substantial interest in the subject matter means: an individual, business, group or other entity that is directly affected by the Commission's administration of the laws within its primary jurisdiction.

Primary jurisdiction of the agency means the agency has a constitutional or statutory grant of authority in the subject matter at issue.

Rule 2.3 Subjects Which May Be Addressed in Declaratory Opinions.

The Commission will issue declaratory opinions regarding the applicability to specified facts of:

A. a statute administered or enforced by the Commission or

B. a rule promulgated by the Commission.

The Commission will not issue a declaratory opinion a statute or rule which is outside the primary jurisdiction of the Commission.

Rule 2.4 Circumstances in Which Declaratory Opinions Will Not Be Issued. The Commission may, for good cause, refuse to issue, a declaratory opinion. T he circumstances in which declaratory opinions will not be issued include, but are not necessarily limited to:

A. Lack of clarity concerning the question presented;

B. There is pending or anticipated litigation, administrative action, or other adjudication which may either answer the question presented by the request or otherwise make an answer unnecessary;

C. The statute or rule on which a declaratory opinion is sought is clear and not in need of interpretation to answer the question presented by the request;

D. The facts presented in the request are not sufficient to answer the question presented;

E. The request fails to contain information required by these rules or the requestor failed to follow the procedure set forth in these rules;

F. The request seeks to resolve issues which have become moot, or are abstract or hypothetical such that the requestor is not substantially affected by the statute or rule on which a declaratory opinion is sought;

G. No controversy exists concerning the issue as the requestor is not faced with existing facts or those certain to arise which raise a question concerning the application of the statute or rule;

H. The question presented by the request concerns the legal validity of a statute or rule;

I. The request is not based upon facts calculated to aid in the planning of future conduct but is, instead, based on past conduct in an effort to establish the effect of that conduct;

J. No clear answer is determinable;

K. The question presented by the request involves the application of a criminal statute or a set of facts which may constitute a crime;

L. The answer to the question presented would require the disclosure of information which is privileged or otherwise protected by law from disclosure;

M. The question is currently the subject of an Attorney General's opinion request or has been answered by an Attorney General's Opinion;

N. A similar request is pending before this agency or any other agency or a proceeding is pending on the same subject matter before any agency, administrative or judicial tribunal, or where such an opinion would constitute the unauthorized practice of law;

O. Where issuance of a declaratory opinion may adversely affect the interests of the State, the Commission or any of their officers or employees in any litigation which is pending or may reasonably be expected to arise;

P. The question involves eligibility for a license, permit, certificate or other approval by the Commission or some other agency, and there is a statutory or regulatory application process by which eligibility for said license, permit, certificate or other approval would be determined.

Rule 2.5 Written Request Required

Each request must be printed or typewritten or must be in legible handwriting.

Each request must be submitted on standard business letter size paper (81/2 inches by 11 inches).

Requests may be in the form of a letter addressed to the Board. Miss.

Rule 2.6 Where to Send Requests.

All requests must be sent to the Commission Administrator,

The Mississippi Real Estate Commission:

(1) by mail at P.O. Box 12685, Jackson, MS 39236; or

(2) delivered to 4780 I-55 North, LeFleur's Bluff Tower, Suite 300,

Jackson, MS 39211; or

(3) sent via facsimile to (601) 321-6955.

All requests must be sent to the attention of Declaratory Opinion Request as follows:

ATTN: DECLARATORY OPINION REQUEST

Rule 2.7 Name, Address, and Signature of Requestor

Each request must include the full name, telephone number and mailing address of the requestor.

All requests shall be signed by the person filing the request, who shall attest that the request complies with the requirements set forth in these rules, including but not limited to a full, complete, and accurate statement of relevant facts and that there are no related proceedings pending before any other administrative or judicial tribunal.

Rule 2.8 Question Presented.

Each request shall contain the following:

A. A clear and concise statement of all facts on which the opinion is requested;

B. A citation to the statute or rule at issue;

C. The question(s) sought to be answered in the opinion, stated clearly;

D. A suggested proposed opinion from the requestor, stating the answers desired by petitioner and a summary of the reasons in support of those answers;

E. The identity of all other known persons involved in or impacted by the described factual situation, including their relationship to the facts, name, mailing address and telephone number; and

F. A statement to show that the person seeking the opinion has a substantial interest in the subject matter.

Rule 2.9 Time for Board Response

Within forty-five (45) days after the receipt of a request for a declaratory opinion which complies with the requirements of these rules, the Commission shall, in writing:

A. Issue a declaratory opinion regarding the specified statute or rule as applied to the specified circumstances;

B. Decline to issue a declaratory opinion, stating the reasons for its action; or

C. Agree to issue a declaratory opinion by a specified time but not later than ninety (90) days after receipt of the written request.

D. The forty-five (45) day period shall begin running on the first State of Mississippi business day on or after the request is received the Board, whichever is sooner.

Rule 2.10 Opinion Not Final for Sixty Days

A declaratory opinion shall not become final until the expiration of sixty (60) days after the issuance of the opinion.

Prior to the expiration of sixty (60) days, the Commission may, in its discretion, withdraw or amend the declaratory opinion for any reason which is not arbitrary or capricious.

Reasons for withdrawing or amending an opinion include, but are not limited to, a determination that the request failed to meet the requirements of these rules or that the opinion issued contains a legal or factual error.

Rule 2.11 Notice by Board to third parties

The Commission may give notice to any person, agency, or entity that a declaratory opinion has been requested, and may receive and consider data, facts arguments and opinions from other persons, agencies or other entities other than the requestor.

Rule 2.12 Public Availability of Requests and Declaratory Opinions

Declaratory opinions and requests for declaratory opinions shall be available for public inspection and copying in accordance with the Public Records Act and the Commission public records request procedure.

All declaratory opinions and requests shall be indexed by name and subject.

Declaratory opinions and requests which contain information which is confidential or exempt from disclosure under the Mississippi Public Records Act or other laws shall be exempt from this requirement and shall remain confidential.

Rule 2.13 Effect of a Declaratory Opinion

The Commission will not pursue any civil, criminal, or administrative action against a person who is issued a declaratory opinion from the Commission and who, in good faith, follows the direction of the opinion and acts in accordance therewith unless a court of competent jurisdiction holds that the opinion is manifestly wrong.

Any declaratory opinion rendered by the Commission shall be binding only on the Mississippi Real Estate Commission and the person to whom the opinion is issued.

Real Estate Training Institute

No declaratory opinion will be used as precedent for any other transaction or occurrence beyond that set forth by the requesting person.

TITLE 30: Professions and Occupations PART 1603: Board Organization and Members

Chapter 1: Board Organization Rule

Members

The Mississippi Real Estate Commission consists of five (5) persons who are appointed by the Governor with the advice and consent of the Senate.

Each appointee shall have been a resident and citizen of Mississippi for at least six (6) years prior to their appointment and shall have been a real estate broker for at least five (5) years.

There shall be at least one (1) Commissioner from each Congressional District, as such Districts are constituted as of July 1, 2002, and one (1) additional Commissioner shall 86 be appointed without regard to residence in any particular Congressional District.

Any member of the Commission may be reappointed by the Governor.

The Commission shall organize by selecting from its members a Chairman and may do all things necessary and convenient to promulgate rules and regulations.

Miss. Code Ann. § 73-50-2

§ 73-50-2. Universal Recognition of Occupational Licenses Act; short title; definitions; licensure

Effective: July 1, 2021

(1) This section shall be known as the "Universal Recognition of Occupational Licenses Act."

(2) As used in this section, the term:

(a)   "License" means any license (other than a privilege license), certificate, registration, permit or other evidence of qualification that an individual is required by the state to obtain before he or she may engage in or represent himself or herself to be a member of a particular profession or occupation.

(b)   "Occupational licensing board" means any state board, commission, department or other agency in Mississippi that is established for the primary purpose of regulating the entry of persons into, and/or the conduct of persons within, a particular profession or occupation, and which is authorized to issue licenses. For the purposes of this section, the State Department of Education shall be considered an occupational licensing board when issuing teacher licenses under Section 37-3-2.

(3) Notwithstanding any other provision of law, an occupational licensing board shall issue a license or government certification in the discipline applied for and at the same practice level to a person who establishes residence in this state if, upon application to an occupational licensing board, the applicant satisfies the following conditions:

(a) The applicant holds a current and valid license in good standing in another state in an occupation with a similar scope of practice, as determined by the occupational licensing board in Mississippi, and has held this license from the occupational licensing board in the other state for at least one (1) year; and

(b) There were minimum education requirements and, if applicable, work experience, examination and clinical supervision requirements in effect, and the other state verifies that the applicant met those requirements in order to be licensed in that state; and

(c) The applicant has not committed any act in the other state that would have constituted grounds for refusal, suspension or revocation of a license to practice that occupation in Mississippi at the time the act was committed, and the applicant does not have a disqualifying criminal record as determined by the occupational licensing board in Mississippi under Mississippi law; and

(d) The applicant did not surrender a license because of negligence or intentional misconduct related to the applicant's work in the occupation in another state; and

(e) The applicant does not have a complaint, allegation or investigation pending before an occupational licensing board or other board in another state that relates to unprofessional conduct or an alleged crime. If the applicant has a complaint, allegation or investigation pending, the occupational licensing board in Mississippi shall not issue or deny a license to the applicant until the complaint, allegation or investigation is resolved, or the applicant otherwise satisfies the criteria for licensure in Mississippi to the satisfaction of the occupational licensing board in Mississippi; and

(f) The applicant pays all applicable fees in Mississippi.

(4) Notwithstanding any other law, the occupational licensing board shall issue a license to an applicant in the discipline applied for and at the same practice level, as determined by the occupational licensing board, to a person who establishes residence in this state based on work experience in another state, if all the following apply:

(a) The applicant worked in a state that does not use a license to regulate a lawful occupation, but Mississippi uses a license to regulate a lawful occupation with a similar scope of practice, as determined by the occupational licensing board;

(b) The applicant worked for at least three (3) years in the lawful occupation; and

(c) The applicant satisfies the provisions of paragraphs (c) through (f) of subsection (3) of this section.

(5)   An occupational licensing board may require an applicant to pass a jurisprudential examination specific to relevant state laws in Mississippi that regulate the occupation if the issuance of a license in Mississippi requires an applicant to pass a jurisprudential examination specific to relevant state statutes and administrative rules in Mississippi that regulate the occupation.

(6)   For purposes of this act, residence may be established by demonstrating proof of a state-issued identification card or one (1) of the following:

(a) Current Mississippi residential utility bill with the applicant's name and address;

(b) Documentation of the applicant's current ownership, or current lease of a residence in Mississippi;

(c) Documentation of current in-state employment or notarized letter of promise of employment of the applicant or his or her spouse; or

(d) Any verifiable documentation demonstrating Mississippi residency.

(7)   A person who receives a license under this section is subject to the laws regulating the person's practice in this state and is subject to the occupational licensing board's jurisdiction.

(8)   A license issued under this section is valid only in this state and does not make the person eligible to be part of an interstate compact.

(9)   The occupational licensing board shall issue or deny the license to the applicant within one hundred twenty (120) days after receiving an application.

If the application requires longer than two (2) weeks to process, the occupational licensing board shall issue a temporary practice permit within thirty (30) days after receiving the application if the applicant submits an affidavit, under penalties of perjury, affirming that he or she satisfies the provisions of subsection (3) or subsection (4) and pays all applicable fees as required by subsection (3)(f) or subsection (4)(f).

The applicant may practice under the temporary permit until a license is granted, or until a notice to deny the license is issued, in accordance with rules adopted by the occupational licensing board. A temporary license will expire in three hundred sixty-five (365) days after its issuance if the applicant fails to satisfy the requirement for licensure in subsections (3) through (5), as applicable.

(10)(a) The applicant may appeal any of the following decisions of an occupational licensing board to a court of general jurisdiction:

(i)   Denial of a license;

(ii) Determination of the occupation;

(iii) Determination of the similarity of the scope of practice of the license issued; or

(iv) Other determinations under this section.

(b) The court shall determine all questions of law, including the interpretation of a constitutional or statutory provision or a rule adopted by an occupational licensing board, without regard to any previous determination that may have been made on the question in any action before the occupational licensing board.

(11) An occupational licensing board shall prominently print the following on all license applications, any communication denying a license, and on the board's website: "Pursuant to the provisions of the Universal Recognition of Occupational Licenses Act, Mississippi shall recognize occupational licenses obtained from other states." An occupational licensing board shall prepare and place on the board's website an annual report detailing the number of applications submitted to the licensing board under this section during a calendar year and the actions taken by the board on the applications.

(12) An occupational licensing board shall adopt rules necessary to implement this section by January 1, 2022. In addition, an occupational licensing board shall make all reasonable efforts to issue a license to an applicant for a license under this section.

(13) Nothing in this section shall be construed to prohibit an applicant for licensure from proceeding under the existing licensure requirements established by an occupational licensing board in Mississippi.

(14) Nothing in this chapter shall be construed to prevent Mississippi from entering into a licensing compact or reciprocity agreement with another state, foreign province, or foreign country. A license issued under this section is valid only in Mississippi. It does not make the person eligible to work in another state under an interstate compact or reciprocity agreement unless otherwise provided in Mississippi law.

(15) Nothing in this section shall be construed to apply to:

(a) The practice of law as regulated under Section 73-3-1 et seq.;

(b) Criteria for an applicant to obtain a license that is established under an interstate compact;

(c) The ability of an occupational licensing board to require an applicant to submit fingerprints in order to access state and federal criminal records information for noncriminal justice purposes;

(d) The practice of medicine by physicians as regulated under Section 73-25-1 et seq.;

(e) The provisions of the Military Family Freedom Act, Section 73-50-1; or

(f) An occupation regulated under Section 73-1-1 et seq. to the extent there is a conflict with a law granting licensure reciprocity under Section 73-1-1 et seq.

Added by Laws 2021, H.B. No. 1263, § 1, eff. July 1, 2021.

Mississippi Real Estate License Law QUIZ

1. Good Faith means:
a. Safe earnest money
b. Honesty
c. Integrity
d. Confidentiality

b. Honesty.

2. Which of the following is not considered real estate in Mississippi?
a. Oil and Gas Leases
b. Condominiums
c. Townhomes
d. Garden Homes

a. Oil and Gas Leases
The term **"real estate"** includes leaseholds as well as any and every interest or estate in land, including timesharing and condominiums, whether corporeal or incorporeal, freehold or non-freehold, and whether said property is situated in this state or elsewhere.

3. Which of the following is not required to hold a real estate license to perform real estate activities for client's and customers.
a. Independent Brokers.
b. Broker's holding a real estate license in another sate.
c. Public officers while performing their duties as such.
d. Cooperating Brokers

c. Public officers while performing their duties as such.

4. Exempt from the licensing requirements shall be any person, partnership, association, or corporation, who, as a bona fide owner, shall perform any aforesaid act with reference to property owned by them, or to the regular employees thereof who are on a stated salary, where such acts are performed in the regular course of business.
The provisions of License Law shall not apply to:
a. Attorneys at law in the performance of primary or incidental duties as such attorneys at law.
b. Any person holding in good faith a duly executed power of attorney from the owner, authorizing the final consummation and execution for the sale, purchase, leasing or exchange of real estate.
c. The acts of any person while acting as a receiver, trustee, administrator, executor, guardian or under court order, or while acting under authority of a deed of trust or will.
d. Public officers while performing their duties as such.
e. Anyone dealing exclusively in oil and gas leases and mineral rights.

d. Public officers while performing their duties as such.

5. Is it possible for a real estate salesperson to prepare a Broker Price Opinion for a client?
a. Only brokers can prepare Broker Price Opinions because it is a Broker product
b. Salespersons can do a Broker Price Opinion but may not collect any compensation.
c. Salespersons and Brokers can prepare Broker Price Opinions for a fee or no fee.
d. Broke Price Opinions are bank products and only bank employees may perform them for the bank that employs them.

c. Salespersons and Brokers can prepare Broker Price Opinions for a fee or no fee.

A salesperson licensed **may prepare a broker's price opinion and charge and collect a fee** for such opinion.

6. Does a Broker Price Opinion determine value?
a.   Yes, it may be used in in conjunction with an appraisal.
b.   Yes, because it is a bank product
c.   No because only an appraiser can determine value.
d.   Yes, but only when an appraiser approves the conditions of the BPO

c. No because only an appraiser can determine value.
Although a BPO can be used in conjunction with an appraisal, it is the appraiser that determines value. Only an appraiser can determine value.
A broker's price opinion may not under any circumstances be referred to as a valuation or appraisal.

7. A real estate licensee has no duty to the seller or purchaser of real property to conduct an independent investigation of the size or area, in square footage or otherwise, of a subject property, or to independently verify the accuracy of any third-party information.
a. True
b. False

a. True

8. Judy, a real estate broker received a copy of an engineering surveyor's report that details the property dimension and lot lines of a farm that her buyers were interested in purchasing. The report was given to the seller's agent by the sellers. And the seller's agent gave it to Judy. Judy delivered the report to her buyer and her buyer made an offer using the survey as the basis for the offer price. After an accepted offer, the buyers decided to perform their own survey of the property to confirm the previous survey report. The new survey had an eight-acre disparity with the original engineering surveyor's report. The first survey indicated the property size was 89 acres. The buyer's survey indicated the property was 97 acres. The new survey was disclosed to the seller's agent as a material fact. When the seller's agent presented the new survey to her seller-clients, the sellers wanted to back out of the deal or have the buyer pay more. The seller's threatened to sue the company that Judy worked for. The seller claimed that the agent committed fraud by not measuring the property before the offer was accepted. If the sellers do attempt to recover damages for fraud, what most likely will happen?
a.   Judy's broker will be sued for misrepresentation and held responsible for actual damages.
b.   Judy will likely be found to have violated the fiduciary duty of care but the ultimate responsibility will be that of the broker.
c.   Nothing will happen because Judy did nothing wrong.
d.   Judy will most likely be sanctioned by the Real Estate Commission and fired from her brokerage.

c. Nothing will happen because Judy did nothing wrong.
A real estate licensee has no duty to the seller or purchaser of real property to conduct an independent investigation of the size or area, in square footage or otherwise, of a subject property, or to independently verify the accuracy of any third-party information.
A real estate licensee who has complied with the requirements of MS License Law, as applicable, shall have no further duties to the seller or purchaser of real property regarding disclosed or undisclosed property size or area information, and shall not be subject to liability to any party for any damages sustained with regard to any conflicting measurements or opinions of size or area, including exemplary or punitive damages.

9. Broker Sam was asked by his wife's father to list land for sale that the father was given from his parents 35 years ago. The father-in-law hasn't visited the property in over 20 years because he moved out of the county. He only kept the property because it was sentimental to him.

Sam and his wife met her parents for lunch. At the restaurant, Sam explained the selling process, had his

Father-in-law sign a **WORKING WITH A REAL ESTATE BROKER AGREEMENT**, a **DUAL AGENCY AGREEMENT** and had his Father-in-law fill in a **PROPERTY CONDITION DISCLOSURE STATEMENT.** The father-in-law also supplied Broker Sam with a copy of a survey that the father received 35 years ago. After lunch, Broker Sam went to his office and imputed the listing information into the MLS. Soon after, three cash offers were delivered to Broker Sam. Sam delivered the offers to his father-in-law as they came in. The father-in-law selected an unrepresented buyer, and all the paperwork was delivered to the closing attorney's office.

Since the buyer was a cash buyer, he did not want to perform a formal survey or inspection even though it was suggested by Sam. Sam required the buyer to acknowledge a **RELEASE OF LIABILITY** for the inspection and survey to protect Sam and the Father-in-Law.

One year later, Broker Sam was served with a lawsuit from the buyer of his Father-in-law's property. The unrepresented buyer stated that Broker Sam did not disclose that seven years ago a hurricane swept away several acres of land and now the property is not the size represented in the survey. What is Broker Sam's liability?
a. The statutes of limitations has expired, and a lawsuit cannot move forward.
b. Sam depended on the information given to him by his father-in-law and requested that the unrepresented buyer get a survey. Sam is not responsible.
c. Sam can move the responsibility for the error to his father-in-law.
d. Sam was not a party to the transaction.

d. Sam was not a party to the transaction.
Although b. is true, d. is more true.
First is that the Purchase Agreement is between the buyer and seller. Sam is not a party in that contract. Second is; real estate licensee has no duty to the seller or purchaser of real property to conduct an independent investigation of the size or area, in square footage or otherwise, of a subject property, or to independently verify the accuracy of any third-party information.

10. How are the Mississippi Real Estate Commissioner chosen?
a. They are appointed by the governor.
b. They are selected by the Mississippi's Realty Department.
c. They are selected by an election and the people of Mississippi chose them.
d. They are selected by realty specialists based on the terms of service to the group.

a. They are appointed by the governor.
The commission shall consist of five (5) persons, to be appointed by the Governor with the advice and consent of the Senate.

11. Two brokers decided to open Two Brothers Real Estate Brokerage. They opened a LLC on advice of their professional advisors. To keep the company in the family, both non-licensed wives were added as owners and partners in the LLC. How will the brokerage be allowed to operate? a. As An LLC and equal four partners.
b. As a partnership of four.
c. As a general partnership for the brothers and a limited interest of the wives.
d. As both brothers as owners.

d. As both brothers as owners.
The owners have to be brokers. The two wives are unlicensed.
A corporation, partnership, company or association shall be granted a license *when individual broker's licenses have been issued to every member*, owner, partner or officer of such partnership, company, association or corporation who actively participates in its brokerage business and when any required fee is paid.

12. In addition to being able to understand the real estate business, what other qualifications must real estate companies prove in order to be approved for a license? a. The ability to display confidentiality and care.

b.   Trustworthiness and competency to transact real estate business.
c.   A business license with the current office and home license of every partner.
d.   A salesperson's license for a minimum of 36 months.

b. Trustworthiness and competency to transact real estate business.
Licenses shall be granted only to persons who present, and to corporations, partnerships, companies or associations whose officers, associates or partners present satisfactory proof to the commission that they are trustworthy and competent to transact the business of a real estate broker or real estate salesperson in such manner as to safeguard the interests of the public.

13. What is the minimum age to apply for a real estate salesperson's license?
      a. 18
      b.   21
      c.   16
      d.   18 and a our year college degree.

a. 18
Every applicant for a resident license as a real estate salesperson shall be age eighteen (18) years or over.

Real Estate Training Institute

PROPERTY DISCLOSURE QUIZ

1. If a consumer requests information on non-material facts
    a.   if known to the property owner or licensee the information shall be disclosed.
    b.   A consumer must file an action with HUD.
    c.   the consumer must request such information from MREC.
    d.   All non-material facts must not be disclosed ever.

a. if known to the property owner or licensee the information shall be disclosed.
Owned or occupied by a person affected or exposed to any disease not known to be transmitted through common occupancy of real estate including, but not limited to, the human immunodeficiency virus (HIV) and the acquired immune deficiency syndrome (AIDS); does not constitute a material fact that must be disclosed in a real estate transaction. A failure to disclose such nonmaterial facts or suspicions shall not give rise to a criminal, civil or administrative action against the owner of such real property, a licensed real estate broker or any affiliated licensee of the broker.
If a consumer requests information on non-material facts, if known to the property owner or licensee the information shall be disclosed.

2. A failure to disclose in any real estate transaction any information that is provided or maintained, or is required to be provided or maintained
    a.   is grounds for suspension and a fine.
    b.   can cause a broker to spend up to 10 months in jail.
    c.   will cause a writ of execution.
    d.   shall not give rise to a cause of action against the owner of real property, a licensed real estate broker or any affiliated licensee of the broker.

d. shall not give rise to a cause of action against the owner of real property, a licensed real estate broker or any affiliated licensee of the broker.
A failure to disclose in any real estate transaction any information that is provided or maintained, or is required to be provided or maintained, *shall not give rise to a cause of action against an owner of real property, a licensed real estate broker* or any affiliated licensee of the broker. Likewise, no cause of action shall arise against any licensed real estate broker or affiliated licensee of the broker for revealing information to a seller or buyer of real estate in accordance with Section 45-33-21 through Section 45-33-57. Any factors related to this paragraph, if known to a property owner or licensee shall be disclosed if requested by a consumer.

3. Failure to disclose nonmaterial facts or suspicions
    a.   gives rise to criminal, civil and administrative action against a transferor and his agent.
    b.   does not give rise to a criminal, civil or administrative action against the owner of such real property, a real estate broker or any affiliated licensee or broker.
    c.   will cause the suspension of the transferor's broker and any affiliated agents.
    d.   will be deemed prima facie.

b. does not give rise to a criminal, civil or administrative action against the owner of such real property, a real estate broker or any affiliated licensee or broker.
Failure to disclose any of the facts or suspicions of facts shall not be grounds for the termination or rescission of any transaction in which real property has been or will be transferred or leased.
A failure to disclose in any real estate transaction any information that is provided or maintained, or is required, shall not give rise to a cause of action against an owner of real property, a licensed real estate broker or any affiliated licensee of the broker. Likewise, no cause of action shall arise against any licensed real estate broker or affiliated licensee of the broker for revealing information to a seller or buyer of real estate. Any factors if known to a property owner or licensee shall be disclosed if requested by a consumer.

4. Not disclosing that a previous tenant has died of HIV/Aids in an apartment of a fourplex;
    a.   constitutes a material fact and the broker may lose his license.

    b.   does not constitute a material fact that must be disclosed in a real estate transaction.

    c.   justifies a Lis pendins.

    d. may have a court exercise a writ of execution.

b. does not constitute a material fact that must be disclosed in a real estate transaction.

Owned or occupied by a person affected or exposed to any disease not known to be transmitted through common occupancy of real estate including, but not limited to, the human immunodeficiency virus (HIV) and the acquired immune deficiency syndrome (AIDS); *does not constitute a material fact that must be disclosed in a real estate transaction.* A failure to disclose such nonmaterial facts or suspicions shall not give rise to a criminal, civil or administrative action against the owner of such real property, a licensed real estate broker or any affiliated licensee of the broker.

5. Which of the following is a material fact that needs to be disclosed?

    a.   illegal drug activity that affects the physical condition of the property.

    b.   a multiple murder site where carpet has been removed.

    c.   A death due to HIV or Aids.

    d.   all of the above.

c. A death due to HIV or Aids.

Owned or occupied by a person affected or exposed to any disease not known to be transmitted through common occupancy of real estate including, but not limited to, the human immunodeficiency virus (HIV) and the acquired immune deficiency syndrome (AIDS); *does not constitute a material fact that must be disclosed in a real estate transaction.* A failure to disclose such nonmaterial facts or suspicions shall not give rise to a criminal, civil or administrative action against the owner of such real property, a licensed real estate broker or any affiliated licensee of the broker

6. Which of the following does not constitute a material fact that needs to be disclosed?

    a. suicide

    b.   HIV or Aids

    c.   homicide

    d.   all of the above.

d. all of the above.

The fact or suspicion that real property is or was:

The site of a natural death, suicide, homicide or felony crime (except for illegal drug activity that affects the physical condition of the property, its physical environment or the improvements located thereon);

The site of an act or occurrence that had no effect on the physical condition of the property, its physical environment or the improvements located thereon;

Owned or occupied by a person affected or exposed to any disease not known to be transmitted through common occupancy of real estate including, but not limited to, the human immunodeficiency virus (HIV) and the acquired immune deficiency syndrome (AIDS); does not constitute a material fact that must be disclosed in a real estate transaction. A failure to disclose such nonmaterial facts or suspicions shall not give rise to a criminal, civil or administrative action against the owner of such real property, a licensed real estate broker or any affiliated licensee of the broker.

7. The Mississippi Real Estate Commission is authorized to enforce the provisions of Real Estate Transfer Disclosure requirements provisions. Any violation shall be treated in the same manner;

    a.   as prima facie criminal activity.

    b.   as a Lis pendins.

    c.   as a writ of execution.

    d.   as a violation of the Real Estate Broker License Law of 1954.

d. as a violation of the Real Estate Broker License Law of 1954.

The Mississippi Real Estate Commission is authorized to enforce the provisions of disclosure law. Any violation of the provisions shall be treated in the same manner as a violation of the Real Estate Broker License Law of 1954, and shall be subject to same penalties as provided in that chapter.

8. Any person who willfully or negligently violates or fails to perform any duty prescribed by any provision of Real Estate Transfer Disclosure requirements
   a. shall be liable in the amount of actual damages suffered by the transferee.
   b. shall be liable in the amount of actual damages to the transferor.
   c. shall be liable for actual damages and a penalty of 100,000.
   d. shall be put in jail for 20 years.

a. shall be liable in the amount of actual damages suffered by the transferee.
Any person who willfully or negligently violates or fails to perform any duty prescribed by any provision of shall be liable in the amount of actual damages suffered by a transferee.

9. No transfer subject to MS Real estate Disclosure Law shall be invalidated
   a. upon the death of the Seller's broker.
   b. upon the foreclosure of the property.
   c. upon the death of the client
   d. solely because of the failure of any person to comply with any provision of real estate transfer disclosure requirement provisions.

d. solely because of the failure of any person to comply with any provision of real estate transfer disclosure requirement provisions.
No transfer shall be invalidated solely because of the failure of any person to comply with any provision of Sections 89-1-501 through 89-1-523.

10. The Real Estate Broker responsible for delivering disclosures;
   a. shall maintain a record of the actions taken to effect compliance.
   b. shall send 2 copies in 10 days to the Commission.
   c. must keep all files for 7 years.
   d. none of the above.

a. shall maintain a record of the actions taken to effect compliance.
A licensed real estate broker responsible for delivering disclosures under this section *shall maintain a record of the action taken to effect compliance.*

11. When a transferee for some reason does not receive the needed disclosures, their Real Estate Broker;
   a. shall do an inspection from the exterior of the property and complete the disclosure.
   b. shall advise in writing of the transferee's rights to the disclosures.
   c. shall look for another property for the customer to purchase.
   d. must turn the other broker into the MREC for license violations.

b. shall advise in writing of the transferee's rights to the disclosures.
If a licensed real estate broker responsible for delivering the disclosures under this section cannot obtain the disclosure document required and does not have written assurance from the transferee that the disclosure has been received, the broker shall advise the transferee in writing of his rights to the disclosure.

12. If more than one licensed broker is acting as an agent in a transaction, the broker who has obtained the offer made by the transferee, shall except otherwise provided,
   a. never deliver disclosures of any kind to the transferor.
   b. deliver the disclosures required to the transferee unless the transferor has given other written instructions for delivery.
   c. by MREC's written approval deliver anything to the transferor.

d. none of the above.

b. deliver the disclosures required to the transferee unless the transferor has given other written instructions for delivery.
If more than one (1) licensed real estate broker is acting as an agent in a transaction subject to Sections 89-1-501 through 89-1-523, the broker who has obtained the offer made by the transferee shall, except as otherwise provided in Sections 89-1-501 through 89-1-523, *deliver the disclosure* required by Sections 89-1-501 through 89-1-523 to the transferee, unless the transferor has given other written instructions for delivery.

13. Any person or entity, other than a duly licensed real estate broker or salesperson acting in the capacity of an escrow agent for the transfer of real property shall not be deemed the agent for the transferee for purpose of the disclosure requirements;
a. ever.
b. unless approved by MREC.
c. unless the person is duly empowered to so act by an express written agreement to that effect.
d. only if their is a 10,000 bond held by that agent.

c. unless the person is duly empowered to so act by an express written agreement to that effect.
Any person or entity, other than a duly licensed real estate broker or salesperson acting in the capacity of an escrow agent for the transfer of real property subject to Sections 89-1-501 through 89-1-523 shall not be deemed the agent of the transferor or transferee for purposes of the disclosure requirements of Sections 89-1-501 through 89-1-523, *unless the person or entity is empowered to so act by an express written agreement to that effect.* The extent of such an agency shall be governed by the written agreement.

14. Delivery to a spouse of a transferee shall be;
a. never an acceptable mode of delivery.
b. notarized.
c. approved by MREC.
d. deemed delivery to the transferee unless provided otherwise by contract.

d. deemed delivery to the transferee unless provided otherwise by contract.
Delivery of disclosure required shall be by personal delivery to the transferee or by mail to the prospective transferee. For the purposes of delivery, *delivery to the spouse of a transferee* shall be deemed delivery to the transferee, unless provided otherwise by contract.

15. Delivery of disclosure required shall be delivered;
a. by personal delivery to the transferee or by mail to the prospective transferee.
b. by certified return receipt United States delivery mail.
c. after approved by The MS Real Estate Commission.
d. once every defect has been corrected.

a. by personal delivery to the transferee or by mail to the prospective transferee.
Delivery of disclosure required shall be by personal delivery to the transferee or by mail to the prospective transferee. For the purposes of Sections 89-1-501 through 89-1-523, delivery to the spouse of a transferee shall be deemed delivery to the transferee, unless provided otherwise by contract.

16. Disclosures may;
a. not be amended once accepted.
b. not be delivered to the transferee before the close of escrow.
c. be amended by the transferor or his agent.
d. be amended by the transferee only.

c. be amended by the transferor or his agent.

Any disclosure made pursuant to Sections 89-1-501 through 89-1-523 may be amended in writing by the transferor or his agent, but the amendment shall be subject to the provisions of Section 89-1-503.

17. Transferors must not;
   a. disclose anything that may be detrimental to the transaction.
   b. use fraud, misrepresentation, or deceit in the transfer transaction.
   c. disclose any known latent conditions.
   d. repair the property before closing.

b. use fraud, misrepresentation, or deceit in the transfer transaction.
The specification of items for disclosure in Sections 89-1-501 through 89-1523 does not limit or abridge any obligation for disclosure created by any other provision of law or which may exist in order to avoid fraud, misrepresentation or deceit in the transfer transaction.

18. "Good Faith" means?
   a. honesty.
   b. a sufficient down payment.
   c. a sufficient deposit
   d. the agency between the buyer and seller.

a. Goof faith means honesty
Each disclosure required and each act which may be performed in making the disclosure, shall be made in good faith. For purposes of MS License Law "good faith" means honesty in fact in the conduct of the transaction.

19. Transferors and their agents must?
   a. allow the broker to fill out the property disclosure statement only.
   b. use the disclosure forms prepared by the Mississippi Real Estate Commission.
   c. use any form available at office supply stores to fill out disclosures
   d. must notarize the final disclosures.

b. use the disclosure forms prepared by the Mississippi Real Estate Commission.
MREC forms can be duplicated in content and size but not altered.

20. If information required to be disclosed and is unknown, the transferor;
   a. must not circumvent the truth.
   b. must use information that is based on the best information available.
   c. may use an approximation of the information, provided the approximation is clearly identified as such.
   d. All the above.

c. may use an approximation of the information, provided the approximation is clearly identified as such.
If at the time the disclosures are required to be made, an item of information required to be disclosed is unknown or not available to the transferor, and the transferor or his agent has made a reasonable effort to ascertain it, the transferor may use an approximation of the information, provided the approximation is clearly identified as such, is reasonable, is based on the best information available to the transferor or his agent, and is not used for the purpose of circumventing or evading Sections 89-1-501 through 89-1-523.

21.   If at the time the disclosures are required to be made, an item of information required to be disclosed is unknown or unavailable;
   a. the transferor and his agent must make reasonable effort to ascertain it.
   b. the agent must file 2 copies in ten days stating thereto.
   c. the agent must temporarily forfeit his license in order to proceed.
   d. the transferor can never transfer title.

   a. the transferor and his agent must make reasonable effort to ascertain it.

If at the time the disclosures are required to be made, an item of information required to be disclosed is unknown or not available to the transferor, and the transferor or his agent has made a reasonable effort to ascertain it, the transferor may use an approximation of the information, provided the approximation is clearly identified as such, is reasonable, is based on the best information available to the transferor or his agent, and is not used for the purpose of circumventing or evading Sections 89-1-501 through 89-1-523.

22.   If information disclosed in accordance with disclosure law is subsequently rendered inaccurate as a result of any act, occurrence or agreement subsequent to the delivery of the required disclosures;
   a.   the inaccuracy resulting therefrom constitutes a punishable violation.
   b.   is forwarded to the Real estate Commission with the license number of the professional.
   c.   is punishable of up to $5000 and 18 months in jail.
   d.   the inaccuracy resulting therefrom does not constitute a violation.

d. the inaccuracy resulting therefrom does not constitute a violation.
If information disclosed is subsequently rendered inaccurate as a result of any act, occurrence or agreement subsequent to the delivery of the required disclosures, the inaccuracy resulting therefrom does not constitute a violation.

23. An expert inspecting a property;
   a.   shall be held liable for any defects in the property.
   b.   shall not be responsible for any verbal statements regarding the condition of the property.
   c.   shall not be responsible for any items of information, or parts thereof, other than those expressly set forth.
   d.   waves his rights to a jury lawsuit and must sign a protection clause.

c. shall not be responsible for any items of information, or parts thereof, other than those expressly set forth.
The delivery of a report or opinion prepared by a licensed engineer, land surveyor, geologist, structural pest control operator, contractor, or other expert, dealing with matters within the scope of the professional's license or expertise, shall be sufficient compliance for application of the exemption provided by subsection (1) if the information is provided to the prospective transferee pursuant to a request therefor, whether written or oral. In responding to such a request, an expert may indicate, in writing, an understanding that the information provided will be used in fulfilling the requirements of Section 89-1-509 and, if so, shall indicate the required disclosures, or parts thereof, to which the information being furnished is applicable. Where such a statement is furnished, the expert shall not be responsible for any items of information, or parts thereof, other than those expressly set forth in the statement.

24. The delivery of any information required to be disclosed to a prospective transferee by a public agency or other expert dealing with matters within their scope of the professionals license or expertise must indicate;
   a.   in writing, an understanding that the information will be used for provisions of MS Real Estate Disclosure law.
   b.   that a Lis pendins may be obtained upon completion.
   c.   a writ of execution stating thereto.
   d.   the technician's cell phone for 24-hour service.

b. In writing, an understanding that the information will be used for provisions of MS Real Estate Disclosure law.
The delivery of a report or opinion prepared by a licensed engineer, land surveyor, geologist, structural pest control operator, contractor, or other expert, dealing with matters within the scope of the professional's license or expertise, shall be sufficient compliance for application of the exemption provided by subsection (1) if the information is provided to the prospective transferee pursuant to a request therefor, whether written or oral. In responding to such a request, an expert may indicate, in writing, an understanding that the information provided will be used in fulfilling the requirements of Section 89-1-509 and, if so, shall indicate the required disclosures, or parts thereof, to which the information being furnished is applicable. Where such a statement is furnished, the expert shall not be responsible for any items of information, or parts thereof, other than those expressly set forth in the statement.

25. The delivery of a report by a contractor or expert dealing within his scope of expertise;

a. must be delivered at least ten days after the transaction recording.
b. must be available in order to give constructive notice to the world.
c. is sufficient compliance for fulfilling requirements for information to hold the transferor an agent not liable for that specific information.
d. all the above.

c. is sufficient compliance for fulfilling requirements for information to hold the transferor an agent not liable for that specific information.

The delivery of a report or opinion prepared by a licensed engineer, land surveyor, geologist, structural pest control operator, contractor, or other expert, dealing with matters within the scope of the professional's license or expertise, shall be sufficient compliance for application of the exemption provided by subsection (1) if the information is provided to the prospective transferee pursuant to a request therefor, whether written or oral. In responding to such a request, an expert may indicate, in writing, an understanding that the information provided will be used in fulfilling the requirements of Section 89-1-509 and, if so, shall indicate the required disclosures, or parts thereof, to which the information being furnished is applicable. Where such a statement is furnished, the expert shall not be responsible for any items of information, or parts thereof, other than those expressly set forth in the statement.

26. The delivery of any information required to be disclosed to a prospective transferee by public agencies
a. will be deemed prima facie.
b. shall relieve the transferor or any listing or selling agent of any duty with respect to that item of information.
c. will relieve the transferor only for all disclosure relating to that property transaction.
d. will be bona fide and notarized.

b. shall relieve the transferor or any listing or selling agent of any duty with respect to that item of information.

The delivery of a report or opinion prepared by a licensed engineer, land surveyor, geologist, structural pest control operator, contractor, or other expert, dealing with matters within the scope of the professional's license or expertise, shall be sufficient compliance for application of the exemption provided by subsection (1) if the information is provided to the prospective transferee pursuant to a request therefor, whether written or oral. In responding to such a request, an expert may indicate, in writing, an understanding that the information provided will be used in fulfilling the requirements of Section 89-1-509 and, if so, shall indicate the required disclosures, or parts thereof, to which the information being furnished is applicable. Where such a statement is furnished, the expert shall not be responsible for any items of information, or parts thereof, other than those expressly set forth in the statement.

27. Neither the transferor nor any listing or selling agent shall be liable for any error, inaccuracy or omission of any information delivered in regards to MS Property Disclosure Law.
a. if the error, inaccuracy, or omission was not within their personal knowledge.
b. was based on timely information provided by public agencies.
c. when ordinary care was taken.
d. all the above.

a. if the error, inaccuracy, or omission was not within their personal knowledge.

Neither the transferor nor any listing or selling agent shall be liable for any error, inaccuracy or omission of any information delivered if the error, inaccuracy or omission was not within the personal knowledge of the transferor or that listing or selling agent, was based on information timely provided by public agencies or by other persons providing information that is required to be disclosed and ordinary care was exercised in obtaining and transmitting it.

28. If a seller fails to deliver the property disclosure statement and the buyer decides to cancel the transaction,
a. the buyer may do so in writing for the cancellation to be enforceable in court.
b. the buyer may do so verbally at any time.
c. the seller may be responsible for action of the courts upon final recordation.
d. the seller's agent may do so at any time.

a. the buyer may do so in writing for the cancellation to be enforceable in court.
Everything in real estate must be in writing to be enforceable in court.

29. If any disclosure or any material amendment of any disclosure required to be made is delivered after the execution of an offer to purchase, the transferee;
    a.   has 10 days to terminate the offer or acceptance.
    b.   the transferee has three days in person or five days after delivery by deposit in the mail to terminate his offer.
    c.   is still bound by the contract and cannot cancel anything acknowledged.
    d.   may sue the broker of the seller.

b. the transferee has three days in person or five days after delivery by deposit in the mail to terminate his offer.
If any disclosure or any material amendment of any disclosure required to be made is delivered after the execution of an offer to purchase, the transferee the transferee has three days in person or five days after delivery by deposit in the mail to terminate his offer.

30. With respect to any transfer, the transferor shall indicate compliance with MS Property Disclosure Law on;
    a.   the receipt for deposit.
    b.   the real property sales contract or lease.
    c.   any addendum attached thereto or on a separate document.
    d.   Any of the above.

d. Any of the above.
With respect to any transfer, the transferor shall indicate compliance either on the receipt for deposit, the real property sales contract, the lease, or any addendum attached thereto or on a separate document.

31. Which of the following transactions does the property condition disclosure be delivered before the making or acceptance of an offer?
    a.   in the case of a transfer by a real sales contract.
    b.   a ground lease coupled with improvements.
    c.   a lease together with an option to purchase.
    d.   all the above.

d. All the above.
The provisions of Sections 89-1-501 through 89-1-523 apply only with respect to transfers by sale, exchange, installment land sale contract, lease with an option to purchase, any other option to purchase or ground lease coupled with improvements, of real property on which a dwelling unit is located, or residential stock cooperative improved with or consisting of not less than one (1) nor more than four (4) dwelling units, when the execution of such transfers is by, or with the aid of, a duly licensed real estate broker or salesperson

32. The written property condition disclosure must be delivered
    a.   after the Real Estate Commission has approved the disclosure.
    b.   up to 15 days after the finalization of the transfer.
    c.   before the courts have declared the sale final.
    d.   in the case of a sale, as soon as practicable before the transfer of title.

d. in the case of a sale, as soon as practicable before the transfer of title.
In the case of a sale, as soon as practicable before transfer of title.

33. The transfer of any real property subject to MS Real Property Disclosure Law
    a.   the transferee must file 2 copies in 10 days with the Real Estate Commission.
    b.   shall deliver to the prospective vendor the written property condition statement required.

    c.   shall deliver to the prospective transferee the written property condition statement required.

c. shall deliver to the prospective transferee the written property condition statement required.
In the case of transfer by a real property sales contract, or by a lease together with an option to purchase, or a ground lease coupled with improvements, as soon as practicable before execution of the contract. For the purpose of this paragraph, execution means the making or acceptance of an offer.

34. Excluded from MS Property Disclosure Law are
    a.   transfers between spouses.
    b.   transfers with no dwelling unit.
    c.   transfers or exchanges to or from any government entity.
    d.   all the above.

d. all the above.
There are specifically excluded from the provisions of Sections 89-1501 through 89-1-523:

- Transfers pursuant to court order, including, but not limited to, transfers ordered by a probate court in administration of an estate, transfers pursuant to a writ of execution, transfers by any foreclosure sale, transfers by a trustee in bankruptcy, transfers by eminent domain, and transfers resulting from a decree for specific performance.
- Transfers to a mortgagee by a mortgagor or successor in interest who is in default, transfers to a beneficiary of a deed of trust by a trustor or successor in interest who is in default, transfers by any foreclosure sale after default, in an obligation secured by a mortgage, transfers by a sale under a power of sale or any foreclosure sale under a decree of foreclosure after default in an obligation secured by a deed of trust or secured by any other instrument containing a power of sale, or transfers by a mortgagee or a beneficiary under a deed of trust who has acquired the real property at a sale conducted pursuant to a power of sale under a mortgage or deed of trust or a sale pursuant to a decree of foreclosure or has acquired the real property by a deed in lieu of foreclosure.
- Transfers by a fiduciary in the course of the administration of a decedent's estate, guardianship, conservatorship or trust.
- Transfers from one co-owner to one or more other co-owners.
- Transfers made to a spouse, or to a person or persons in the lineal line of consanguinity of one or more of the transferors.
- Transfers between spouses resulting from a decree of dissolution of marriage or a decree of legal separation or from a property settlement agreement incidental to such a decree.
- Transfers or exchanges to or from any governmental entity.
- Transfers of real property on which no dwelling is located.

35. When a dwelling unit is transferred from one co-owner to one or more other co-owners;
    a.   all property disclosure must be made before transfer.
    b.   two copies must be sent in ten days to the commission.
    c.   Property Disclosure law does not apply.
    d.   A copy of the property disclosure must be notarized.

c. Property Disclosure law does not apply.
Transfers from one co-owner to one or more other co-owners.

36. Which of the following does Disclosure not apply to?
    a.   Transfers by a fiduciary in the course of the administration of a decedent's estate.
    b.   Transfers of cooperatives of units with not less than 1 and no more than 4.
    c.   Transfers from Land coupled with improvements on which a dwelling unit is located.
    d.   Transfers of a dwelling unit involving a licensed agent or broker.

a. Transfers by a fiduciary in the course of the administration of a decedent's estate.

The provisions apply only with respect to transfers by sale, exchange, installment land sale contract, lease with an option to purchase, any other option to purchase or ground lease coupled with improvements, of real property on which a dwelling unit is located, or residential stock cooperative improved with or consisting of not less than one (1) nor more than four (4) dwelling units, when the execution of such transfers is by, or with the aid of, a duly licensed real estate broker or salesperson

37. When a property is transferred by "deed in lieu of foreclosure";
    a.   the court must determine the validity of the deed.
    b.   disclosure law does not apply.
    c.   disclosure is mandatory always.
    d.   MS disclosure law applies to out of state property.

b. disclosure law does not apply.
Transfers pursuant to court order, including, but not limited to, transfers ordered by a probate court in administration of an estate, transfers pursuant to a writ of execution, transfers by any foreclosure sale, transfers by a trustee in bankruptcy, transfers by eminent domain, and transfers resulting from a decree for specific performance.

38. Excluded from MS Disclosure law are transfers;
    a.   by writ of execution, foreclosure sale and transfer by bankruptcy.
    b.   eminent domain and transfers from a decree for specific performance.
    c.   court order and probate.
    d.   all the above.

d. All the above.
There are specifically excluded from the provisions of Sections 89-1501 through 89-1-523:
- Transfers pursuant to court order, including, but not limited to, transfers ordered by a probate court in administration of an estate, transfers pursuant to a writ of execution, transfers by any foreclosure sale, transfers by a trustee in bankruptcy, transfers by eminent domain, and transfers resulting from a decree for specific performance.
- Transfers to a mortgagee by a mortgagor or successor in interest who is in default, transfers to a beneficiary of a deed of trust by a trustor or successor in interest who is in default, transfers by any foreclosure sale after default, in an obligation secured by a mortgage, transfers by a sale under a power of sale or any foreclosure sale under a decree of foreclosure after default in an obligation secured by a deed of trust or secured by any other instrument containing a power of sale, or transfers by a mortgagee or a beneficiary under a deed of trust who has acquired the real property at a sale conducted pursuant to a power of sale under a mortgage or deed of trust or a sale pursuant to a decree of foreclosure or has acquired the real property by a deed in lieu of foreclosure.
- Transfers by a fiduciary in the course of the administration of a decedent's estate, guardianship, conservatorship or trust.
- Transfers from one co-owner to one or more other co-owners.
- Transfers made to a spouse, or to a person or persons in the lineal line of consanguinity of one or more of the transferors.
- Transfers between spouses resulting from a decree of dissolution of marriage or a decree of legal separation or from a property settlement agreement incidental to such a decree.
- Transfers or exchanges to or from any governmental entity.
- Transfers of real property on which no dwelling is located.

39. Disclosure law applies when;
    a.   a homeowner is selling their property FSBO.
    b.   a homeowner is selling with the aid of a duly licensed real estate broker or salesperson.
    c.   a property consists of more than 4 units but not less than 9.
    d.   none of the above.

b. a homeowner is selling with the aid of a duly licensed real estate broker or salesperson.
With the duly licensed real estate professional, MREC requirements are valid.

40. MS Disclosure law applies to transfers by;

  a. all options to purchase, installment land sale contract coupled with improvements on which a dwelling is located.
  b. sales exchange, installment land sales, lease with an option to purchase.
  c. ground lease coupled with improvements on which a dwelling is located, residential stock cooperative consisting of not less than 1 an not more than 4 dwelling units.
  d. all the above.

d. all the above.

There are specifically excluded from the provisions of Sections 89-1501 through 89-1-523:

- Transfers pursuant to court order, including, but not limited to, transfers ordered by a probate court in administration of an estate, transfers pursuant to a writ of execution, transfers by any foreclosure sale, transfers by a trustee in bankruptcy, transfers by eminent domain, and transfers resulting from a decree for specific performance.

- Transfers to a mortgagee by a mortgagor or successor in interest who is in default, transfers to a beneficiary of a deed of trust by a trustor or successor in interest who is in default, transfers by any foreclosure sale after default, in an obligation secured by a mortgage, transfers by a sale under a power of sale or any foreclosure sale under a decree of foreclosure after default in an obligation secured by a deed of trust or secured by any other instrument containing a power of sale, or transfers by a mortgagee or a beneficiary under a deed of trust who has acquired the real property at a sale conducted pursuant to a power of sale under a mortgage or deed of trust or a sale pursuant to a decree of foreclosure or has acquired the real property by a deed in lieu of foreclosure.

- Transfers by a fiduciary in the course of the administration of a decedent's estate, guardianship, conservatorship or trust.

- Transfers from one co-owner to one or more other co-owners.

- Transfers made to a spouse, or to a person or persons in the lineal line of consanguinity of one or more of the transferors.

- Transfers between spouses resulting from a decree of dissolution of marriage or a decree of legal separation or from a property settlement agreement incidental to such a decree.

- Transfers or exchanges to or from any governmental entity.

Transfers of real property on which no dwelling is located.

Mississippi: Conducting Business Quiz

1. The Broker is responsible for;
    a.   all activities of his agents.
    b.   fixing commissions.
    c.   keeping the licensees up to date with their license.
    d.   the real estate practices of his licensees.

d. the real estate practices of his licensees.
A responsible broker must maintain an office and display the license therein. If the broker has more than one office, the broker shall display a branch office license in each branch office. The broker is responsible for the real estate practices of those licensees.

2. If the Broker has more than one office,
    a.   the Broker must display the branch office license in each branch office.
    b.   the Broker must set commission fees equally.
    c.   must have one receptionist for each office.
    d.   none of the above.

a. the Broker must display the branch office license in each branch office.
A responsible broker must maintain an office and display the license therein. If the broker has more than one office, the broker shall display a branch office license in each branch office. The broker is responsible for the real estate practices of those licensees.

3. A responsible broker must maintain an office and;
    a.   demand all independent contractors show up at 9AM to keep their license.
    b.   display the license therein.
    c.   follow office procedure in regards to state mandatory laws.
    d.   set commission fees.

b. display the license therein.

4. How many days does the MS Cooperating Broker have to send in the Cooperating Broker Agreement?
    a. 10 days.
    b.   5 days.
    c.   7 days.
    d.   30 days.

a. 10 days.
Two copies of the Cooperating Broker Agreement must be sent to MREC within ten days.

5. How many years does a Broker need to keep on hand, complete records relating to any real estate transaction?
    a.   5 years.
    b.   3 years.
    c.   7 years.
    d.   9 years.

b. 3 years
A real estate broker must keep on file for three years following its consummation, complete records relating to any real estate transaction. This includes, but is not limited to: listings, options, leases, offers to purchase, contracts of sale, escrow records, agency agreements and copies of all closing statements.

6. No licensee shall represent to a lender or any interested party, either verbally or through the preparation of a false sales contract,
    a.   an amount in excess less than the true value.
    b.   an amount in excess of the true and actual selling price.
    c.   an amount including the additions that shall be made upon close.
    d.   all of the above.

b. an amount in excess of the true and actual selling price.
No licensee shall represent to a lender or any other interested party, either verbally or through the preparation of a false sales contract, an amount in excess of the true and actual selling price.

7. Every contract must reflect whom the broker represents by a statement;
    a.   over the signatures of the parties involved.
    b.   under the signatures of the parties involved.
    c.   to the left of the signatures to the parties involved.
    d.   on the right side of the signatures of the parties involved.

b. over the signatures of the parties involved.
Every real estate contract must reflect whom the broker represents by a statement over the signatures of the parties to the contract.

8. When the Seller has received more than one offer;
    a.   he should accept only the highest offer.
    b.   he should reject all offers.
    c.   the Broker shall tell the buyers the lowest price a seller will accept.
    d.   the Broker should caution the Seller against countering on more than one offer at a time.

d. the Broker should caution the Seller against countering on more than one offer at a time.
In the event that more than one written offer is made before the owner has accepted an offer, any other written offer received by the listing broker, whether from a prospective purchaser or from another licensee cooperating in a sale, shall be presented to the owner unless the listing broker has specific, written instructions from the owner to postpone the presentation of other offers. Broker should caution the seller against countering on more than one offer at the same time

9. All offers;
    a.   must be presented to the Seller.
    b.   may be presented as long as the seller has rejected offers already.
    c.   may not be presented if higher offers have been presented already.
    d.   must be presented only if the buyer has joint tenancy.

a. must be presented to the Seller.
Present all offers.

10. An Exclusive Buyer Representation Agreement shall clearly indicate in the body of the document;
    a. that dual agency is an option contract.
    b.   that it is such an agreement.
    c.   that land sales constitute a Lis pendins.
    d.   that such an agreement is with the agent only and not his broker.

b. that it is such an agreement.
All exclusive buyer representation agreements shall be in writing and properly identify the terms and conditions under which the buyer will rely on the broker for the purchase of real estate; including the sales price, the considerations to be paid, the signatures of all parties to the agreement, and a definite date of expiration. The buyer may terminate the agreement upon fifteen (15) calendar days written notice to the buyer's exclusive agent. An

Exclusive Buyer Representation agreement shall clearly indicate in the body of the document *that it is such an agreement.*

11. The Buyer may terminate the Buyer Agreement;
    a.   upon 15 calendar days written notice to the buyer's exclusive agent.
    b.   upon 10 days written notice to the buyer's exclusive agent.
    c.   upon 30 calendar days written notice to the buyer's exclusive agent.
    d.   never.

a. upon 15 calendar days written notice to the buyer's exclusive agent.
The buyer may terminate the agreement *upon fifteen (15) calendar days* written notice to the buyer's exclusive agent. An Exclusive Buyer Representation agreement shall clearly indicate in the body of the document that it is such an agreement.

12. No Listing Agreement shall contain any provision requiring the listing party to notify the Broker of their intention to cancel the listing;
    a.   before any expiration date.
    b.   without financing first.
    c.   after such definite expiration date.
    d.   without the signature of the buyer.

c. after such definite expiration date.
No listing agreement shall contain any provision requiring the listing party to notify the broker of their intention to cancel the listing after such definite expiration date.

13. All exclusive Listing Agreements shall;
    a.   properly identify the property to be sold
    b.   contain all the conditions under which the transaction is to be consummated.
    c.   a definite date of expiration, sales price, consideration, and signatures.
    d.   all the above.

d. all the above.
All exclusive listing agreements shall be in writing, properly identify the property to be sold, and contain all of the terms and conditions under which the transaction is to be consummated; including the sales price, the considerations to be paid, the signatures of all parties to the agreement, and a definite date of expiration.

14. All Exclusive Listing Agreements;
    a.   shall be allowed to be verbal with relatives.
    b.   shall be in writing.
    c.   shall be an instrument for financing.
    d.   belongs to the sales agent.

b. shall be in writing.
All exclusive listing agreements shall be in writing, properly identify the property to be sold, and contain all of the terms and conditions under which the transaction is to be consummated; including the sales price, the considerations to be paid, the signatures of all parties to the agreement, and a definite date of expiration.

15. A real estate licensee shall deliver a true and correct copy of any instrument to any party or parties executing the same;
    a.   immediately at the time of signing.
    b.   within 5 days.
    c.   within 10 days.
    d.   by delivery in person only.

a. immediately at the time of signing.
A real estate licensee shall **immediately (at the time of signing)** deliver a true and correct copy of any instrument to any party or parties executing the same.

16. When an agent sells his own property;
    a.   the licensee is exempt from Disclosure Law.
    b.   the licensee is exempt from Agency Relationship.
    c.   the licensee has jurisdiction.
    d.   the licensee is not exempt from disciplinary actions by the commission.

d. the licensee is not exempt from disciplinary actions by the commission.
A real estate licensee shall not be exempt from disciplinary actions by the commission when selling property owned by the licensee.

17. Brokers shall document and date an acceptance or rejection of an offer;
    a. and upon written request, shall provide a copy of such document to the person making the offer.
    b. in order to violate insurable title.
    c.   for novation.
    d.   for all the above.

a. and upon written request, shall provide a copy of such document to the person making the offer.
When an offer is made on property owned by a party with whom a broker has entered into a listing agreement, such broker shall document and date the seller's personal acceptance or rejection of the offer and upon written request, shall provide a copy of such document to the person making the offer.

18. A Real Estate Broker or Salesperson in the ordinary course of his business may give an opinion as to the price of real estate for the purpose of a prospective listing or sale;
    a.   unless they are a credentialed Real Estate Appraiser.
    b.   unless they fall within the jurisdiction of Federal Appraisal Regulations.
    c.   however, this opinion as to the listing price or the sale price shall not be referred to as an appraisal.
    d.   never.

c. however, this opinion as to the listing price or the sale price shall not be referred to as an appraisal.
A real estate broker or salesperson in the ordinary course of business may give an opinion as to the sales price of real estate for the purpose of a prospective listing or sale; however, this opinion as to the listing price or the sale price shall not be referred to as an appraisal and must be completed in compliance with Section 73-354 of the Real Estate Broker's License Act and must conform to the Standards established by the National Association of Broker Price Opinion Professionals (NABPOP).

19. Any person who fails in a timely manner to respond to official MS Real Estate Commission written communication or who fails or neglects to abide by Mississippi Real Estate Commission Rules and Regulations shall be deemed;
    a.   innocent of wrongdoing for another 30 days.
    b.   prima facie, to be guilty of improper dealing.
    c.   guilty of a civil crime.
    d.   guilty of a federal offense.

b. prima facie, to be guilty of improper dealing.
Any licensee who fails in a timely manner to respond to official Mississippi Real Estate Commission written communication or who fails or neglects to abide by Mississippi Real Estate Commission's Rules and Regulations shall be deemed, *prima facie, to be guilty of improper dealing.*

20. A licensee that has changed to inactive status or who has transferred to another responsible broker may receive compensation from the previous responsible broker;

    a.   if the commission was generated from activity during the time that the licensee was under the supervision of that responsible broker.

    b.   never.

    c.   for all activities after transfer.

    d.   all of the above.

a. if the commission was generated from activity during the time that the licensee was under the supervision of that responsible broker.

A licensee who has changed to inactive status or who has transferred to another responsible broker may receive compensation from the previous responsible broker if the commission was generated from activity during the time that the licensee was under the supervision of that responsible broker.

21. No Broker shall pay a licensee a commission or other compensation knowingly if,

    a.   a licensee has earned it.

    b.   a licensee was an agent in a single agency agreement.

    c.   the licensee will pay a portion to a person who does not hold a real estate license.

    d.   the licensee was an agent in a dual agency.

c. the licensee will pay a portion to a person who does not hold a real estate license.

No licensee shall knowingly pay a commission, or other compensation to a licensed person knowing that licensee will in turn pay a portion or all of that which is received to a person who does not hold a real estate license.

22. No licensee shall pay any part of a fee, commission, or other compensation;

    a.   to another licensee except through that licensee's responsible Broker.

    b.   to another licensee without the expressed acceptance of their client.

    c.   without Due Diligence.

    d.   without the specific knowledge of their Broker.

a. to another licensee except through that licensee's responsible Broker.

No licensee shall pay any part of a fee, commission, or other compensation received by such licensee in buying, selling, exchanging, leasing, auctioning, or renting any real estate except to another licensee through the licensee's responsible broker.

23. How many copies of the cooperating agreement needs to be sent to MREC.

    a.   2 copies

    b.   1 copy

    c.   3 copies

    d.   4 copies

a. 2 copies

The responsible nonresident broker cannot place any sign on real property located in the state of Mississippi without the written consent of the cooperating responsible Mississippi broker. When the consent is obtained, the sign of the responsible Mississippi broker must be placed in a prominent place and in close proximity to the responsible nonresident broker's sign. Any licensed responsible Mississippi broker assisting or cooperating in the sale, lease, property management, rental or auction of real property within the state of Mississippi with a responsible nonresident broker who fails or refuses to list his or her name in such advertisement, or fails or refuses to cross-list such property with him or her, in writing, shall be deemed in violation of Section 73-35-11 of the Real Estate Broker's License Act, and shall be subject to a revocation or suspension of his or her license. In such instance herein where a responsible Mississippi broker enters into a cooperative agreement with a responsible nonresident broker pertaining to the sale of real property within the state of Mississippi, the responsible Mississippi broker must *file two copies of the cooperating agreement* with the Mississippi Real Estate Commission.

24. Equal prominence in regards to signs placement means that signs?

    a.   must not be placed at all.

   b.   must be placed side by side.
   c.   only one sign can be placed.
   d.   any of the above.

b. must be placed side by side.
The responsible nonresident broker cannot place any sign on real property located in the state of Mississippi without the written consent of the cooperating responsible Mississippi broker. When the consent is obtained, the sign of the responsible Mississippi broker must be placed in a prominent place and in close proximity to the responsible nonresident broker's sign.

25. When consent for signs is granted to the nonresident Broker, the MS Broker's signs must be;
   a. be larger.
   b.   be attached to the out of state Broker sign.
   c.   of equal prominence.
   d.   smaller.

b. of equal prominence.
The responsible nonresident broker cannot place any sign on real property located in the state of Mississippi without the written consent of the cooperating responsible Mississippi broker. When the consent is obtained, the sign of the responsible Mississippi broker must be placed in a prominent place and in close proximity to the responsible nonresident broker's sign.

26. A nonresident broker;
   a.   may place a sign on any property listed.
   b.   cannot place any sign on real property located in the state of MS without the written consent of the MS cooperating broker.
   c.   may place a sign on any property the out of state broker has listed without any permission.
   d.   can do any of the above.

b. cannot place any sign on real property located in the state of MS without the written consent of the MS cooperating broker.
The responsible nonresident broker cannot place any sign on real property located in the state of Mississippi without the written consent of the cooperating responsible Mississippi broker. When the consent is obtained, the sign of the responsible Mississippi broker must be placed in a prominent place and in close proximity to the responsible nonresident broker's sign.

27. A Mississippi Broker is ;
   a.   A nonresident or resident broker whose license was issued by MREC.
   b.   is a real estate Broker whose license is on active status and whose license was issued by MREC.
   c.   c. a nonresident Broker.
   d. all the above.

b. is a real estate Broker whose license is on active status and whose license was issued by MREC.

28. An active, licensed real estate Broker of another state who does not possess an active nonresident real estate license issued by MREC is the definition of;
   a.   a nonresident alien.
   b.   non licensed Broker.
   c.   a non-licensed agent employed by a Broker..
   d.   a nonresident Broker.

d. a nonresident Broker.

A responsible (principal) nonresident broker described herein is defined as an active, licensed responsible real estate broker of another state who does not possess an active responsible nonresident real estate broker's license issued by the Mississippi Real Estate Commission (MREC). A Mississippi broker described herein is a responsible (principal) real estate broker whose license is on active status and whose license was issued by MREC either as a responsible resident Mississippi broker or as a responsible nonresident Mississippi broker.

29. The commission or compensation derived from an agreement with the Mississippi Broker and a Out of State Broker shall be divided;
   a.   according to the set fees of MREC.
   b.   on a negotiable basis between the MS Broker and the out of state Broker.
   c.   after approval by the local board of Realtors.
   d.   according to the set fees in place set by the Commissioners.

b. on a negotiable basis between the MS Broker and the out of state Broker.
The commissions or other compensation resulting from the sale/rent/lease/property management or auction of the Mississippi real property and which are earned during the period the cooperative agreement is in force shall be divided on a negotiable basis between the Mississippi broker and the nonresident broker.

30. In a Cooperating Agreement, the listing or property management agreement for the Mississippi Real Estate Listing must;
   a.   remain in the name of the Mississippi Broker.
   b.   remain in the name of the out of state Broker if they were the procuring cause.
   c.   include any intestate interests.
   d.   a clause to invalidate the contract based on implied agency.

a. remain in the name of the Mississippi Broker.
A licensed Mississippi broker may cooperate with a broker licensed in another state who does not hold a Mississippi license through the use of a cooperative agreement. A separate cooperative agreement must be filed for each property, prospective user, or transaction with said writing reflecting the compensation to be paid to the Mississippi licensed broker. The listing or property management agreement for the Mississippi real property shall in such cases remain in the name of the Mississippi licensed broker.

31. When Mississippi Broker files a Cooperating Agreement with an out of state Broker, the Mississippi Broker must include;
   a.   the guaranteed sale plan.
   b.   the compensation to be paid to the out of state Broker.
   c.   the compensation to be paid to the Mississippi Broker.
   d.   a copy of the grant deed.

c. the compensation to be paid to the Mississippi Broker.
A licensed Mississippi broker may cooperate with a broker licensed in another state who does not hold a Mississippi license through the use of a cooperative agreement. A separate cooperative agreement must be filed for each property, prospective user, or transaction with said writing reflecting the *compensation to be paid to the Mississippi* licensed broker. The listing or property management agreement for the Mississippi real property shall in such cases remain in the name of the Mississippi licensed broker.

32. When cooperating with an non Mississippi Broker;
   a.   a separate cooperative agreement must be filed for each property, prospective user, or transaction.
   b.   The outside Broker must file for Homestead Protection.
   c.   the Mississippi Broker must file for Homestead Protection.
   d.   an habendum clause must be inserted.

a. a separate cooperative agreement must be filed for each property, prospective user, or transaction.

A licensed Mississippi broker may cooperate with a broker licensed in another state who does not hold a Mississippi license through the use of a cooperative agreement. A separate cooperative agreement must be filed for each property, prospective user, or transaction with said writing reflecting the *compensation to be paid to the Mississippi licensed broker.* The listing or property management agreement for the Mississippi real property shall in such cases remain in the name of the Mississippi licensed broker.

33. A licensed Mississippi Broker may cooperate with a broker licensed in another state who does not hold a Mississippi license through the use of a;
   a. novation.
   b. cooperative agreement.
   c. grant deed.
   d. holographic will.

b. cooperative agreement.
A licensed Mississippi broker may cooperate with a broker licensed in another state who does not hold a Mississippi license through the use of a cooperative agreement.

34. Upon the termination of an approved affiliated broker's real estate activities outside the scope of his employing broker's license, the responsible broker must;
   a. file a 1099 S
   b. give the broker a 1099misc for the transaction.
   c. immediately notify the Commission in writing upon the termination of such relationship.
   d. allow the affiliated broker 2 weeks off to recover.

c. immediately notify the Commission in writing upon the termination of such relationship.
However, should the responsible broker agree that a broker under his supervision may perform certain real estate services outside the responsible broker's supervision or direction the responsible broker shall notify the Commission in writing as to the exact nature of such relationship and the names of the broker or brokers involved. The responsible broker shall immediately notify the Commission in writing upon the termination of such relationship.

Real Estate Teams or Groups

1. When does the terms "Team or Group" be used in Mississippi Real Estate?
    a.   When a real estate brokerage advertises in Mississippi.
    b.   When two or more active real estate licensees represent themselves to the public as being part of a single entity.
    c.   When a developer registers their company with MREC
    d.   When an LLC is used for real estate purposes.

b. When two or more active real estate licensees represent themselves to the public as being part of a single entity.
A "Team or Group" shall mean a collective name used by two or more active real estate licensees who represent themselves to the public as being part of a single entity which is organized with the written approval of a Principal Broker to perform licensable real estate activity.

2. To qualify as a "Real Estate Team or Group" the active real estate licensees must be working together and each must work under the direct supervision of the same Principal Broker.
    a. True
    b.   False

a. True

To qualify as a "Real Estate Team or Group" the active real estate licensees must be working together and each must

(a) work under the direct supervision of the same Principal Broker,

(b) work together on real estate transactions to provide real estate brokerage services,

(c) must represent themselves to the public as being part of a Team or Group,

(d) must be designated by a specific team or group name, and (e) must conduct all real estate activity from the primary office or branch office where their individual licenses are displayed.

3. To qualify as a "Real Estate Team or Group" the active real estate licensees must be working together and each must?
    a.   work under the direct supervision of the same Principal Broker.
    b.   work together on real estate transactions to provide real estate brokerage services.
    c.   must represent themselves to the public as being part of a Team or Group.
    d.   must be designated by a specific team or group name, and (e) must conduct all real estate activity from the primary office or branch office where their individual licenses are displayed. E
    e.   . All the above.

e. All the above.

To qualify as a "Real Estate Team or Group" the active real estate licensees must be working together and each must (a) work under the direct supervision of the same Principal Broker, (b) work together on real estate transactions to provide real estate brokerage services, (c) must represent themselves to the public as being part of a Team or Group, (d) must be designated by a specific team or group name, and (e) must conduct all real estate activity from the primary office or branch office where their individual licenses are displayed.

4. All Principal Brokers must have specific information on each Team operating within their Brokerage and must
    a. Set up the team with an LLC.

    c.   Register each Team with the Real Estate Commission
    d.   File a new business license with the state of Mississippi
    e.   Assign all members their daily duties

b. Register each Team with the Real Estate Commission
All Principal Brokers must have specific information on each Team operating within their Brokerage and must register each Team with the Real Estate Commission on forms provided for that purpose; to include a detailed list indicating all approved Team names, the name of the Team Leader, the name of the individual Team members and the name of any unlicensed employee(s) of the Team.

5. The working team list(s) should indicate the dates that Team members are added to or deleted from any Team and should enable the Principal Broker and/or the Real Estate Commission to determine
    a.   Team membership at any point in time.
    b.   Licensees other business licenses.
    c.   Whether each member could qualify for a specific team.
    d.   All the above.

a. Team membership at any point in time.
All Principal Brokers must have specific information on each Team operating within their Brokerage and must register each Team with the Real Estate Commission on forms provided for that purpose; to include a detailed list indicating all approved Team names, the name of the Team Leader, the name of the individual Team members and the name of any unlicensed employee(s) of the Team. The working list(s) should indicate the dates that Team members are added to or deleted from any Team and should enable the Principal Broker and/or the Real Estate Commission to determine Team membership at any point in time.

6. Adjustments to a Team should be filed with the Real Estate Commission within _____ working day of any change and should be on forms provided by the Commission.
    a.   Twenty (20)
    b.   Fifteen (15)
    c.   Thirty (30)
    d.   Ten (10)

d. Ten (10)
Adjustments to a Team should be filed with the Real Estate Commission within ten (10) working day of any change and should be on forms provided by the Commission.

67 Who must a team within a brokerage appoint?
    a.   A listing agent
    b.   A broker
    c.   A team leader
    d.   A selling agent

c. A team leader
All teams must appoint a Team Leader.

8 What level license does a Team Leader have?
    a.   A Salesperson of three years.
    b.   A Broker Associate with a minimum of one year experience.
    c.   A new broker with less than one year experience.
    d.   A Registered office manager.

b. Broker Associate with a minimum of one year experience.
All teams must appoint a Team Leader, who will be a Broker Associate with a minimum of one years' real estate experience and will have supervisory responsibility (under the supervision of the Principal Broker) over the Team

members. The Team Leader may be subject to disciplinary action for violations of the Mississippi Real Estate Brokers Act by Team members under their supervision.

9. With the written approval of the Principal Broker and the Team Leader a Team name may
   a. Be registered as an S-corp
   b. Be registered with the Office of Business Licenses
   c. Be allowed to use a separate trust account from their broker that does not fall under the jurisdiction of MREC
   d. Be allowed to advertise using the team name along with the brokerage name.

d. Be allowed to advertise using the team name along with the brokerage name.
A Team Name may, with the written approval of the Principal Broker and the Team Leader, be used in any type of advertising. Any individual whose name is displayed in any advertisement must be an active licensee who is sponsored by the Principal Broker. All advertising must fully comply with the guidelines established in MREC Administrative Rule 3.3.

10. What does the principle broker of the brokerage and the team do before team advertising can be used by the team?
   a. Confirm that the name of the Principal Broker or the Brokerage Firm and their telephone number is prominently displayed on all advertising.
   b. Confirm that MREC is notified of the advertisement.
   c. Indicate and list all the members of the team.
   d. List the Team Leader in all advertisements.

a. Confirm that the name of the Principal Broker or the Brokerage Firm and their telephone number is prominently displayed on all advertising
Principal Brokers and Team Leaders must confirm that the name of the Principal Broker or the Brokerage Firm and their telephone number is prominently displayed on all advertising. The name of the Team must be situated near the name of the Brokerage Firm and shall be identified with the same sized or smaller print as that of the Brokerage.

11. Neither team names nor team advertising should suggest that the team is an independent real estate brokerage. Team names must not include terms such as
   a. real estate brokerage.
   b. realty.
   c. real estate.
   d. company.
   e. All the above.

e. All the above

Match

1. Real estate broker	Association of Real Estate License Law Officials.
2. Real estate	The person to whom the agent owes a fiduciary duty.
3. Real estate salesperson	A type of license that is not subject to renewal.
4. Automated valuation method	A surveyor developer's plan prepared by a licensed surveyor; A tax assessor's public record; or A builder's plan used to construct or market the property.
5. Broker price opinion	An agent representing both parties to a real estate transaction with the informed consent of both parties, with written understanding of specific duties and representation to be afforded each party.
6. Third-party information	A collective name used by two or more active real estate licensees who represent themselves to the public as being part of a single entity which is organized with the written approval of a Principal Broker to perform licensable real estate activity.
7. ARELLO	Leaseholds as well as any and every interest or estate in land, including timesharing and condominiums, whether corporeal or incorporeal, freehold, or non-freehold, and whether said property is situated in this state or elsewhere
8. Temporary license	The duties due the principal (client)
9. Advertising	That person not represented in a real estate transaction.
10. Team or Group	Persons, partnerships, associations and corporations, foreign and domestic, who for a fee, commission or other valuable consideration, or who with the intention or expectation of receiving or collecting the same, list, sell, purchase, exchange, rent, lease, manage or auction any real estate, or the improvements thereon, including options; or who negotiate or attempt to negotiate any such activity; or who advertise or hold themselves out as engaged in such activities; or who direct or assist in the procuring of a purchaser or prospect calculated or intended to result in a real estate transaction.
11. Agency	A fee paid to a broker for the rendering of services. Compensation, when considered alone, is not the determining factor in an agency relationship.
12. Agent	The use of any oral, written, visual, printed or electronically generated advertisement by a real estate licensee or other person on behalf of a real estate licensee.
13. Client	Any person employed or engaged by or on behalf of a licensed real estate broker.
14. Compensation"	One who is authorized to act on behalf of and represent another.
15. Customer	The relationship created when one person, the Principal (client), delegates to another, the agent, the right to act on his behalf in a real estate transaction and to exercise some degree of discretion while so acting.

Real Estate Training Institute

| 16. Disclosed Du al Agent | An estimate prepared by a real estate broker, agent, or salesperson that details the probable selling price of a particular piece of real estate property and provides a varying level of detail about the property's condition, market, and neighborhood, and information on comparable sales. |
| 17.Fiduciary Responsibilities | Any computerized model used by mortgage originators and secondary market issuers to determine the collateral worth of a mortgage secured by a consumer's principal dwelling. |

Answer Key

1. Real estate broker	Persons, partnerships, associations and corporations, foreign and domestic, who for a fee, commission or other valuable consideration, or who with the intention or expectation of receiving or collecting the same, list, sell, purchase, exchange, rent, lease, manage or auction any real estate, or the improvements thereon, including options; or who negotiate or attempt to negotiate any such activity; or who advertise or hold themselves out as engaged in such activities; or who direct or assist in the procuring of a purchaser or prospect calculated or intended to result in a real estate transaction.
2. Real estate	Leaseholds as well as any and every interest or estate in land, including timesharing and condominiums, whether corporeal or incorporeal, freehold, or non-freehold, and whether said property is situated in this state or elsewhere.
3. Real estate salesperson	Any person employed or engaged by or on behalf of a licensed real estate broker.
4. Automated valuation method	Any computerized model used by mortgage originators and secondary market issuers to determine the collateral worth of a mortgage secured by a consumer's principal dwelling.
5. Broker price opinion	An estimate prepared by a real estate broker, agent, or salesperson that details the probable selling price of a particular piece of real estate property and provides a varying level of detail about the property's condition, market, and neighborhood, and information on comparable sales.
6. Third-party information	A surveyor developer's plan prepared by a licensed surveyor; A tax assessor's public record; or A builder's plan used to construct or market the property.
7. ARELLO	Association of Real Estate License Law Officials.
8. Temporary license	A type of license that is not subject to renewal.
9. Advertising	The use of any oral, written, visual, printed or electronically generated advertisement by a real estate licensee or other person on behalf of a real estate licensee.
10. Team or Group	A collective name used by two or more active real estate licensees who represent themselves to the public as being part of a single entity which is organized with the written approval of a Principal Broker to perform licensable real estate activity.
11. Agency	The relationship created when one person, the Principal (client), delegates to another, the agent, the right to act on his behalf in a real estate transaction and to exercise some degree of discretion while so acting.

12. Agent	One who is authorized to act on behalf of and represent another.
13. Client	The person to whom the agent owes a fiduciary duty.
14. Compensation"	Fee paid to a broker for the rendering of services. Compensation, when considered alone, is not the determining factor in an agency relationship.
15. Customer	That person not represented in a real estate transaction.
16. Disclosed Du al Agent	An agent representing both parties to a real estate transaction with the informed consent of both parties, with written understanding of specific duties and representation to be afforded each party.
17.Fiduciary Responsibilities	Duties due the principal (client)

Mississippi Real Estate License Law QUIZ

1. Who are exempt from having a real estate license?

a. Brokers

b. A Public Official holding an auction.

c. A Licensee selling her own home.

d. None of the above.

b. A Public Official holding an auction.

Exclusions

1. Attorneys at law in the performance of primary or incidental duties as such attorneys at law.

2. Any person holding in good faith a duly executed power of attorney from the owner, authorizing the final consummation and execution for the sale, purchase, leasing or exchange of real estate.

3. The acts of any person while acting as a receiver, trustee, administrator, executor, guardian or under court order, or while acting under authority of a deed of trust or will.

4. *Public officers while performing their duties as such.*

Anyone dealing exclusively in oil and gas leases and mineral rights.

5.Life insurance companies and their representatives from negotiating or attempting to negotiate loans secured by mortgages on real estate, nor shall these companies or their representatives be required to qualify as real estate brokers or agents under this chapter.

6. Activities of mortgagees approved by the Federal Housing Administration or the United States Department of Veterans Affairs, banks chartered under the laws of the State of Mississippi or the United States, savings and loan associations chartered under the laws of the State of Mississippi or the United States, licensees under the Small Loan Regulatory Law, and under the Small Loan Privilege Tax Law, being Sections 75-67-201 through 75-67-243, small business investment companies licensed by the Small Business Administration and chartered under the laws of the State of Mississippi, or any of their affiliates and subsidiaries, related to the making of a loan secured by a lien on real estate or to the disposing of real estate acquired by foreclosure or in lieu of foreclosure or otherwise held as security. No director, officer, or employee of any such financial institution shall be required to qualify as a real estate broker or agent under this chapter when engaged in the aforesaid activities for and on behalf of such financial institution.

2. The following people may be excluded from holding a real estate license except

a. Attorneys and Public officers performing their duties as such.

b. A person holding a duly executed power of attorney from the owner and a receiver, trustee, administrator, executor, guardian or under court order or while acting under authority of a deed of trust or will.

c. Anyone dealing in oil and gas leases and mineral rights.

d. A person who places an ad on the internet under their responsible broker.

d. A person who places an ad on the internet under their responsible broker.

1. Attorneys at law in the performance of primary or incidental duties as such attorneys at law.

2. Any person holding in good faith a duly executed power of attorney from the owner, authorizing the final consummation and execution for the sale, purchase, leasing or exchange of real estate.

3. The acts of any person while acting as a receiver, trustee, administrator, executor, guardian or under court order, or while acting under authority of a deed of trust or will.

4. Public officers while performing their duties as such.

Anyone dealing exclusively in oil and gas leases and mineral rights.

5.Life insurance companies and their representatives from negotiating or attempting to negotiate loans secured by mortgages on real estate, nor shall these companies or their representatives be required to qualify as real estate brokers or agents under this chapter.

6. Activities of mortgagees approved by the Federal Housing Administration or the United States Department of Veterans Affairs, banks chartered under the laws of the State of Mississippi or the United States, savings and loan associations chartered under the laws of the State of Mississippi or the United States, licensees under the Small Loan Regulatory Law, and under the Small Loan Privilege Tax Law, being Sections 75-67-201 through 75-67-243, small

business investment companies licensed by the Small Business Administration and chartered under the laws of the State of Mississippi, or any of their affiliates and subsidiaries, related to the making of a loan secured by a lien on real estate or to the disposing of real estate acquired by foreclosure or in lieu of foreclosure or otherwise held as security. No director, officer, or employee of any such financial institution shall be required to qualify as a real estate broker or agent under this chapter when engaged in the aforesaid activities for and on behalf of such financial institution.

3. The five Commissioners appointed by the Governor with advise and consent from the Senate have the power to do all of the following except;
a. Appoint a commissioner.
b. Give 15 days' notice of a hearing to a licensee when the licensee has a violation charged against him.
c. Issue subpoenas for the attendance of witnesses and the production of books and papers.
d. d. Both 1 and 3.

a. Appoint a commissioner.
There is hereby created the Mississippi Real Estate Commission. The commission shall consist of five (5) persons, to be appointed by the Governor with the advice and consent of the Senate. Each appointee shall have been a resident and citizen of this state for at least six (6) years prior to his appointment, and his vocation for at least five (5) years shall have been that of a real estate broker. One (1) member shall be appointed for the term of one (1) year; two (2) members for terms of two (2) years; two (2) members for terms of four (4) years; thereafter, the term of the members of said commission shall be for four (4) years and until their successors are appointed and qualify. There shall be at least one (1) commissioner from each congressional district, as such districts are constituted as of July 1, 2002. The commissioners appointed from each of the congressional districts shall be bona fide residents of the district from which each is appointed. One (1) additional commissioner shall be appointed without regard to residence in any particular congressional district. Members to fill vacancies shall be appointed by the Governor for the unexpired term. The Governor may remove any commissioner for cause. The State of Mississippi shall not be required to furnish office space for such commissioners. The provisions of this section shall not affect persons who are members of the Real Estate Commission as of January 1, 2002. Such members shall serve out their respective terms, upon the expiration of which the provisions of this section shall take effect. Nothing provided herein shall be construed as prohibiting the reappointment of any member of the said commission.

4. Can the Real Estate Commissioners issue subpoenas?
a. No because it is a legal matter.
b. Yes, because it is within the authority of the Commission's power.
c. No because they need to contact the appropriate local public official to issue such subpoenas.
d. Yes, but only if there is proof of a crime being committed.

b. Yes because it is within the authority of the Commission's power.
The commission is hereby authorized and empowered to issue subpoenas for the attendance of witnesses and the production of books and papers. The process issued by the commission shall extend to all parts of the state, and such process shall be served by any person designated by the commission for such service. The person serving such process receive such compensation as may be allowed by the commission, not to exceed the fee prescribed by law for similar services. All witnesses who are subpoenaed and who appear in any proceedings before the commission receive the same fees and mileage as allowed by law, and all such fees shall be taxed as part of the costs in the case.

5. A broker applicant who has not held a salesperson license for a period of 12 months immediately prior to submitting an application, must;

  a. have a master's degree from a college or university as approved by the Southern Association of Colleges and Schools.

  b. have successfully completed 120 classroom hours in real estate courses, which courses are acceptable by the Commissioners.

  c. have successfully completed 150 classroom hours in real estate courses, which courses are acceptable for credit toward a degree at a college or university as approved by the Southern Association of Colleges and Schools. d. have attended a college that is approved by the Southern Association of Colleges and Schools.

c. have successfully completed 150 classroom hours in real estate courses, which courses are acceptable for credit toward a degree at a college or university as approved by the Southern Association of Colleges and Schools. d. have attended a college that is approved by the Southern Association of Colleges and Schools.
An applicant who has not held an active real estate salesperson's license for a period of at least thirty-six (36) months prior to submitting an application shall have successfully completed a minimum of one hundred fifty (150) classroom hours in real estate courses, which courses are acceptable for credit toward a degree at a college or university as approved by the Southern Association of Colleges and Schools.

6. A nonresident may apply for a nonresident's license in Mississippi provided the individual is a licensed broker or is a broker salesperson or salesperson affiliated with a resident or nonresident Mississippi broker.
a. provided a nonresident who applies for a broker's license and who will maintain an office in Mississippi.
b. provided the nonresident not maintain a place of business within Mississippi provided he is regularly actively
c. engaged in the real estate business and maintains a place of business in the other state.
d. All the above.

d. All the above.
The nonresident need not maintain a place of business within Mississippi provided he is regularly actively engaged in the real estate business and maintains a place of business in the other state.

7. It is unlawful to carry out the business of a broker or salesperson without;
a. A high school diploma.
b. The approval of your county's supervisors.
c. a license.
d. being 21 or older.

c. a license.
It shall be unlawful for any person, partnership, association, or corporation to engage in or carry on, directly or indirectly, or to advertise or to hold himself, itself, or themselves out as engaging in or carrying on the business, or act in the capacity of, a real estate broker, or a real estate salesperson, within this state, without first obtaining a license.

8. The following may be exempt from having a license;
a. Attorneys and executed power of attorney.
b. Receiver, trustee, administrator, and public Officers.
c. Those dealing in oil/gas leases and mineral rights.
d. All the above.

d. All the above.
Exclusions
1. Attorneys at law in the performance of primary or incidental duties as such attorneys at law.
2. Any person holding in good faith a duly executed power of attorney from the owner, authorizing the final consummation and execution for the sale, purchase, leasing or exchange of real estate.
3. The acts of any person while acting as a receiver, trustee, administrator, executor, guardian or under court order, or while acting under authority of a deed of trust or will.

4. Public officers while performing their duties as such.
Anyone dealing exclusively in oil and gas leases and mineral rights.

5. Life insurance companies and their representatives from negotiating or attempting to negotiate loans secured by mortgages on real estate, nor shall these companies or their representatives be required to qualify as real estate brokers or agents under this chapter.

6. Activities of mortgagees approved by the Federal Housing Administration or the United States Department of Veterans Affairs, banks chartered under the laws of the State of Mississippi or the United States, savings and loan associations chartered under the laws of the State of Mississippi or the United States, licensees under the Small Loan Regulatory Law, and under the Small Loan Privilege Tax Law, being Sections 75-67-201 through 75-67-243, small business investment companies licensed by the Small Business Administration and chartered under the laws of the State of Mississippi, or any of their affiliates and subsidiaries, related to the making of a loan secured by a lien on real estate or to the disposing of real estate acquired by foreclosure or in lieu of foreclosure or otherwise held as security. No director, officer, or employee of any such financial institution shall be required to qualify as a real estate broker or agent under this chapter when engaged in the aforesaid activities for and on behalf of such financial institution.

9. Licensee following notification of action resulting from a Commissioner hearing;
a. has 30 days to appeal any ruling and post a required $500 bond for any costs which may be adjudged against him.
b. has 60 days to appeal any ruling and post a required $1000 bond for any expenses that may be incurred. c. has 15 days to appeal, and no bond is required.
d. has 30 days to appeal, and no bond is required.

a. has 30 days to appeal any ruling and post a required $500 bond for any costs which may be adjudged against him.
Notice of appeals shall be filed in the office of the clerk of the court who shall issue a writ of certiorari directed to the commission commanding it, within thirty (30) days after service thereof, to certify to such court its entire record in the matter in which the appeal has been taken. The appeal shall thereupon be heard in due course by said court, without a jury, which shall review the record and make its determination of the cause between the parties.
Any person taking an appeal shall post a satisfactory bond in the amount of Five Hundred Dollars ($500.00) for the payment of any costs which may be adjudged against him.

10. Whenever a Mississippi broker enters into a cooperating agreement with a nonresident broker, the Mississippi broker;
a. must file two copies of the cooperating agreement within 10 days with the Mississippi Real Estate Commission.
b. Does not need to file anything with the Commission since the broker has his own business license.
c. must file a copy of the agreement with the Department of Real Estate.
d. must contact the Commission in the state where the nonresident broker resides.

a. must file two copies of the cooperating agreement within 10 days with the Mississippi Real Estate Commission.
Whenever a Mississippi broker enters into a cooperative agreement under this section, the Mississippi broker shall file two (2) copies within ten (10) days with the commission a copy of each such written agreement.

11. When a broker has an agreement with a nonresident broker, involving a property located in Mississippi all advertising must have the name and telephone number of the Mississippi broker.
a. and the address of the nonresident broker
b. and the Mississippi broker shall be given equal prominence.
c. and the nonresident broker's signs are the only signs allowed on the property for sale.
d. none of the above.

b. and the Mississippi broker shall be given equal prominence.

In all advertising of real estate located in Mississippi, the name and telephone number of the Mississippi broker shall appear and shall be given equal prominence with the name of the nonresident broker who is not licensed in this state.

12. When both the nonresident broker and the Mississippi broker have their company signs on a property listed together, the signs
a. should be placed with the nonresident broker sign in front of the Mississippi broker's signs as a courtesy.
b. of the nonresident broker should be at least 10 times the size of the Mississippi Broker.
c. should have equal prominence and be placed side by side.
d. It doesn't matter where the signs are placed.

c. should have equal prominence and be placed side by side.
The showing of property located in Mississippi and negotiations pertaining thereto shall be supervised by the Mississippi broker. In all advertising of real estate located in Mississippi, the name and telephone number of the Mississippi broker shall appear and shall be given equal prominence with the name of the nonresident broker who is not licensed in this state.

13. The Mississippi broker in a nonresident cooperating broker agreement
a. shall be liable for all acts of the cooperating broker
b. shall be liable for his own acts.
c. shall be liable for his own acts only.
d. Both a and b.

d. Both a and b.
The Mississippi broker shall be liable for all acts of the above cooperating broker, as well as for his own acts, arising from the execution of any cooperative agreement.

14. An earnest money deposit pertaining to a cooperative agreement must be held in escrow;
a. by the nonresident broker unless both buyer and seller agree otherwise.
b. can be held by either of the brokers depending on who has a more secure trust account.
c. by the Mississippi broker unless both the buyer and seller agree in writing to relieve the Mississippi broker of this responsibility.
d. The Seller holds the earnest money deposit.

c. by the Mississippi broker unless both the buyer and seller agree in writing to relieve the Mississippi broker of this responsibility.
All earnest money pertaining to a cooperative agreement must be held in escrow by the Mississippi broker unless both the buyer and seller agree in writing to relieve the Mississippi broker of this responsibility.

15. All to a real estate salesperson or broker salesperson;
a. shall designate the responsible broker of such salesperson or broker salesperson.
b. shall designate the home phone number and home address of each person.
c. both a and b.
d. neither a nor b.

b. shall designate the home phone number and home address of each person.
All licenses issued to a real estate salesperson or broker-salesperson shall designate the responsible broker of such salesperson or broker-salesperson. Prompt notice in writing, within three (3) days, shall be given to the commission by any real estate salesperson of a change of responsible broker, and of the name of the principal broker into whose agency the salesperson is about to enter; and a new license shall thereupon be issued by the commission to such salesperson for the unexpired term of the original license upon the return to the commission of the license previously issued.

16. Notice in writing shall be given to the Commission by any real estate salesperson with a change of responsible broker within;
a. 5 days
b. 3 days
c. Two weeks
d. no notice is required.

b. 3 days
The change of responsible broker or employment by any licensed real estate salesperson without notice to the commission as required shall automatically cancel his license. Upon termination of a salesperson's agency, the responsible broker shall within three (3) days return the salesperson's license to the commission for cancellation. It shall be unlawful for any real estate salesperson to perform any of the acts contemplated by this chapter either directly or indirectly after his agency has been terminated and his license has been returned for cancellation until his license has been reissued by the commission.

17. When within 3 days a salesperson notifies the Commission of a change of broker.
a. The salesperson must give the name of his responsible broker and the name of the principal broker into whose agency the salesperson is about to enter.
b. The salesperson does not need to name the broker the salesperson is transferring to until the first of the year.
c. The salesperson is not allowed to change brokers more than three times a year.
d. The salesperson must include the names of his bank in case a suit is brought against him.

a. The salesperson must give the name of his responsible broker and the name of the principal broker into whose agency the salesperson is about to enter.
Prompt notice in writing, within three (3) days, shall be given to the commission by any real estate salesperson of a change of responsible broker, and of the name of the principal broker into whose agency the salesperson is about to enter; and a new license shall thereupon be issued by the commission to such salesperson for the unexpired term of the original license upon the return to the commission of the license previously issued. The change of responsible broker or employment by any licensed real estate salesperson without notice to the commission as required shall automatically cancel his license.

18. When changing responsible brokers;
a. The Commission shall issue a new license for a period of one year and when the agent completes the mandatory hours of continuing education will issue a license for 4 more years.
b. The Commission has no more than 30 days to issue a new license.
c. A new license shall thereupon be issued by the Commission to such salesperson for the unexpired term of the original license upon the return to the Commission of the license previously issued.
d. The Commission doesn't care if a salesperson changes responsible broker and no notice needs be submitted.

c. A new license shall thereupon be issued by the Commission to such salesperson for the unexpired term of the original license upon the return to the Commission of the license previously issued.
Prompt notice in writing, within three (3) days, shall be given to the commission by any real estate salesperson of a change of responsible broker, and of the name of the principal broker into whose agency the salesperson is about to enter; and a new license shall thereupon be issued by the commission to such salesperson for the unexpired term of the original license upon the return to the commission of the license previously issued.

19. Brokers may give legal advice;
a. When a client asks how to take title.
b. When a client is getting a divorce.
c. When the client is under 18.
d. Never.

d. Never.
NEVER EVER FOREVER

No real estate broker shall practice law or give legal advice directly or indirectly unless said broker be a duly licensed attorney under the laws of this state. He shall not act as a public conveyancer nor give advice or opinions as to the legal effect of instruments nor give opinions concerning the validity of title to real estate; nor shall he prevent or discourage any party to a real estate transaction from employing the services of an attorney; nor shall a broker undertake to prepare documents fixing and defining the legal rights of parties to a transaction. However, when acting as a broker, he may use an earnest money contract form. A real estate broker shall not participate in attorney's fees unless the broker is a duly licensed attorney under the laws of this state and performs legal services in addition to brokerage services.

20. Licensees may obtain errors and omissions coverage independently if the coverage contained in the policy follows the minimum requirement of;
a. a per claim limit is not less than $1,000.
b. a per claim limit is not less than $10,000.
c. a per claim limit is not less than $100,000.
d. There is no minimum limit.

c. a per claim limit is not less than $100,000.
All activities contemplated under this chapter are included as covered activities;
A per-claim limit is not less than One Hundred Thousand Dollars ($100,000.00);
An annual aggregate limit is not less than One Hundred Thousand Dollars ($100,000.00);
Limits apply per licensee per claim.
Maximum deductible is Two Thousand Five Hundred Dollars ($2,500.00) per licensee per claim for damages; Maximum deductible is One Thousand Dollars ($1,000.00) per licensee per claim for defense costs; and The contract of insurance pays, on behalf of the injured person(s), liabilities owed.

21. All (5) five commissioners appointed by the Governor with advise and consent of the Senate;
a. Must be a resident for 6 years and a managing broker for 5 years.
b. Must be a resident for 6 years and a salesperson/broker for 5 years.
c. Must be a college graduate and scored over 89% on the broker's exam.
d. Can be a nonresident if he has been a managing broker for 5 years.

a. Must be a resident for 6 years and a managing broker for 5 years.
There is hereby created the Mississippi Real Estate Commission. The commission shall consist of five (5) persons, to be appointed by the Governor with the advice and consent of the Senate. Each appointee shall have been a resident and citizen of this state for at least six (6) years prior to his appointment, and his vocation for at least five (5) years shall have been that of a real estate broker.

22. Commissioners are vested with power of court to issue and enforce subpoenas; levy fines and;
a. Appoint other commissioners.
b. Set commission fee limits brokers can charge a client.
c. Levy jail terms.
d. None of the above.

c. Levy jail terms.
In addition to the authority granted to the commission as hereinabove set forth, the commission is hereby vested with the authority to bring injunctive proceedings in any appropriate forum against any violator or violators of this chapter, and all judges or courts now having the power to grant injunctions are specifically granted the power and jurisdiction to hear and dispose of such proceedings.

23. All license fee funds must be submitted to the State Treasury with detailed explanation;
a. on a monthly basis.
b. on a quarterly basis.
c. on a daily basis.
d. on a weekly basis.

4. on a weekly basis.
All fees charged and collected under this chapter shall be paid by the administrator at least once a week, accompanied by a detailed statement thereof, into the treasury of the state to credit of a fund to be known as the "Real Estate License Fund," which fund is hereby created. All monies which shall be paid into the State Treasury and credited to the "Real Estate License Fund" are hereby appropriated to the use of the commission in carrying out the provisions of this chapter including the payment of salaries and expenses, printing an annual directory of licensees, and for educational purposes. Maintenance of a searchable, internet-based web site shall satisfy the requirement for publication of a directory of licensees under this section.

24. Real Estate Commissioners;
a. are from each congressional district and one at large.
b. are from North, South, East and West Mississippi with one at large.
c. are two democrats and two republicans and one independent.
d. All the above.

a. are from each congressional district and one at large.
There shall be at least one (1) commissioner from each congressional district, as such districts are constituted as of July 1, 2002. The commissioners appointed from each of the congressional districts shall be bona fide residents of the district from which each is appointed. One (1) additional commissioner shall be appointed without regard to residence in any congressional district.

25. Any applicant or licensee or person aggrieved shall have the right of appeal from any adverse or order or decision the Commission to the circuit court of the county of the residence of the applicant, licensee, or person or of the First Judicial District of Hinds County within _____ days from the service of notice of the action of the Commission.
a. five
b. ten
c. twenty
d. thirty

d. thirty
Any applicant or licensee or person aggrieved shall have the right of appeal from any adverse ruling or order or decision of the commission to the circuit court of the county of residence of the applicant, licensee, or person, or of the First Judicial District of Hinds County, within thirty (30) days from the service of notice of the action of the commission upon the parties in interest.

26. Any person charged with a violation shall be given _____ days' notice of the hearing upon the charges filed, together with a copy of the complaint.
a. Three days
b. Five days
c. Fifteen days
d. Thirty days

c. Fifteen days
The commission is hereby authorized and directed to take legal action against any violator of this chapter. Upon complaint initiated by the commission or filed with it, the licensee or any other person charged with a violation of this chapter shall be *given fifteen (15) days' notice* of the hearing upon the charges filed, together with a copy of the complaint. The applicant or licensee or other violator shall have an opportunity to be heard in person or by counsel,

to offer testimony, and to examine witnesses appearing in connection with the complaint. Hearings shall be held at the offices of the Mississippi Real Estate Commission, or at the commission's sole discretion, at a place determined by the commission.

27. Any person taking appeal shall post a satisfactory bond in the amount of _____dollars for the payment of any costs which may be adjudged against him.
a. $100
b. $200
c. $400
d. $500

d. $500
Any person taking an appeal shall post a satisfactory bond in the amount of *Five Hundred Dollars ($500.00)* for the payment of any costs which may be adjudged against him.

28. Funds received by the Commission are used to;
a. fund Mississippi Real Estate Commission operations.
b. fund highway projects.
c. fund referral fees.
d. fund kickbacks.

a. fund Mississippi Real Estate Commission operations.
All fees charged and collected under this chapter shall be paid by the administrator at least once a week, accompanied by a detailed statement thereof, into the treasury of the state to credit of a fund to be known as the "Real Estate License Fund," which fund is hereby created. All monies which shall be paid into the State Treasury and credited to the "Real Estate License Fund" are hereby appropriated to the use of the commission in carrying out the provisions of this chapter including the payment of salaries and expenses, printing an annual directory of licensees, and for educational purposes. Maintenance of a searchable, internet-based web site shall satisfy the requirement for publication of a directory of licensees under this section.

29. Licensees who do not show proof of E and O Insurance have 30 days to correct the deficiency. If the deficiency is not corrected within the 30 days;
a. the Commission will fine the responsible broker.
b. the licensees' licenses will be placed on inactive status.
c. the Commission will close the office of the licensee.
d. the Commission will do nothing.

b. the licensees' licenses will be placed on inactive status.
For licensees not submitting proof of insurance necessary to continue active licensure, the commission shall be responsible for sending notice of deficiency to those licensees. Licensees who do not correct the deficiency within thirty (30) days shall have their licenses placed on inactive status. The commission shall assess fees for inactive status and for return to active status when errors and omissions insurance has been obtained.

30. All monies which shall be paid into the state treasury are credited;
a. to the "real estate license fund".
b. to the state general fund.
c. are not credited anywhere.
d. none of the above.

a. to the "real estate license fund".
All fees charged and collected under this chapter shall be paid by the administrator at least once a week, accompanied by a detailed statement thereof, into the treasury of the state to credit of a fund to be known as the "Real Estate License Fund," which fund is hereby created.

31. Monies from the "real estate license fund" are used for;
a. salaries and expenses.
b. printing an annual directory of licensees.
c. educational purposes and maintenance of a searchable internet-based web site which shall satisfy the requirement for publication of a directory of licensees.
d. All the above.

d. All the above.
All monies which shall be paid into the State Treasury and credited to the "Real Estate License Fund" are hereby appropriated to the use of the commission in carrying out the provisions of this chapter including the payment of salaries and expenses, printing an annual directory of licensees, and for educational purposes. Maintenance of a searchable, internet-based web site shall satisfy the requirement for publication of a directory of licensees under this section.

32. No fee, commission or other valuable consideration may be paid to a person for real estate brokerage activities unless the person provides evidence of;
a. a social security number and ID.
b. a license or a cooperating agreement.
c. a personal bank account or a trust account.
d. none of the above.

b. a license or a cooperating agreement.
No fee, commission or other valuable consideration may be paid to a person for real estate brokerage activities unless the person provides evidence of licensure or provides evidence of a cooperative agreement.

33. A broker wants to pay his neighbor a referral fee for sending the broker the neighbor's sister who purchased a home through that broker.
a. The broker cannot pay his neighbor a fee unless the neighbor is a licensed real estate agent and then the broker would need to pay his broker.
b. The broker can pay his neighbor a referral fee because no one will find out.
c. The broker can pay his neighbor by automatic deposit.
d. None of the above.

a. The broker cannot pay his neighbor a fee unless the neighbor is a licensed real estate agent and then the broker would need to pay his broker.
No fee, commission or other valuable consideration may be paid to a person for real estate brokerage activities unless the person provides evidence of licensure or provides evidence of a cooperative agreement.

34. IREBEA (Interest on Real Estate Broker's Escrow Accounts) is;
a. mandatory
b. voluntary
c. based on the amount of deposits on hand
d. depends on how long a broker has been in business.

b. voluntary
The IREBEA program shall be a voluntary program based upon willing participation by real estate brokers, whether proprietorships, partnerships, or professional corporations.

35. The determination of whether a client's funds are nominal in amount or to be held for a short period of time;
a. rest in the judgment of the client.
b. rest in the sound judgment of each broker, and no charge of ethical impropriety or other breach of professional conduct shall attend a broker's exercise of judgment in that regard.
c. is regulated by the Senate.

d. Both 1 and 3.

b. rest in the sound judgment of each broker, and no charge of ethical impropriety or other breach of professional conduct shall attend a broker's exercise of judgment in that regard.

The determination of whether clients' or customers' funds are nominal in amount or to be held for a short period of time rests in the sound judgment of each broker, and no charge of ethical impropriety or other breach of professional conduct shall attend a broker's exercise of judgment in that regard.

36. The interest in a IREBEA account for nominal or short-term deposits shall be made quarterly to;
a. the Real Estate Commission.
b. the State Treasury.
c. the Mississippi Housing Opportunity Fund.
d. the Mississippi Legal Help Foundation.

c. the Mississippi Housing Opportunity Fund.

House Bill 196

AN ACT TO ESTABLISH THE MISSISSIPPI AFFORDABLE HOUSING OPPORTUNITY FUND; TO CREATE SECTION 43-33-801, MISSISSIPPI CODE OF 1972, TO DEFINE CERTAIN TERMS RELATED TO *THE HOUSING OPPORTUNITY FUND*; TO CREATE SECTION 43-33-803, MISSISSIPPI CODE OF 1972, TO ESTABLISH AND PROVIDE FOR THE ADMINISTRATION OF THE HOUSING OPPORTUNITY FUND; TO CREATE SECTION 43-33-805, MISSISSIPPI CODE OF 1972, TO AUTHORIZE MISSISSIPPI HOME CORPORATION TO IMPLEMENT AND ADMINISTER THE HOUSING OPPORTUNITY FUND; TO CREATE SECTION 43-33-807, MISSISSIPPI CODE OF 1972, TO ESTABLISH THE MISSISSIPPI AFFORDABLE HOUSING OPPORTUNITY FUND ADVISORY COUNCIL; TO CREATE SECTION 43-33-809, MISSISSIPPI CODE OF 1972, TO PROVIDE FOR THE PERCENTAGE OF FUNDING AVAILABLE TO CERTAIN PERSONS OR TO CERTAIN ACTIVITIES; TO CREATE SECTION 43-33-811, MISSISSIPPI CODE OF 1972,
TO ESTABLISH MINIMUM AFFORDABILITY PERIODS FOR APPLICANTS; TO CREATE SECTION 43-33-813, MISSISSIPPI CODE OF 1972, TO PROVIDE MINIMUM STANDARDS FOR THE HOUSING OPPORTUNITY FUND APPLICATION PROCESS; TO CREATE SECTION 43-33-815, MISSISSIPPI CODE OF 1972, TO AUTHORIZE MISSISSIPPI HOME CORPORATION TO ADMINISTER THE HOUSING OPPORTUNITY FUND IN COMPLIANCE WITH STATE AND FEDERAL HOUSING PROGRAMS; TO AMEND SECTION 27-65-75, MISSISSIPPI CODE OF 1972, TO PROVIDE THAT 2.5% OF ALL TAXES COLLECTED BY THE DEPARTMENT OF REVENUE ON LUMBER AND BUILDING MATERIALS SHALL BE CREDITED TO THE MISSISSIPPI AFFORDABLE HOUSING OPPORTUNITY FUND; AND FOR RELATED PURPOSES.

37. Participation in IREBEA is accomplished by;
a. A broker written notice to an authorized financial institute.
b. A broker verbal notice to an authorized financial institute.
c. The broker opening a company account.
d. All the above is sufficient.

a. A broker written notice to an authorized financial institute.

Notification to clients or customers whose funds are nominal in amount or to be held for a short period of time is unnecessary for those brokers who choose to participate in the program. Participation in the IREBEA program is accomplished by the *broker's written notification to an authorized financial institution*. That communication shall contain an expression of the broker's desire to participate in the program and, if the institution has not already received appropriate notification, advice regarding the Internal Revenue Service's approval of the taxability of earned interest or dividends to a chair of real estate, or a local affiliate of Habitat for Humanity International, Inc., or local affiliate of Fuller Center for Housing, Inc.

38. Transfer Disclosures are mandatory for all the following except;
a. Transfer of a Duplex.
b. Transfer of a four-unit apartment building.
c. A transfer from one co-owner to one or more other co-owners.
d. All the above.

c. A transfer from one co-owner to one or more other co-owners.
Transfers pursuant to court order, including, but not limited to, transfers ordered by a probate court in administration of an estate, transfers pursuant to a writ of execution, transfers by any foreclosure sale, transfers by a trustee in bankruptcy, transfers by eminent domain, and transfers resulting from a decree for specific performance. Transfers to a mortgagee by a mortgagor or successor in interest who is in default, transfers to a beneficiary of a deed of trust by a trustor or successor in interest who is in default, transfers by any foreclosure sale after default, in an obligation secured by a mortgage, transfers by a sale under a power of sale or any foreclosure sale under a decree of foreclosure after default in an obligation secured by a deed of trust or secured by any other instrument containing a power of sale, or transfers by a mortgagee or a beneficiary under a deed of trust who has acquired the real property at a sale conducted pursuant to a power of sale under a mortgage or deed of trust or a sale pursuant to a decree of foreclosure or has acquired the real property by a deed in lieu of foreclosure.
Transfers by a fiduciary in the course of the administration of a decedent's estate, guardianship, conservatorship or trust.
Transfers from one co-owner to one or more other co-owners.
Transfers made to a spouse, or to a person or persons in the lineal line of consanguinity of one or more of the transferors.
Transfers between spouses resulting from a decree of dissolution of marriage or a decree of legal separation or from a property settlement agreement incidental to such a decree.
Transfers or exchanges to or from any governmental entity.
Transfers of real property on which no dwelling is located.

39. The transferor of a duplex shall deliver to the prospective transferee the written property disclosure statement;
a. within 3 days
b. within 5 days after the close of escrow.
c. when the transferor meets with the transferee.
d. as soon as practicable before the transfer of title.

d. as soon as practicable before the transfer of title.
In the case of a sale, *as soon as practicable* before transfer of title.
In the case of transfer by a real property sales contract, or by a lease together with an option to purchase, or a ground lease coupled with improvements, *as soon as practicable* **before** execution of the contract. For the purpose of this paragraph, execution means the making or acceptance of an offer.
With respect to any transfer the transferor shall indicate compliance either on the receipt for deposit, the real property sales contract, the lease, or any addendum attached thereto or on a separate document.
If any disclosure, or any material amendment of any disclosure, is delivered after the execution of an offer to purchase, the transferee shall have three (3) days after delivery in person or five (5) days after delivery by deposit in the mail, to terminate his or her offer by delivery of a written notice of termination to the transferor or the transferor's agent.

40. In the case of transfer by a real property sales contract, or by a lease together with an option to purchase, or a ground lease coupled with improvements, delivery of the Transfer Disclosure Statement is delivered;
a. as soon as practicable after the execution of the contract.
b. as soon as practicable before the execution of the contract.
c. after the contract has been voided.
d. None of the above.

b. as soon as practicable *before* the execution of the contract.
In the case of transfer by a real property sales contract, or by a lease together with an option to purchase, or a ground lease coupled with improvements, *as soon as practicable before* execution of the contract. For the purpose of this paragraph, execution means the making or acceptance of an offer.

41. The transferor shall indicate delivery of the Property Disclosure Statement on ;
a. The receipt for deposit or the real property sales contract or the lease.
b. Any addendum attached thereto or on a separate document.
c. Both a and/or b.
d. Neither a or b

c. Both a and/or b.
With respect to any transfer the transferor shall indicate compliance either on the receipt for deposit, the real property sales contract, the lease, or any addendum attached thereto or on a separate document.

42. Delivery of the Real Estate Transfer Disclosure is mandatory in all the following cases except ;
a. a transfer of a one-to-four-unit dwelling.
b. a transfer between neighbors.
c. a transfer to a government entity.
d. a transfer of a single-family home.

c. a transfer to a government entity.
Transfers pursuant to court order, including, but not limited to, transfers ordered by a probate court in administration of an estate, transfers pursuant to a writ of execution, transfers by any foreclosure sale, transfers by a trustee in bankruptcy, transfers by eminent domain, and transfers resulting from a decree for specific performance. Transfers to a mortgagee by a mortgagor or successor in interest who is in default, transfers to a beneficiary of a deed of trust by a trustor or successor in interest who is in default, transfers by any foreclosure sale after default, in an obligation secured by a mortgage, transfers by a sale under a power of sale or any foreclosure sale under a decree of foreclosure after default in an obligation secured by a deed of trust or secured by any other instrument containing a power of sale, or transfers by a mortgagee or a beneficiary under a deed of trust who has acquired the real property at a sale conducted pursuant to a power of sale under a mortgage or deed of trust or a sale pursuant to a decree of foreclosure or has acquired the real property by a deed in lieu of foreclosure.
Transfers by a fiduciary in the course of the administration of a decedent's estate, guardianship, conservatorship or trust.
Transfers from one co-owner to one or more other co-owners.
Transfers made to a spouse, or to a person or persons in the lineal line of consanguinity of one or more of the transferors.
Transfers between spouses resulting from a decree of dissolution of marriage or a decree of legal separation or from a property settlement agreement incidental to such a decree.
Transfers or exchanges to or from any governmental entity.
Transfers of real property on which no dwelling is located.

43. If any disclosure, or any material amendment of any disclosure, required to be made is delivered after the execution of an offer to purchase;
a.   the transferee shall have three (3) days after delivery in person or five (5) days after delivery by deposit in mail to terminate his or her offer by delivery of a written notice of termination to the transferor or the transferor's agent.
b.   the transferee shall have 3 days after delivery in person or 5 days after delivery by mail to terminate his or her offer by making verbal cancellations.
c.   both a and b are acceptable.
d.   neither a or b is acceptable.

a. the transferee shall have three (3) days after delivery in person or five (5) days after delivery by deposit in mail to terminate his or her offer by delivery of a written notice of termination to the transferor or the transferor's agent.

If any disclosure, or any material amendment of any disclosure, required to be made is delivered after the execution of an offer to purchase, the transferee shall have three (3) days after delivery in person or five (5) days after delivery by deposit in the mail, to terminate his or her offer by delivery of a written notice of termination to the transferor or the transferor's agent.

44. Neither the transferor nor any listing or selling agent shall be liable for an error, inaccuracy or omission of information delivered.
a. if the seller lives on the property.
b. if the error, inaccuracy, or omission was not within their personal knowledge.
c. if the buyer doesn't seem to care.
d. all of the above.

b. if the error, inaccuracy, or omission was not within their personal knowledge.

Neither the transferor nor any listing or selling agent shall be liable for any error, inaccuracy or omission of any information delivered if the error, inaccuracy, or omission was not within the personal knowledge of the transferor or that listing or selling agent, was based on information timely provided by public agencies or by other persons providing information that is required to be and ordinary care was exercised in obtaining and transmitting it. The delivery of any information required to be disclosed to a prospective transferee by a public agency or other person providing information required to be disclosed shall be deemed to comply with the and shall relieve the transferor or any listing or selling agent of any further duty with respect to that item of information.

45. An agent without personal knowledge will not be held responsible for an error when the error was by a;
a. licensed engineer, land surveyor or geologist.
b. structural pest operator or contractor
c. experts dealing in matters within the scope of the professional's license or expertise.
d. All the above.

d. All the above.

The delivery of a report or opinion prepared by a licensed engineer, land surveyor, geologist, structural pest control operator, contractor, or other expert, dealing with matters within the scope of the professional's license or expertise, shall be sufficient compliance for application of the exemption provided by subsection (1) if the information is provided to the prospective transferee pursuant to a request therefor, whether written or oral. In responding to such a request, an expert may indicate, in writing, an understanding that the information provided will be used in fulfilling requirements and, if so, shall indicate the required disclosures, or parts thereof, to which the information being furnished is applicable. Where such a statement is furnished, the expert shall not be responsible for any items of information, or parts thereof, other than those expressly set forth in the statement.

46. Delivery to a spouse of a property disclosure transferee;
a. shall not be deemed delivery to the transferee.
b. shall be deemed delivery to the transferee unless provided otherwise in the contracts.
c. shall only be deemed a delivery to the transferee if they were married within the state of Mississippi before 1981.
d. shall never be deemed delivery to the transferee under any circumstances.

b. shall be deemed delivery to the transferee unless provided otherwise in the contracts.

Delivery of disclosure shall be by personal delivery to the transferee or by mail to the prospective transferee. For the purposes delivery to the spouse of a transferee shall be deemed delivery to the transferee, unless provided otherwise by contract.

47. Any person who willfully and negligently does not deliver the needed disclosures shall be liable
a. and if the seller, must take his property back uncontested.

b. in the amount of actual damages suffered by a transferee.
c. for up to $100,000.
d. for no more than $100,000.

b. in the amount of actual damages suffered by a transferee.
No transfer shall be invalidated solely because of the failure of any person to comply with any provision. However, any person who willfully or negligently violates or fails to perform any duty prescribed by any provision shall be liable in the amount of actual damages suffered by a transferee.

48. Real Estate Transfer Disclosures are needed for
a. office buildings when a real estate professional is involved.
b. shopping centers.
c. residential stock cooperatives of one to four units when a real estate professional is involved.
d. none of the above.

c. residential stock cooperatives of one to four units when a real estate professional is involved.
The provisions apply only with respect to transfers by sale, exchange, installment land sale contract, lease with an option to purchase, any other option to purchase or ground lease coupled with improvements, of real property on which a dwelling unit is located, or residential stock cooperative improved with or consisting of not less than one (1) nor more than four (4) dwelling units, when the execution of such transfers is by, or with the aid of, a duly licensed real estate broker or salesperson.

49. A nonmaterial fact which need not be disclosed is
a. illegal drug activity that affects the physical condition of the property.
b. the seller or any resident of the property died or is sick from AIDS.
c. the foundation of the house has shifted, and it is built on a hill that's sliding.
d. the property is located below a runway path for the local airport and the house shakes so bad the buyer will have to replace several windows a year from noise vibration breakage.

b. the seller or any resident of the property died or is sick from AIDS.
Failure to disclose nonmaterial fact regarding property as site of death or felony crime, as site of act or occurrence having no effect on physical condition of property, or as being owned or occupied by persons affected or exposed to certain diseases; failure to disclose information provided or maintained on registration of sex offenders
The fact or suspicion that real property is or was:
The site of a natural death, suicide, homicide or felony crime (except for illegal drug activity that affects the physical condition of the property, its physical environment or the improvements located thereon);
The site of an act or occurrence that had no effect on the physical condition of the property, its physical environment or the improvements located thereon;
Owned or occupied by a person affected or exposed to any disease not known to be transmitted through common occupancy of real estate including, but not limited to, the human immunodeficiency virus (HIV) and the acquired immune deficiency syndrome (AIDS); does not constitute a material fact that must be disclosed in a real estate transaction. A failure to disclose such nonmaterial facts or suspicions shall not give rise to a criminal, civil or administrative action against the owner of such real property, a licensed real estate broker or any affiliated licensee of the broker.
A failure to disclose in any real estate transaction any information that is provided or maintained, or is required to be provided or maintained, in accordance with Section 45-33-21 through Section 45-33-57, shall not give rise to a cause of action against an owner of real property, a licensed real estate broker or any affiliated licensee of the broker. Likewise, no cause of action shall arise against any licensed real estate broker or affiliated licensee of the broker for revealing information to a seller or buyer of real estate in accordance with Section 45-33-21 through Section 45-33-57. Any factors related to this paragraph, if known to a property owner or licensee shall be disclosed if requested by a consumer.
Failure to disclose any of the facts or suspicions of facts described in subsections (1) and (2) shall not be grounds for the termination or rescission of any transaction in which real property has been or will be transferred or leased. This provision does not preclude an action against an owner of real estate who makes intentional or fraudulent

misrepresentations in response to a direct inquiry from a purchaser or prospective purchaser regarding facts or suspicions that are not material to the physical condition of the property including, but not limited to, those factors listed in subsections (1) and (2).

50. A salesperson has a listing with his responsible broker, Broker A.   The salesperson decided to transfer to a new broker before the listing expires. When the agent moves to the new broker, who owns the listing?
a. The agent.
b. The listing automatically gets cancelled.
c. The listing moves to the salesperson's new broker.
d. Broker A

d. Broker A
A licensee who has changed to inactive status or who has transferred to another responsible broker may receive compensation from the previous responsible broker if the commission was generated from activity during the time that the licensee was under the supervision of that responsible broker.

51. It is not the duty of the responsible broker;
a. to instruct the licensees licensed under that broker in the fundamentals of real estate practice.
b. to instruct the licensees licensed under that broker in ethics of the profession and the Mississippi Real Estate Law.
c. to exercise supervision of his licensees of their real estate activities.
d. to make sure each agent has completed their post licensing education and kept their license current.

d. to make sure each agent has completed their post licensing education and kept their license current.
It shall be the duty of the responsible broker to instruct the licensees licensed under that broker in the fundamentals of real estate practice, ethics of the profession and the Mississippi Real Estate License Law and to exercise supervision of their real estate activities for which a license is required.

52. An affiliated broker cannot act independently of his employing broker;
a. without the full consent and knowledge of his employing broker.
b. without full disclosure of his client.
c. without full consent and knowledge of both the buyer and seller.
d. ever, once employed by his responsible broker.

a. without the full consent and knowledge of his employing broker.
A real estate broker who operates under the supervision of a responsible broker must not at any time act independently as a broker. The responsible broker shall at all times be responsible for the action of the affiliated broker to the same extent as though that licensee were a salesperson and that affiliated broker shall not perform any real estate service without the full consent and knowledge of his employing or supervising broker.

53. Applicants for a real estate license
a. must have a responsible broker before applying for their license.
b. may take the exam but have ten days to find a responsible broker.
c. may not take the exam without a responsible broker.
d. may not send in the license fee.

b. may take the exam but have ten days to find a responsible broker.
A person who passes the license exam has 10 days to find a broker.

54. A change of responsible broker requires the salesperson;
a. to within 3 days give written notice to the Commission
b. call the commission and tell them.
c. to take all his listings with him.
d. All the above.

a. to within 3 days give written notice to the Commission

Prompt notice in writing, within three (3) days, shall be given to the commission by any real estate salesperson of a change of responsible broker, and of the name of the principal broker into whose agency the salesperson is about to enter; and a new license shall thereupon be issued by the commission to such salesperson for the unexpired term of the original license upon the return to the commission of the license previously issued. The change of responsible broker or employment by any licensed real estate salesperson without notice to the commission as required shall automatically cancel his license. Upon termination of a salesperson's agency, the responsible broker shall within three (3) days return the salesperson's license to the commission for cancellation. It shall be unlawful for any real estate salesperson to perform any of the acts contemplated by this chapter either directly or indirectly after his agency has been terminated and his license has been returned for cancellation until his license has been reissued by the commission.

55. A licensed Mississippi broker may cooperate with a broker licensed in another state who does not hold a Mississippi license;

a. as long as it's agreed upon by both brokers.
b. as long as the buyer and seller know.
c. through the use of a cooperative agreement.
d. never.

c. through the use of a cooperative agreement.

A licensed Mississippi broker may cooperate with a broker licensed in another state who does not hold a Mississippi license through the use of a cooperative agreement. A separate cooperative agreement must be filed for each property, prospective user, or transaction with said writing reflecting the compensation to be paid to the Mississippi licensed broker. The listing or property management agreement for the Mississippi real property shall in such cases remain in the name of the Mississippi licensed broker.

56. A separate cooperating agreement must be filed for each property, prospective user, or transaction with said writing;

a. reflecting the relationship of the brokers.
b. reflecting the compensation to be paid to the Mississippi licensed broker.
c. reflecting the price of the property.
d. reflecting the client(s).

b. reflecting the compensation to be paid to the Mississippi licensed broker.

A licensed Mississippi broker may cooperate with a broker licensed in another state who does not hold a Mississippi license through the use of a cooperative agreement. A separate cooperative agreement must be filed for each property, prospective user, or transaction with said writing reflecting the compensation to be paid to the Mississippi licensed broker. The listing or property management agreement for the Mississippi real property shall in such cases remain in the name of the Mississippi licensed broker.

The commissions or other compensation resulting from the sale/rent/lease/property management or auction of the Mississippi real property and which are earned during the period the cooperative agreement is in force shall be divided on a negotiable basis between the Mississippi broker and the nonresident broker.

57. When there is a cooperative agreement with a non-resident broker, the listing or property management agreement for the Mississippi property;

a. must remain in the name of the Mississippi broker.
b. must remain in the name of both brokers.
c. must remain in the name of the out of state broker.
d. must remain with no name.

a. must remain in the name of the Mississippi broker.

A licensed Mississippi broker may cooperate with a broker licensed in another state who does not hold a Mississippi license through the use of a cooperative agreement. A separate cooperative agreement must be filed for each property, prospective user, or transaction with said writing reflecting the compensation to be paid to the Mississippi licensed broker. The listing or property management agreement for the Mississippi real property shall in such cases remain in the name of the Mississippi licensed broker.

58. How many copies of a cooperative agreement must a Mississippi broker file with the Mississippi Real Estate Commission?
a. one
b. two
c. three
d. four

b. two
Two copies in ten days

59. The nonresident broker cannot place any sign on real property located in Mississippi without the written consent of the cooperating Mississippi broker. When both brokers place signs on the property.
a. The Mississippi broker's sign must be larger.
b. The out of state broker can only use vinyl signs.
c. They should be placed side by side in a prominent place and in close proximity.
d. Only one broker's sign can be placed.

c. They should be placed side by side in a prominent place and in close proximity.
In all advertising of real estate located in Mississippi, the name and telephone number of the Mississippi broker shall appear and shall be given equal prominence with the name of the nonresident broker who is not licensed in this state.

60. When advertising a property shared by an out of state broker;
a. the name of the Mississippi broker must be listed.
b. the name of the seller must be listed.
c. the Mississippi broker must contact the Real Estate Commission.
d. None of the above.

a. the name of the Mississippi broker must be listed.
In all advertising of real estate located in Mississippi, the name and telephone number of the Mississippi broker shall appear and shall be given equal prominence with the name of the nonresident broker who is not licensed in this state.

61. A responsible broker must maintain an office and display the license therein. If the broker has more than one office
a. the broker need not display licenses in branch offices.
b. the broker shall display a branch office license in each branch office.
c. there are no branch offices allowed.
d. None of the above.

b. the broker shall display a branch office license in each branch office.
A responsible broker must maintain an office and display the license therein. If the broker has more than one office, the broker shall display a branch office license in each branch office. The broker is responsible for the real estate practices of those licensees.

62. No licensee shall pay any part of a fee, commission or other compensation received by such licensee in buying, selling, exchanging, leasing, auctioning, or renting any real estate except
a. to a licensee through the licensee's responsible broker.
b. to the customer directly as a referral fee.
c. to your neighbor for getting his brother to list with you.

d. all the above

a. to a licensee through the licensee's responsible broker.
No licensee shall pay any part of a fee, commission, or other compensation received by such licensee in buying, selling, exchanging, leasing, auctioning, or renting any real estate except to another licensee through the licensee's responsible broker.

63. The responsible broker must
a. hold meetings every Tuesday.
b. tell agents the hours they must make phone calls.
c. hang in the office all licenses of the licensees he is responsible for.
d. take Fridays off.

c. hang in the office all licenses of the licensees he is responsible for.
A responsible broker must maintain an office and display the license therein. If the broker has more than one office, the broker shall display a branch office license in each branch office. The broker is responsible for the real estate practices of those licensees.

64. Peggy, a salesperson for broker Bob listed and sold a property. Before being paid for that executed transaction, Peggy changed responsible brokers. Broker Bob
a. owes Peggy nothing.
b. must only pay Peggy's new responsible broker.
c. can pay Peggy her commission directly.
d. owes Peggy interest.

c. can pay Peggy her commission directly.
A licensee who has changed to inactive status or who has transferred to another responsible broker may receive compensation from the previous responsible broker if the commission was generated from activity during the time that the licensee was under the supervision of that responsible broker.

65. Any licensee who fails in a timely manner to respond to official Mississippi Real Estate Commission written communication or who fails or neglects to abide by Mississippi Real Estate Commission Rules and Regulations shall be deemed;
a. too irresponsible to sell real estate.
b. prima facie, to be guilty of improper dealing.
c. to be harboring a criminal.
d. on vacation.

b. prima facie, to be guilty of improper dealing.
Any licensee who fails in a timely manner to respond to official Mississippi Real Estate Commission written communication or who fails or neglects to abide by Mississippi Real Estate Commission's Rules and Regulations shall be deemed, prima facie, to be guilty of improper dealing.

66. A real estate broker or salesperson in the ordinary course of his business may give an opinion as to the price of real estate for the purpose of a prospective listing or sale, however this opinion as to the listing price or sale price;
a. must not refer to this as an appraisal.
b. must not take compensation.
c. both 1 and 2
d. neither 1 or 2

a. must not refer to this as an appraisal.
Only an appraiser can determine value with an opinion.

67. When an offer is made on a property owned by a party with whom the broker has entered into a listing agreement, such broker shall document and date an acceptance or rejection of the offer and;
a. make five copies.
b. then show his salespeople how he documented the information.
c. upon written request, shall provide a copy of such document to the person making the offer.
d. upon verbal request, shall provide a copy of such document to the person refusing the offer.

c. upon written request, shall provide a copy of such document to the person making the offer.
When an offer is made on property owned by a party with whom a broker has entered into a listing agreement, such broker shall document and date the seller's personal acceptance or rejection of the offer and upon written request, shall provide a copy of such document to the person making the offer.

68. A real estate licensee shall deliver a true and correct copy of any instrument to any party or parties executing the same;
a. within five days.
b. within 3 days.
c. immediately (at the time of signing).
d. no copies need to be given to any party.

c. immediately (at the time of signing).
A real estate licensee shall **immediately (at the time of signing)** deliver a true and correct copy of any instrument to any party or parties executing the same.

69. All exclusive listing agreements shall be in writing, properly identify the property to be sold and contain all of the terms and conditions under which the transaction is to be consummated including the sales price, the considerations to be paid, the signatures of all parties to the agreement and;
a. a provision requiring the listing party to notify the broker of their intention to cancel the listing.
b. a definite date of expiration.
c. both 1 and 2.
d. neither 1 or 2.

b. a definite date of expiration.
All exclusive listing agreements shall be in writing, properly identify the property to be sold, and contain all of the terms and conditions under which the transaction is to be consummated; including the sales price, the considerations to be paid, the signatures of all parties to the agreement, and a definite date of expiration. No listing agreement shall contain any provision requiring the listing party to notify the broker of their intention to cancel the listing after such definite expiration date. An "Exclusive Agency" listing or "Exclusive Right to Sell" listing shall clearly indicate in the listing agreement that it is such an agreement.

70. All exclusive buyer representation agreements shall be in writing and properly identify the terms and conditions under which the buyer will rely on the broker for the purchase of real estate including the sales price, the considerations to be paid, the nature of all parties to the agreement and a definite date of expiration.
a. The exclusive buyer agreement does not have to indicate in the document that it is such an agreement.
b. Copies of the exclusive buyers agreement do not have to be given to the buyer after signing.
c. The buyer may terminate the agreement upon fifteen (15) calendar days written notice to the buyer's exclusive agent.
d. The exclusive buyer agreement must not clearly state that the agreement is such.

c. The buyer may terminate the agreement upon fifteen (15) calendar days written notice to the buyer's exclusive agent.
All exclusive buyer representation agreements shall be in writing and properly identify the terms and conditions under which the buyer will rely on the broker for the purchase of real estate; including the sales price, the considerations to be paid, the signatures of all parties to the agreement, and a definite date of expiration. The buyer

may terminate the agreement upon fifteen (15) calendar days written notice to the buyer's exclusive agent. An Exclusive Buyer Representation agreement shall clearly indicate in the body of the document that it is such an agreement.

71. Broker Bob received an offer this morning for a property he has listed. Bob promptly called his client and then faxed the offer to his client. Later that day Bob received a second offer that was lower and had bad credit terms for financing. What should Broker Bob do?
a. Not present the second offer because the first offer is higher.
b. Present the second offer because the seller has not accepted the first offer and any other written offer received by the broker in a sale shall be presented to the owner.
c. Hold off on presenting the second offer until his client accepts the first offer.
d. Both 1 and 3.

b. Present the second offer because the seller has not accepted the first offer and any other written offer received by the broker in a sale shall be presented to the owner.
In the event that more than one written offer is made before the owner has accepted an offer, any other written offer received by the listing broker, whether from a prospective purchaser or from another licensee cooperating in a sale, shall be presented to the owner unless the listing broker has specific, written instructions from the owner to postpone the presentation of other offers. Broker should caution the seller against countering on more than one offer at the same time.

72. Every contract must reflect whom the broker represents by a statement;
a. under the signatures of the parties to the contract.
b. over the signatures of the parties to the contract.
c. on the side in a handwritten statement.
d. All the above.

b. over the signatures of the parties to the contract.
Every real estate contract must reflect whom the broker represents by a statement over the signatures of the parties to the contract.

73. A real estate broker must keep on file following its consummation complete records relating to any real estate transaction for;
a. one year.
b. two years.
c. three years.
d. five years.

c. three years.
A real estate broker must keep on file for three years following its consummation, complete records relating to any real estate transaction. This includes, but is not limited to: listings, options, leases, offers to purchase, contracts of sale, escrow records, agency agreements and copies of all closing statements.

74. The use of any copyrighted term or insignia on stationary, office signs, or in advertisement by any licensee not authorized to do so, will be considered;
a. as "substantial misrepresentation" and cause for refusal, suspension, or revocation of the license.
b. as a "substantial material fact" and cause for refusal, suspension, or revocation of the license.
c. as a "substantial misrepresentation" and cause for a penalty of up to $2,000.
d. as a "substantial misrepresentation" and cause for a penalty of no more than $10,000.

a. as "substantial misrepresentation" and cause for refusal, suspension, or revocation of the license.
Grounds for refusing to issue or suspending or revoking license; hearing;
The commission may, upon its own motion and shall upon the verified complaint in writing of any person, hold a hearing for the refusal of license or for the suspension or revocation of a license previously issued, or for such other

action as the commission deems appropriate. The commission shall have full power to refuse a license for cause or to revoke or suspend a license where it has been obtained *by false or fraudulent representation*, or where the licensee in performing or attempting to perform any of the acts mentioned herein, is deemed to be guilty of:

A broker shall advertise in the name in which the license is issued. A broker may use a descriptive term after the broker's name to indicate the occupation in which engaged, for example, "realty", "real estate" or "property management". If advertising in any other form, a partnership, trade name, association, company, or corporation license must be obtained prior to advertising in that manner.

Principal Brokers are required to verify and determine that their name or the name of the Brokerage Firm is prominently displayed on all advertising and that the name of any real estate licensee or any approved real estate Team or Group is situated near the name of the Brokerage Firm. The Broker or the Brokerage Firm must be identified by using the same size or larger print as that of a Licensee or a Team in all advertising. All advertising must include the telephone number of the Principal Broker or the Brokerage Firm.

No Principal Broker or licensee sponsored by said broker shall in any way advertise property or place a sign on any such property offering the property for sale or rent without first obtaining the written authorization to do so by all owners of the property or by any appointed person or entity who also has full authority to convey the property.

When a licensee is advertising their own property for sale, purchase or exchange which is not listed with a broker, the licensee must indicate that he or she is licensed. The disclosure of licensee's status must be made in all forms of advertising enumerated in Rule 3.3 (A), including the "for sale" sign.

In addition to disclosing their licensed status in all advertisements, licensees are required to disclose their licensed status on all real estate contracts in which they have an ownership interest.

A licensee shall not advertise to sell, buy, exchange, auction, rent or lease property in a manner indicating that the offer to sell, buy, exchange, auction, rent, or lease such property is being made by a private party who is not engaged in the real estate business. No advertisement shall be inserted by a licensee in any publication where only a post office box number, telephone number, e-mail address or street address appears. Every licensee, when advertising real estate in any publication, shall indicate that the party advertising is licensed in real estate; whether on active or inactive status.

75. A salesperson wants to advertise on an internet web page.
a. He may do so without checking with his broker first.
b. He does not need to specify that he is an agent.
c. All advertising must be under the direct supervision and in the name of the responsible broker or in the name of the real estate firm.
d. The internet doesn't fall under the terms of advertising.

c. All advertising must be under the direct supervision and in the name of the responsible broker or in the name of the real estate firm.

All advertising must be under the direct supervision and in the name of the Principal Broker or in the name of the real estate Brokerage Firm and must prominently display the name of the Principal Broker or the name of the Brokerage Firm in such a manner that it is conspicuous, discernible, and easily identifiable by a member of the public.

Advertisement" means any oral, written, visual, printed or electronic media advertisement and encompasses any correspondence, mailing, newsletter, brochure, business card, for sale or for lease signage or sign rider, promotional items, automobile signage, telephone directory listing, radio and television broadcasts, telephone solicitation and electronic media to include e-mails, text messaging, *public blogs, social media networking websites*, and/or *internet displays.*

76. When a licensee is advertising their own property for sale, purchase or exchange which is not listed with a broker, the licensee must?
a. The licensee is not allowed to sell his own property without his broker listing it.
b. The licensee does not have to state he or she is an agent.
c. The licensee must indicate he or she is licensed.
d. The licensee must not tell his broker.

c. The licensee must indicate he or she is licensed.

When a licensee is advertising their own property for sale, purchase or exchange which is not listed with a broker, the licensee must indicate that he or she is licensed. The disclosure of licensee's status must be made in all forms of advertising, including the "for sale" sign.

A licensee shall not advertise to sell, buy, exchange, auction, rent or lease property in a manner indicating that the offer to sell, buy, exchange, auction, rent, or lease such property is being made by a private party who is not engaged in the real estate business. No advertisement shall be inserted by a licensee in any publication where only a post office box number, telephone number, e-mail address or street address appears. Every licensee, when advertising real estate in any publication, shall indicate that the party advertising is licensed in real estate; whether on active or inactive status.

77. In addition to disclosing their licensed status on all advertisements, licensees are required to disclose their license status
a. on all contracts for real estate in which they have an ownership interest.
b. on all contracts regardless.
c. on all receipts they receive.
d. never.

a. on all contracts for real estate in which they have an ownership interest.
In addition to disclosing their licensed status in all advertisements, licensees are required to disclose their licensed status *on all real estate contracts in which they have an ownership interest.*

78. An agent made real estate signs to put in the front yard of his client's home. He did not put the name of his responsible broker or name of his real estate firm on the sign.
a. It's OK to have signs called "Blind Ads".
b. This is a "Blind Ad" and is in violation.
c. The agent can't put up signs.

b. This is a "Blind Ad" and is in violation.
This is a blind ad. The broker and a number must be listed on the sign.

79. Earnest money accepted by the broker or any licensee for which the broker is responsible and upon acceptance of a mutually agreeable contract is required to deposit the money;
a. Into his personal account.
b. Into a trust account within three business days.
c. Into a safe deposit box in his office.
d. Into a trust account prior to the close of business of the next banking day.

d. Into a trust account prior to the close of business of the next banking day.
The responsible broker is responsible at all times for earnest money deposits. Earnest money accepted by the broker or any licensee for which the broker is responsible and upon acceptance of a mutually agreeable contract is required to deposit the money into a trust *account prior to the close of business of the next banking day.* The responsible broker is required to promptly account for and remit the full amount of the deposit or earnest money at the consummation or termination of transaction. A licensee is required to pay over to the responsible broker all deposits and earnest money immediately upon receipt thereof. Earnest money must be returned promptly when the purchaser is rightfully entitled to same allowing reasonable time for clearance of the earnest money check. In the event of uncertainty as to the proper disposition of earnest money, the broker may turn earnest money over to a court of law for disposition. Failure to comply with this regulation shall constitute grounds for revocation or suspension of license.

80. When a broker is agent for the seller and for any reason the seller fails or is unable to consummate the transaction, the broker has no right to any portion of the money deposited by the purchaser;
a. is a false statement because the commission was earned.
b. even if the commission was earned.
c. is just plain wrong.

d. 1 and 3 are correct.

b. even if the commission was earned.
When the broker is the agent for the seller and for any reason the seller fails or is unable to consummate the transaction, the broker has no right to any portion of the earnest money deposited by the purchaser, even if a commission has been earned. The entire amount of the earnest money deposit must be returned to the purchaser and the broker should look to the seller for compensation.

81. When the broker is agent for the seller and for any reason the seller fails or is unable to consummate the transaction, the broker has no right to any portion of the money deposited by the purchaser, even if the commission has been earned. The money must be returned to the purchaser and the broker;
a. must under no circumstance receive payment for his actions.
b. must sue the seller for specific performance.
c. must sue the buyer's agent for specific performance.
d. should look to the seller for compensation.

d. should look to the seller for compensation.
When the broker is the agent for the seller and for any reason the seller fails or is unable to consummate the transaction, the broker has no right to any portion of the earnest money deposited by the purchaser, even if a commission has been earned. The entire amount of the earnest money deposit must be returned to the purchaser and the broker should look to the seller for compensation.

82. Monies received in a trust account on behalf of clients or customers are not assets of the broker; however, a broker may deposit and keep in each escrow account or rental account some personal funds for the express purpose;
a. of paying his office bills.
b. of paying commission
c. of covering service charges and other bank debits related to each account.
d. none of the above.

c. of covering service charges and other bank debits related to each account.
Accurate records shall be kept on escrow accounts of all monies received, disbursed, or on hand. All monies shall be individually identified as to a particular transaction. Escrow records shall be kept in accordance with standard accounting practices and shall be subject to inspection at all times by the Commission.
Monies received in a trust account on behalf of clients or customers are not assets of the broker; however, a broker may deposit and keep in each escrow account or rental account some personal funds for the express purpose of covering service charges and other bank debits related to each account.

83. If a broker, as escrow agent, accepts a check and later finds that such check has not been honored by the bank on which it was drawn, the broker shall;
a. immediately notify all parties involved in the transaction.
b. call the check writer and ask for a cashier's check.
c. immediately close the books on that transaction.
d. sue the bad check writer for specific performance.

a. immediately notify all parties involved in the transaction.
If a broker, as escrow agent, accepts a check and later finds that such check has not been honored by the bank on which it was drawn, the broker shall immediately notify all parties involved in the transaction.

84. Special situations, where unusual facts exist or where one or more parties involved are especially vulnerable, could require additional disclosures not contemplated. In such cases, brokers;
a. should not accept to represent any party.
b. should be extra careful.

c. should seek legal advice prior to entering into an agency relationship.

d. should make sure that a notary public verifies the identity of all parties.

c. should seek legal advice prior to entering into an agency relationship.

Consumers shall be fully informed of the agency relationships in real estate transactions. This rule places specific requirements on Brokers to disclose their agency relationship. This does not abrogate the laws of agency as recognized under common law and compliance with the prescribed disclosures will not always guarantee that a Broker has fulfilled all of his responsibilities under the common law of agency. Compliance will be necessary in order to protect licensees from impositions of sanctions against their license by the Mississippi Real Estate Commission. *Special situations, where unusual facts exist or where one or more parties involved are especially vulnerable, could require additional disclosures not contemplated by this rule.* In such cases, Brokers should seek legal advice prior to entering into an agency relationship.

85. "Disclosed Dual Agent" is when

a. an agent representing both parties to a real estate transaction with the verbal commitment to do one's best.

b. an agent representing both parties to a real estate transaction with the informed consent of both parties, with written understanding of specific duties and representation to be afforded each party.

c. an agent representing the seller and two parties making offers on the same property on the same day.

d. an agent representing two sellers at the same time with written informed consent of both parties and the understanding of specific duties to both.

b. an agent representing both parties to a real estate transaction with the informed consent of both parties, with written understanding of specific duties and representation to be afforded each party.

"Disclosed Dual Agent" shall mean that agent representing both parties to a real estate transaction with the informed consent of both parties, with written understanding of specific duties and representation to be afforded each party. There may be situations where disclosed dual agency presents conflicts of interest that cannot be resolved without breach of duty to one party or another.

87. Brokers who practice disclosed dual agency

a. should do so with the utmost care to protect consumers from other brokers who may violate common law standards.

b. are in violation of Mississippi Real Estate Law and their license may be suspended or revoked.

c. should do so with the utmost caution to protect consumers and themselves from inadvertent violation of demanding common law standards of disclosed dual agency.

d. are in violation of National Real Estate Law and may be fined of no more than $500,000.

c. should do so with the utmost caution to protect consumers and themselves from inadvertent violation of demanding common law standards of disclosed dual agency.

Brokers who practice disclosed dual agency should do so with the utmost caution to protect consumers and themselves from inadvertent violation of demanding common law standards of disclosed dual agency.

88. "Fiduciary Responsibility" are those duties due the principal (client) in a real estate transaction are

a. Care, Honesty and Due Diligence.

b. Honest and Fair Dealing.

c. Full Accounting, Disclosure, Honest Dealings and Care.

d. Loyalty, Obedience, Disclosure, Confidentiality, Reasonable Skill, Care and Diligence and Full Accounting.

d. Loyalty, Obedience, Disclosure, Confidentiality, Reasonable Skill, Care and Diligence and Full Accounting.

"Fiduciary Responsibilities" are those duties due the principal (client) in a real estate transaction are:

'Loyalty' - the agent must put the interests of the principal above the interests of the agent or any third party.

'Obedience' - the agent agrees to obey any lawful instruction from the principal in the execution of the transaction that is the subject of the agency.

'Disclosure' - the agent must disclose to the principal any information the agent becomes aware of in connection with the agency.

'Confidentiality' - the agent must keep private information provided by the principal and information which would give a customer an advantage over the principal strictly confidential unless the agent has the principal's permission to disclose the information. This duty lives on after the agency relationship is terminated.

'Reasonable skill, care and diligence' - the agent must perform all duties with the care and diligence which may be reasonably expected of someone undertaking such duties.

'Full accounting' - the agent must provide a full accounting of any money or goods coming into the agent's possession which belong to the principal or other parties.

89. When the broker is the agent for the seller, "first substantive meeting" shall be before or just immediately prior to the first of any of the following

a. showing the property, eliciting confidential information and the execution of any agreements.

b. showing the property, telephone communication and first meeting in the office.

c. showing the property, before any chit chat or small talk.

d. before any small talk.

a. showing the property, eliciting confidential information and the execution of any agreements.

In a real estate transaction in which the Broker is the agent for the seller, first substantive meeting shall be before or just immediately prior to the first of any of the following:

Showing the property to a prospective buyer.

Eliciting confidential information from a buyer concerning the buyers' real estate needs, motivation, or financial qualifications.

The execution of any agreements governed by Section 73-35-3 of the Mississippi Code of 1972 Annotated.

90. For the seller's agent, the first substantive meeting does not include

a. a bona fide open house where the customer asks specific questions about finance terms or down payment assistance programs.

b. eliciting confidential information.

c. a bona fide open house or model home showing, small talk concerning price range, location and property styles and responding to general factual questions.

d. none of the above.

c. a bona fide open house or model home showing, small talk concerning price range, location and property styles and responding to general factual questions.

For the seller's agent, the definition shall not include:

A bona fide "open house" or model home showing.

Preliminary conversations or "small talk" concerning price range, location, and property styles.

Responding to general factual questions from a prospective buyer concerning properties that have been advertised for sale or lease.

91. When the broker is the agent for the buyer, first substantive meeting is;

a. Showing the property of a seller to a represented buyer.

b. Eliciting any confidential information from a seller concerning their real estate needs, motivation, or financial qualifications.

c. The execution of any agreements.

d. All the above.

d. All the above.

In a real estate transaction in which the Broker is the agent for the buyer, first substantive meeting shall be at the initial contact with a seller or a seller's agent or before or just immediately prior to the first of any of the following:

Eliciting any confidential information from a seller concerning their real estate needs, motivation, or financial qualifications.
The execution of any agreements governed by Section 73-35-3 of the MS Code.

92. For the buyer's agent, the first substantial meeting shall not include ;
a. a bona fide open house or model home.
b. preliminary conversations or small talk concerning price range, location, and property styles.
c. responding to general factual questions from a prospective buyer concerning properties that have been advertised for sale or lease.
d. all the above.

d. all the above.
For the buyer's agent, the definition shall not include:
A bona fide "open house" or model home showing. Preliminary conversations or "small talk: concerning price range, location and property styles
Responding to general factual questions from a prospective buyer concerning properties that have been advertised for sale or lease.

93. In dual agency;
a. the buyer shall give his/her consent by modifying the MREC Single Agency Agreement to reflect the dual agency.
b. the buyer shall give his/her consent by signing the MREC Dual Agency Confirmation Form which shall be attached to the offer to purchase.
c. the buyer shall give his/her consent by meeting the seller to pass papers.
d. none of the above.

b. the buyer shall give his/her consent by signing the MREC Dual Agency Confirmation Form which shall be attached to the offer to purchase.
The buyer, at the time an agreement for representation is entered into between the broker and buyer, gives written consent to dual agency by signing the Consent To Dual Agency portion of MREC Form A.
The Broker must confirm that the buyer(s) understands and consents to the consensual dual agency relationship prior to the signing of an offer to purchase. The buyer shall give his/her consent by signing the MREC Dual Agency Confirmation Form which shall be attached to the offer to purchase. The Broker must confirm that the seller(s) also understands and consents to the consensual dual agency relationship prior to presenting the offer to purchase. *The seller shall give his/her consent by signing the MREC Dual Agency Confirmation Form attached to the buyer's offer. The form shall remain attached to the offer to purchase regardless of the outcome of the offer to purchase.*

94. In the event the agency relationship changes between the parties to a real estate transaction;
a. the original disclosure shall be modified to document the changes
b. addendums to the original disclosures' forms must be acknowledged by all parties to the transaction.
c. new disclosure forms will be acknowledged by all parties involved.
d. the original disclosures are legal.

c. new disclosure forms will be acknowledged by all parties involved.
In the event the agency relationship changes between the parties to a real estate transaction, new disclosure forms will be acknowledged by all parties involved.

95. In the event one or more parties are not available to sign one or more disclosures forms, the disclosure will be accomplished orally. The applicable form will be so noted by the broker and said forms will be forwarded for signatures as soon as possible.
a. written electronic transmission will not fulfill the legal requirement.
b. both a and d.
c. written electronic transmission will fulfill this requirement.
d. written electronic transmission will not fulfill this requirement.

c. written electronic transmission will fulfill this requirement.

In the event one or more parties are not available to sign one or more of the Disclosure Forms, the disclosure will be accomplished orally. The applicable form will be so noted by the Broker and said forms will be forwarded for signature(s) as soon as possible. Written electronic transmission will fulfill this requirement.

96. The Commission mandated disclosure form;
a. may be altered to fit the terms of the transaction.
b. may be altered and duplicated before presenting copies to all parties involved in the transaction.
c. may be duplicated in content and size but not altered.
d. may be duplicated in content and altered, but not in size.

c. may be duplicated in content and size but not altered.

The Commission mandated disclosure form may be duplicated in content and size but not altered.

97. Every licensee shall notify the Real Estate Commission of any adverse court decisions in which the licensee appeared as a defendant.
a. within 10 days
b. within 30 days
c. within 24 hours
d. never

a. within 10 days

Every licensee shall, *within ten days*, notify the Real Estate Commission of any adverse court decisions in which the licensee appeared as a defendant.

98. The expiration, suspension or revocation of a responsible broker's license shall automatically suspend the license of every real estate licensee currently under the supervision of that broker. In such cases;
a. all licensees will automatically lose their licenses.
b. a licensee may transfer to another responsible broker.
c. a licensee cannot transfer to another broker until the original responsible broker acquires a new license.
d. a licensee must avoid the responsible broker whose license has been suspended at all costs.

b. a licensee may transfer to another responsible broker.

The expiration, suspension or revocation of a responsible broker's license shall automatically suspend the license of every real estate licensee currently under the supervision of that broker. In such cases, a licensee may transfer to another responsible broker.

99. Any seller of a timeshare plan with the state of Mississippi must be a licensed Real Estate Broker or Real Estate Salesperson except;
a. There are no exceptions.
b. The developer and his regular employees.
c. Everyone must be licensed.
d. Both a and c

b. The developer and his regular employees.

Any seller, other than the developer and its regular employees, of a timeshare plan within the State of Mississippi must be a licensed Real Estate Broker or Real Estate Salesperson pursuant to and subject to Mississippi Law and the Rules and Regulations of the Mississippi Real Estate Commission.

100. A person who offers a timeshare plan located outside of Mississippi in a national publication or by electronic media, which is not directed to or targeted to any individual located in Mississippi and contains appropriate disclaimers;
a. must register with the state of Mississippi.

b. is exempt from licensee requirements.
c. is exempt from the registration requirements.
d. none of the above.

c. is exempt from the registration requirements.
A person is exempt from the registration requirements under the following circumstances.
An owner of a timeshare interest who has acquired the timeshare interest from another for the owner's own use and occupancy and who later offers it for resale; or
A managing entity or an association that is offering to sell one or more timeshare interests acquired through foreclosure, deed in lieu of foreclosure or gratuitous transfer, if such acts are performed in the regular course of or as incident to the management of the association for its own account in the timeshare plan; or
The person offers a timeshare plan located outside of Mississippi in a national publication or by electronic media, which is not directed to or targeted to any individual located in Mississippi and contains appropriate disclaimers

101. A purchaser of a time share may cancel the contract;
a. within 3 months after receiving the public offering
b. within 7 calendar days of signing the contract or 7 calendar days of receiving the public offering statement.
c. after the first visit if the purchaser decides they no longer want it.
d. none of the above.

b. within 7 calendar days of signing the contract or 7 calendar days of receiving the public offering statement.
A cancellation period of at least seven (7) calendar days

102. The MREC will issue a (timeshare) preliminary permit in 20 days;
a. if the developer resides within the state of Mississippi.
b. unless deficiencies are found on the application.
c. unless the developer has over 15 employees.
d. unless the Commission is overworked.

b. unless deficiencies are found on the application.
Preliminary permit. A preliminary permit shall be issued within twenty (20) calendar days after receipt of a properly completed application unless the Commission provides to the applicant a list of deficiencies in the application. A preliminary permit shall be issued within fifteen (15) calendar days after receipt by the Commission of the information listed in the deficiencies in the application.

103. Developers of timeshares and any of his agents cannot practice timeshare;
a. without meeting registration requirements of the MREC.
b. without the developer and his employees pass a Mississippi real estate license exam.
c. unless the developer becomes a responsible broker.
d. within the state of Mississippi.

a. without meeting registration requirements of the MREC.
Developer registration; offer or disposal of interest. - A developer, or any of its agents, shall not sell, offer or dispose of a timeshare interest in the state unless *all necessary registration requirements are completed and approved* by the Mississippi Real Estate Commission, or the sale, offer, or disposition is otherwise permitted by or exempt from these rules. A developer, or any of its agents, shall not sell, offer, or dispose of a timeshare interest in the state while an order revoking or suspending a registration is in effect.

104. The responsible broker must report any licensee for whom that broker is responsible to the commission if;
a. he/she believes the agent scored low on the real estate exam.
b. he/she believes that a licensee has let his/her license expire.

c. he/she believes that a licensee is slacking.
d. he/she believes that a licensee has violated laws rules or regulations.

d. he/she believes that a licensee has violated laws rules or regulations.
The responsible broker is responsible for the real estate activities of their associated salespersons. If a salesperson has broken any laws, the broker needs to contact MREC.

105. A licensee shall not be required to comply with disclosure requirements when engaged in transactions with;
a. corporation, nonprofit corporation, professional corporation
b. professional association, limited liability company, partnership, real estate investment trust, business trust, charitable trust, family trust
c. any governmental entity in transactions involving real estate.
d. All the above.

d. All the above.
There are specifically excluded from the provisions of Sections 89-1501 through 89-1-523:
Transfers pursuant to court order, including, but not limited to, transfers ordered by a probate court in administration of an estate, transfers pursuant to a writ of execution, transfers by any foreclosure sale, transfers by a trustee in bankruptcy, transfers by eminent domain, and transfers resulting from a decree for specific performance.
Transfers to a mortgagee by a mortgagor or successor in interest who is in default, transfers to a beneficiary of a deed of trust by a trustor or successor in interest who is in default, transfers by any foreclosure sale after default, in an obligation secured by a mortgage, transfers by a sale under a power of sale or any foreclosure sale under a decree of foreclosure after default in an obligation secured by a deed of trust or secured by any other instrument containing a power of sale, or transfers by a mortgagee or a beneficiary under a deed of trust who has acquired the real property at a sale conducted pursuant to a power of sale under a mortgage or deed of trust or a sale pursuant to a decree of foreclosure or has acquired the real property by a deed in lieu of foreclosure.
Transfers by a fiduciary in the course of the administration of a decedent's estate, guardianship, conservatorship or trust.
Transfers from one co-owner to one or more other co-owners.
Transfers made to a spouse, or to a person or persons in the lineal line of consanguinity of one or more of the transferors.
Transfers between spouses resulting from a decree of dissolution of marriage or a decree of legal separation or from a property settlement agreement incidental to such a decree.
Transfers or exchanges to or from any governmental entity.
Transfers of real property on which no dwelling is located.

106. Every applicant for a resident license as a real estate salesperson shall be;
a. 21 years of age and a resident of Mississippi for 5 years.
b. 18 years of age or older and be a bona fide resident of the state of Mississippi prior to filing his application.
c. 16 years of age and a resident of Mississippi.
d. none of the above.

b. 18 years of age or older and be a bona fide resident of the state of Mississippi prior to filing his application.
Every applicant for a resident license as a real estate salesperson shall be age eighteen (18) years or over, shall be a bona fide resident of the State of Mississippi prior to filing his application, shall have successfully completed a minimum of sixty (60) hours in courses in real estate as hereafter specified, and shall have successfully completed the real estate salesperson's examination as hereafter specified.

107. Legal action by the Commission for a violation may take the form of a fine of not more than $1,000 and or up to 90 days in jail, or both. The second violation can be;
a. up to 2 years in jail.
b. a fine of $5,000.

c. up to a $2,000 fine and up to 6 months in jail or both.
d. none of the above.

c. up to a $2,000 fine and up to 6 months in jail or both.
The second violation is double from the first violation.

108.What was the primary reason for the Mississippi Real Estate Commission was established?
a. To create jobs
b. **To** safeguard the public
c. To have a system in place for fines
d. For all the above reasons.

b. To safeguard the public
The Real Estate Brokers License Law of 1954 was established to protect the consumer.

109. The extent of cooperation of reciprocity with other states.
a. vary
b. are all the same.
c. neither
d. all the above.

a. vary
Each state determines their own reciprocity.

110. Failure to renew your license on time will result in a penalty of double fee. 30 days late, will result;
a. in triple penalty.
b. in having to retake the real estate exam.
c. in having to participate with an extra 30 hours of post licensing.
d. in the license being cancelled.

d. in the license being cancelled.
Failure to renew your license on time will result in a double fee. 30 days late, will result in the license being cancelled.

112. What year was the Mississippi Real Estate Commission established?
a. 1945
b. 1959
c. 1954
   d.   1899

c. 1954
MREC was established in 1954 to safeguard the public

113. When a buyer acknowledges a Dual Agency Agreement, must a notary be available to attest to the signature?
a. Yes, because the Dual Agency Agreement has to be notarized when the buyer signs it.
b. Yes, because when the seller accepts the dual agency, the notarized signature makes the contract valid. c. No because it is not required.
d. No because the seller must notarize the form.

c. No because it is not required.
There is no requirement for a notarized signature on the dual agency agreement.

114. When an agent transfers to a new broker and within 3 days gives written notice to the Commission the name of the principal broker into whose agency he is about to enter
a. the agent makes a notation on his license and gives it to the new broker.
b. he mails his license to the Commission and a new license will be issued for the unexpired term of the original license.
c. needs to attend more ethics classes.
d. mails his license to his new broker.

b. he mails his license to the Commission and a new license will be issued for the unexpired term of the original license.
When an agent transfers to a new broker and within 3 days gives written notice to the Commission the name of the principal broker into whose agency, he is about to enter he mails his license to the Commission and a new license will be issued for the unexpired term of the original license.

Real Estate Training Institute

THE NUMBER GAMES

GAME ONE

1. The number of photographs to accompany each application for license	
2. The year MREC was established	
3. The number of Mississippi real estate commissioners	
4. The number of years a real estate commissioner must be a resident of Mississippi	
5. The number of commissioners from each congressional district	
6. Qualification age for a broker's license	
7. The number of congressional districts in Mississippi	
8. Qualification age for a salesperson's license	
9. The number of months a broker applicant must have been an active salesperson.	
10. The number of hours a broker candidate must have in real estate education	
11. The number of months a broker must have had since the issuance of a salesperson's license to qualify for hiring agents	
12. On a real estate license applicant how many real estate owners must be included	
13. The application fee for a broker's license	
14. Home many times you can take the state exam before you have to wait to take it again.	
15. The hours of education a candidate for a salesperson's license must take	
16. The number of days a new salesperson has to find a broker after passing their exam	
17. A company application fee	
18. The score a salesperson has to obtain to pass the national section of the exam	
19. The number of days you have to prove that you have E&O insurance to MREC after the activation of your license	

ANSWER KEY

1. The number of photographs to accompany each application for license	**2**
2. The year MREC was established	1954
3. The number of Mississippi real estate commissioners	5
4. The number of years a real estate commissioner must be a resident of Mississippi	6
5. The number of commissioners from each congressional district	1

6. Qualification age for a broker's license	21
7. The number of congressional districts in Mississippi	4
8. Qualification age for a salesperson's license	18
9. The number of months a broker applicant must have been an active salesperson.	12
10. The number of hours a broker candidate must have in real estate education	120
11. The number of months a broker must have had since the issuance of a salesperson's license to qualify for hiring agents	36
12. On a real estate license applicant how many real estate owners must be included	3
13. The application fee for a broker's license	150
14. Home many times you can take the state exam before you have to wait to take it again.	2
15. The hours of education a candidate for a salesperson's license must take	60
16. The number of days a new salesperson has to find a broker after passing their exam	10
17. A company application fee	75
18. The score a salesperson has to obtain to pass the national section of the exam	70
19. The number of days you have to prove that you have E&O insurance to MREC after the activation of your license	30

1954 MREC Establishes
5 Commissioners
Six years a citizen and Five years a broker license
One commissioner from each congressional district and one at large.

Real Estate Broker License
21 years or older
Have held a active salesperson's license for 12 months
120 hours of real estate classes
Can't hire salesperson until 36 months after their salesperson's license was issued
Homeowners for three years and known for three years
Application fee: $150.

Exam
Any individual who fails to pass the broker's examination upon two (2) occasions, shall be ineligible for a similar examination until after the expiration of six (6) months from the time such individual last took the examination, and then only upon making application as in the first instance.
Score: 75 National and 80 State
Real Estate Salesperson License
18 years or older
60 hours in education

Application
3 property owners for three years and known for one month is on the application
3 business people known for five years
2 photographs
Asking for social security number
Application fee: $120.

Exam
Any individual who fails to pass the examination for salesperson upon two (2) occasions, shall be ineligible for a similar examination, until after the expiration of three (3) months from the time such individual last took the examination
10 days after passing the exam to find a broker
National 70 and State 75

1. The number of Cooperating Broker Agreements the Mississippi Broker makes.	
2. The monetary fine for a first violation that the amount can be up to	
3. The number of days the Mississippi Real Estate Broker has to send in the cooperating Broker Agreement to MREC.	
4. Upon complaint, the number of days **a licensee will be given notice of a hearing upon a charge files fifteen (15) days' notice** of the hearing upon the charges filed,	
5. The number of Cooperating Broker Agreements that the Mississippi Broker sends to MREC.	
6. The monetary amount for a second violation can be up to	
7. The number of days for a first violation that a licensee could be held in jail	
8. The number of months for a second violation that a licensee could be held in jail	
9. The number of hours needed every two years for continuing education	
10. The two-year renewal fee (2021)	
11. The number hours of a post license course	
12. The amount of the bond to file an appeal	
13. Number of days a timeshare buyer has to cancel	
1. The number of Cooperating Broker Agreements the Mississippi Broker makes.	4
2. The monetary fine for a first violation that the amount can be up to	1000
3. The number of days the Mississippi Real Estate Broker has to send in the cooperating Broker Agreement to MREC.	10
4. Upon complaint, the number of days **a licensee will be given notice of a hearing upon a charge files fifteen (15) days' notice** of the hearing upon the charges filed,	15
5. The number of Cooperating Broker Agreements that the Mississippi Broker sends to MREC.	2
6. The monetary amount for a second violation can be up to	2000
7. The number of days for a first violation that a licensee could be held in jail	90

8. The number of months for a second violation that a licensee could be held in jail	6
9. The number of hours needed every two years for continuing education	16
10. The two-year renewal fee (2021)	120
11. The number hours of a post license course	30
12. The amount of the bond to file an appeal	500
13. Number of days a timeshare buyer has to cancel	7

Upon complaint, licensees shall be given **fifteen (15) days' notices** of the hearing upon the charges filed
3 days to change broker

Violations
First is up to 1000 and 90 days in jail
Second is up to $2000 and 6 months in jail
Cooperating Broker Agreement
Four copies in all
Two copies are sent to MREC in ten days.

Renew license every two years $120 and 16 hours of CE

Post License
A temporary license shall be valid for a period of **one (1) year following the first day of the month after its issuance. 30-hour course.**

Appeals 30 days and $500 bond.
Timeshare cancelation 7 days

Thank you for trusting the Real Estate Training Institute. ♥

Made in the USA
Columbia, SC
17 May 2023

16826913R00109